SALEM COUNTY WILLS

Recorded in the Office of the Surrogate at
Salem, New Jersey

Abstracted by
H. STANLEY CRAIG

1831-1860

Southern Historical Press, Inc.
Greenville, South Carolina

This volume was reproduced from
An 1932 edition located in the
Publisher's private Library
Greenville, South Carolina

All rights reserved. No part of this publication may be reproduced,
stored in a retrieval system, transmitted in any form, posted
on to the web in any form or by any means without
the prior written permission of the publisher.

Please direct all correspondence and orders to:

www.southernhistoricalpress.com
or
SOUTHERN HISTORICAL PRESS, Inc.
PO Box 1267
375 West Broad Street
Greenville, SC   29601
southernhistoricalpress@gmail.com

Originally published: Merchantville, NJ, 1932
Copyright 1932 by H. Stanley Craig
ISBN #0-89308-727-0
All rights Reserved.
Printed in the United States of America

PREFACTORY NOTE

In a previous volume we abstracted the wills recorded from 1804 to and including 1830, by the Surrogate of Salem County. In this volume we continue the abstracts to 1860.

It has been our purpose to make these books of interest from a genealogical standpoint, therefor we have paid particular attention to the relationship between the testators and persons mentioned in the wills.

The letter and figures following the abstract indicate the book and page on which the will is recorded. Further details may be had by reference thereto.

SALEM COUNTY WILLS

1831, Apr. 9—JAMES LIPPINCOTT, Mannington. To sons Isaac, English and Thomas, and daus. Emily and Caroline, all real estate equally. Exec. Robert Robinson. Wit. Thomas Yarrow, Ann Robinson and Hannah Kelty. Proved Apr. 26, 1831. C-437

1831, Apr. 9—JOSHUA THOMPSON, Lower Alloways Creek. To son Joseph 1/2 of drained meadow in Alloways Creek Bank Co. and 1/2 of bonds and mortgages held against estate of David Bradway, dec'd. To dau. Elizabeth Nicholson, remainder of said meadow, bonds and mortgage and the house and lot where she resides. To gr. son Joshua Thompson house and land in Lower Alloways Creek and woodland in Upper Alloways Creek; my son William to have use thereof until Joshua is of age. To son William my plantation which he occupies, in Elsinborough, and the residue of my personal estate. Exec. John Mason and William Carpenter. Wit. Jeremiah Powell, Josiah Thompson and John Powell. Proved May 7, 1831. C-438

1828, Nov. 27—JEREMIAH POLSON, Pilesgrove. Profits of farm until March 25, 1831; then executor shall sell farm and pay my neice Ann Polson $100. Remainder of money from the sale and movable estate to wife Elizabeth and William Stratton, a young man who lives with me, when he is 21 years of age. Exec. wife and William Stratton. Wit. Joseph Davis, Abraham Eggman and Ephraim Watson. Proved Aug. 19, 1831. C-140

1831, Sept. 13—JACOB FOX, Mannington. Personal estate to be sold. To son Jacob the plantation in Lower Penns Neck; at his death to his sons Jacob and Henry. Plantation in Mannington to be sold. To son Frederick $2000. To son Jeremiah the property which he now occupies, the field on the opposite side of the road, and 1/2 of woodland in Mannington. To dau. Ann Ware $800. To children of son Isaac, dec'd, $1500 To children of dau. Margaret Mulford, dec'd, $1500. Executors to sell land in Lower Penns Neck adjoining the Delaware River, land on the Hook in Upper Penns Neck, land in Mannington, and woodland in Upper Alloways Creek. Money arising from sale to children and grandchildren. Executor to sell land on Salem Creek in Wyatt Marsh Co. in Mannington. Exec. Thomas Sinnickson and Lot Hinchman. Wit. Joseph Bassett, Jr., Benjamin Bassett and Thomas Yarrow. Proved Oct. 1, 1831. C-441

1828, Nov. 27—REBECCA THOMPSON, Salem. To dau. Ann Firth, meadow in Town Marsh. To said dau. and granddau. Rebecca Garrison, meadow near the old Salem Bridge. To daus. Ann Firth, Hannah Sayre and Rachel Archer, all my upland in Salem. To dau. Hannah Sayre, land and buildings where George Fox lives. To dau. Jane Smith, house and lot where she lives, in Salem. To dau. Mary Thompson, during life, land on street leading to the Presbyterian church, in Salem, To dau. Rachel Archer, land on Old Bridge street and land near Hagar Town, in Lower Alloways Creek. To granddau. Rebecca Garrison, the house and lot where Elisha Collins lives. To my grandchildren, Rebecca Ann Anderson, Rebecca F. Garrison, and Rebecca H. Thompson, land near the Court House, in Salem. To grandchildren, Richard P. Thompson, Thomas Thompson and Mary Thompson, woodland in Haines Neck, near the Methodist church. To dau. Jane Smith, my eight-day clock; at her death, to Ann Firth. To Rachel Archer, my silver teapot. To John Firth, $30. To Rebecca Garrison, silver cream cup and teaspoons. Remainder of real estate to daus Ann Firth, Hannah Sayre, Ann Smith, Rachel Archer and granddau. Rebecca Garrison, said daus. to pay annually to dau. Mary Thompson, $12. Exec. Joseph Bassett and Benjamin Archer. Wit. Thomas Sinnickson, Jesse Bond and Daniel Garrison.

1828, Nov. 27. Codicil—The devise of meadow near old Salem Bridge to Ann Firth and Rebecca Garrison is revoked; same is given to Rebecca alone. Woodland devised to Richard, Thomas and Mary Thompson is revoked; same is given to grandchildren Richard, Thomas, Mary, Joseph and Rebecca Thompson. Wit.

Jesse Bond, Thomas Catttell and William I. Shinn.   Proved Nov. 1, 1831.   C-444

1829, June 16—AMOS PETERSON, Pilesgrove. Apparel to son William. To grandsons Stacy and Joseph, sons of Amos Peterson, each a chest. Remainder of estate to all my children. Exec. son Amos. Wit. Joseph Davis and Joseph Barnes. Proved Nov. 3 1831.   C-449

1831, May 27—SAMUEL MORGAN, Pilesgrove. To son Joseph, the farm where he lives, land bot. of Joseph Sharp and Thomas Gillingham, and cedar swamp on Reed's Branch. To grandson Morgan, son of William Coles the farm bot. of Josiah Tatum, when 22 years of age. To son Samuel, the plantation where he lives and the old home plantation, and other land. To dau. Rebecca, wife of William Coles, the plantation where they live; they to pay my son Samuel $400. Son Samuel to pay the following legacies; To dau. Ann Horner, $800, and $50 to each of her children at 21 years of age: to dau. Margaret Coles $300, and to her dau. Martha, $100 at 21 years of age: and $50 yearly to my dau. Ann Morgan. To grandson Morgan Coles. my desk, high drawers and corner cupboard. To granddaus Rebecca and Martha Ann Coles. each bedding. Remainder of household goods to my daus. Remainder of movables to my sons. Exec. sons Joseph and Samuel. Wit. Joseph Davis, James Richman and Moses Richman, Jr. Proved Nov. 3, 1831.   C-450

1831, Oct. 11—SAMUEL M. JOHNSON, Lower Alloways Creek. To wife Ann, real and movable estate during life; then to Lot, son of Jacob and Elizabeth Bacon. Exec. James Butcher. Wit. John W. Maskell, James Harris and Job Tharp. Proved Nov. 11, 1831.   C-452

1828, June 26—BATHSHEBA VANMETER, Pittsgrove. To son Dr. James VanMeter of Salem, land devised to him by his grandfather, and meadow adjoining Mary Craig. To grandson Thomas I. VanMeter, woodland adjoining above. To dau. Bathsheba Mayhew, 1/2 of personal estate. To dau. Ann VanMeter, $400. Remaining real estate to dau. Bathsheba Mayhew during life; then to grand-lau Ann Johnson. To son Dr. Robert H Van-Meter of Salem, 6 sheep. To son Erasmus Van Meter, 6 cents and no more. Dr. James VanMeter trustee of estate left to dau. Ann. Exec. son-in-law William Mayhew. Wit. Alphonso L. Eakin, and David Johnson.

Codicil—To son Dr. James VanMeter, 12 acres of woodland additional, my black horse and $40 to be paid by him for funeral expenses. To Maria Richman, dau. of William Mayhew, my riding wagon and harness. Wit. Alphonso L. Eakin, David Johnson and Elizabeth Garrison. Proved Nov. 19, 1831. C-453

1831, Mar. 15—JOB FINLEY, Lower Penns Neck. To wife Ann, a cow, furniture, wheat, provisions, and use of farm in Upper Penns Neck while remaining my widow. If she is not satisfied, I give to Horatio, son of John Finley, dec'd, remainder of property after debts are paid, an if she is satisfied, I give all property remaining to (her sons) Benjamin, John and Furman Lloyd To John Lloyd, my gold watch. Exec. William A. Dick. Wit. H. W. Snitcher, William S. Hewitt and Benjamin Hewitt, Jr. Proved Nov. 21, 1831. C-456

1828, Aug. 5—REBECCA WALKER. To Thomas Brown Armstrong, son of William Armstrong, late of Salem County, $50. All my movables at my bro. William Walker's. except my watch, chain, key and seal, I dispose of as follows: To said bro. 1/2 doz. teaspoons marked HF; the residue of them to Phebe Bilderback, Sarah Ann Flanagin and Hannah Williams. The residue, including watch, chain, key and seal to the Third Baptist Church of Philadelphia. Exec. Wm. Darman of Philadelphia Wit. B. G. Mitchell and James Dalrymple. Proved in Philadelphia, Nov. 19, 1831. C-458

1829, Aug. 27—OBADIAH ROBBINS, Pilesgrove. Estate to b sold; receipts to wife Sarah after debts are paid. Exec. sons Obadiah and George Robbins and Thomas Yarrow. Wit. Wm. Morris, Charles Swing and Burdin Cranmer. Proved Jan. 2, 1832.
C-462

1829, June 7—JOHN MAY, Pittsgrove. To grandchildren

SALEM COUNTY WILLS 9

John and Eunes Langley, $25 each. To grandchildren William and Joseph, sons of my dau. Sarah Holdskins, $25 each. Remainder of estate to sons and daus. George and John May, Margaret Elwell, Catharine Garrison and Jacob May. Exec. son John May. Wit. Jonathan Richman and Cornelius Hulick. Proved Jan. 10, 1832. C-463

1832, Jan. 6—ABRAHAM HUDSON, Pitnsgrove. To son Abraham, my silver watch (if he will give his watch to my grandson, Samuel Hudson) and my gray colt. To grandson Samuel Hudson, my gun. To son Abraham and grandson Samuel, all my gold and silver peases that was my father's. To dau. Mary Martin, my small brass kittle. Exec. to sell personal estate and pay debts; residue of money and real estate to son Abraham and grandson Samuel. Exec. Jonathan Richman and son Abraham Hudson. Wit. James Fish, Richard Kirby and Clarra Davis. Proved Jan. 10, 1832. C-465

Not Dated—LYDIA MILLER, Mannington. To sister Mary Sheppard and my neices Mary M. Wood, Priscilla W. Reeve and Mary M. Sheppard, apparel. To nephew and neices, $200 each. To bro. William Miller, who is appointed executor, residue of estate after debts are paid.
1832, Jan. 20—Elizabeth W. Miller, being duly affirmed, declared that Lydia Miller on or about the 28th of July, 1829, put in her hands the annexed paper, and informed her that it contained her will.
1832, Jan. 20—Sarah W. Acton, being duly affirmed, declared she is acquainted with the handwriting of Lydia Miller, and that the annexed instrument is in the handwriting of said deceased.
C-466

1831, Dec. 19—ISAAC BIDDLE, Upper Penns Neck. To wife Sarah, a cow and furniture. To son John Milton Biddle, all real estate. To dau Evelina Biddle, $200. Exec. wife Sarah and Richard Somers. Wit. William Strimple, George Peterson and Benjamin Allwas. Proved Jan. 28, 1832. C-468

1832, Jan. 23—WILLIAM CLARK, Pilesgrove. To Rachel

Carney, $550 and furniture. To Sarah Ann Carter, $50. To Thomas McCalister, land on lane leading to Sculltown. To bro. George Clark during life, the house and farm where I live; at his death, to his son Thomas. To George Clark, woodland In Pilesgrove during life; then to Thomas McCalister, Jr. To Deborah, wife of Thomas McCalister, Mary Clark and Jane Ann, wife of James Turner, each a double coverlet. To Thomas McCalister, Sr., all remaining personal estate. Exec. Thomas McCalister and Thomas Yarrow. Wit. Isaac Lewis, Sr., Smith Hewitt and Michael Null. Proved Feb. 20, 1832. C-469

1831, Oct. 27—BENJAMIN HEWARD, Pittsgrove. To children Richard, Joseph and Mary, all movable estate after debts are paid. Plantation to be sold and receipts divided between said children. Exec. sons Richard and Joseph. Wit. Jeremiah DuBois, Rachel DuBois and Hope M. DuBois. Proved March 6, 1832.
C-471

1829, Aug. 7—MARY MINCH, Upper Alloways Creek. To neices Mary, Rachel and Sarah McConner, daus. of William and Rachel McConner, furniture, To nephew Clement McConner, my silver watch and bureau. To nephew Matthias Kiger McConner, $10. To Rachel McConner, apparel. To Mary Elizabeth, dau. of Peter and Jane String my new looking-glass. To Margaret, wife of Peter Shimp, my sunbonnets and caps, Exec. Stacy Lloyd. Wit. Nathan DuBois, David English and Zacheus Ray. Proved Mar. 7, 1832. C-473

1832, Feb. 15—JOSEPH PATTERSON, Pilesgrove. To wife Elizabeth, all personal estate, in trust for benefit of her and my children. Exec. Robert P. Robinson. Wit. Thomas Yarrow and Rachel Goforth. Proved Mar. 20, 1832. C-475

1828, Apr. 24—ELIZABETH BEE, Upper Alloways Creek. To son George Bee, bedding and $300 when of age; if he dies before becoming of age, to my children, John Mowers, Eliza Remster, Margaret Applegate, Joseph Mowers and Catharine Mowers. To my youngest dau., Catharine Mowers and my grandson Adam M. Couch, each a house and land at Allowaystown; the latter house where Enoch Applegate lives, my dau. Margaret Applegate to have use of same during life. To granddau. Elizabeth, B. Mowers, land in Allowaystown, her parents to have use of same during life. Residue of estate to be sold and receipts divided among my children. Exec. and grdn. of son George E. Bee, Stacy Lloyd. Wit. Jno. H. Lambert, Christiana Ayres and Zacheus Ray. Proved Apr. 17, 1832.   C-477

1831, July 21—SUSANNAH BRADWAY, Salem, Executor to pay debts out of cash I have on hand; remainder, 2 3 to Militon, wife of John Hance and remainder to Rebecca, wife of Joseph Noblet. My land to Rebecca Noblet; after her death, to her bro. Joseph Barber. No charge shall be brought against Waddington or Adna Bradway for arrearages due me. Exec. John Hance. Wit. David Bacon, Mary White and Wm. White   Proved Apr. 25, 1832.
   C-479

1831, Aug. 10—PRUDENCE SMITH, Salem   To neice Elizabeth Dennis, 2/3 of personal estate; remainder to neices Rachel and Lucy Ann Dennis and Lucy Kirby. To sister Elizabeth Black, during life, my share in my sister Lucy Smith's estate; at her death, to my nephews, Albert Dennis, Henry, Nicholas C., William, Samuel and Hill Smith Kirby. Exec. Aaron Waddington and Samuel C. Atkinson. Wit. Morris Hancock Charles Hopkins and Jervis Butcher. Proved May 5, 1832.   C-480

1832, Apr. 25—THOMAS REEVE, Pilesgrove. To wife Sophia, $100   To Elizabeth Coombs, $20. To grandson Scull Reeves, my watch. To son Micajah, family Bible. To son Abraham, apparel. To sons Thomas and Isaac, $700 in trust for my son Abraham. To grandsons Anthony and Elwood Reeve, $50 each. Exec. Jonathan Cawley. Wit. David Davis, Samuel Young and Joseph Davis. Proved May 29, 1832.   C-482

1832, Mar. 23—HENRY KIGER, Mannington, Executors to sell real estate and divide receipts between my children: Henry, John, Adam. Daniel, Nathan, Rebecca, Margaret and Barbara. Exec. sons Henry, John and Adam. Wit. Lot Hinchman, Joshua H. Reeves and Thomas Yarrow. Proved June 25, 1832.   C-485

1832, June 13—JOHN KIRBY, Upper Penns Neck, To sister Deborah Kirby, $65. To my children, Ebenezer, Chalkley, Jacob, Emily and Robert, the proceeds of my property after debts are paid. Richard Somers and Asa Kirby grdns. of children. Exec. Richard Somers. Wit. Thomas Yarrow, Hudson Springer and Hannah Kirby. Proved Aug. 8, 1832. C-487

1832, Aug. 18—MERIAM CUFF (signed Merion Cuff), Lower Alloways Creek. To daus. Mary Gould and Sarah Murry, each $1. To dau. Emma Ann Cuff, the house where I live. Exec. Joseph Harris. Wit. James H. Young, Joseph Baker and Ezekiel Loper. Proved Aug. 25, 1832. C-489

1823, Dec. 30—ANN WALMSLEY, (spinster) Mannington. To Samuel Hackett, my right to land in Mannington and Penns Neck. To Rebecca, wlfe of John Gibbs, apparel. To nephew William W. Hackett, $100. If my nephew Samuel Hackett dies intestate or without heir, lands devided to him shall be sold and receipts divided between William W., Edward, Emily Ellen, Mary Ann and Sarah Ann, children of Jonathan and Hope Hackett. Exec. Samuel Hackett. Wit. Ann Hall, Margaret Smith and Sarah Vanneman. Proved Sept. 26, 1832. C-490

1827, June 4—JOSIAH WOOD, Pittsgrove. To wife Hannah, land in Pittsgrove. Exec. wife Hannah. Wit. Jacob Newkirk, Daniel Hutchinson and John Wood. Proved Oct. 1, 1832. C-492

1831, July 25—ELISHA STRETCH, Lower Alloways Creek. To son Joshua, $20. To wife Mary D., 1/3 of remainder of estate. To oldst Children William B. Stretch, Ann Stewart and Job Stretch, 4/16 of the remaining 2/3 of estate. To three youngest children, Bulah, Mary D. and Sarah, remainder of estate. Exec. Mary D. Stretch and John Stewart. Wit. Edward Waddington, Benjamin Harris and Charles Thompson. Proved Oct. 2, 1832. C-494

1832, June 12—FRANCIS DAVIS, Pilesgrove. Part of land to be sold and debts paid; residue of estate to wife Elizabeth.

SALEM COUNTY WILLS 13

Exec. Thomas Edwards. Wit. Isaac Ballenger, Josiah Ballenger and Isaac Ballenger, Jr. Proved Oct. 24, 1832. C-496

1832, Sept. 19—ABRAHAM SWING, Pittsgrove Wife Hannah, during life, occupancy of dwelling, use of a horse light wagon and harness, 2 cows and use of farm in possession of son Leonard. To son Jonathan, land bot of William Lambert, and a note against him for $50 To son-in-law David DuBois, in right of his wife, Ruth, proceeds of the timber standing on my woodlands on the north side of Cumberland Road. The home farm to be divided and one share set off to each, my son Leonard, son-in-law Ebenezer Harris and his wife Sarah, son Nathaniel, dau. Hannah and son Samuel. Exec. sons Jonathan and Nathaniel. Wit. George W. Janvier, Thomas DuBois and Susannah Whitaker. Proved Nov. 5, 1832. C-497

1832, July 25—REBECCA BLACKWOOD, Salem. To son John, $800; to his children, $200 each. To grandson Joseph, son of son William, dec'd, $700 at 21 years of age. To children of son Samuel, dec'd, $200 each. To dau. Rebecca Wilson, $1000; to her sons Joseph and William Wilson, $200 each at 21 years of age. To granddaus Sarah S. Wilson, $500; Rebecca Ann Cooper, $1000; and Sarah Boon, dau. of dau. Beulah Blackwood, dec'd, $200. Residue of estate to son Joseph. Exec. sons John and Joseph. Wit. John Simpson, John N. Cooper and Rachel Denn. Proved Nov. 15, 1832. C-500

1832, Oct. 16—SAMUEL PANCOAST, Elsinborough. Executor to sell farm in Elsinboro and divide receipts between my children, Joseph, Elizabeth, Eliakim, Hannah Hilliard, James, William, Dorcas, Josiah, Charles, Ann and Samuel. Wife Dorcas to have the interest on $1500, annually. Exec. sons Joseph and Eliakim. Wit. John Powell, William Peterson and George Kirk. Proved Nov. 16, 1832. C-502

1830 Aug. 26—SAMUEL BRICK, JR., Lower Alloways Creek. To sister Deborah Brick, who is named executrix, all my lands. Wit. Samuel Pancoast, William Peterson and Dorcas Pancoast, Jr. Proved Nov. 24, 1832. C-504

SALEM COUNTY WILLS

1826, Sept. 15—CHRISTOPHER MIRES, Upper Alloways Creek. To dau. Margaret, wife of Peter Stanger, all personal estate and the house in which I live. Exec. Peter Stanger. Wit. William Dickinson, Nicholas Bright and J. F. Risley. Proved Dec. 3, 1832. C-505

1830, Feb. 26—ELIRABETH CHRISTOPHER, Upper Penns Neck. To Mary Keen and her dau. Rebecca Keen, the remainder of estate after debts are paid. Exec. Samuel Lineh and David Scull. Wit. David Linch, Abel Burdsall and Samuel Bolton. Proved Jan. 11, 1833. C-507

1832, June 28—OLIVER SMITH, Upper Alloways Creek. To son William, the farm where I live, and marsh in Lower Alloways Creek. To son Oliver, the house and lot where he lives, the wharf and landing, orchard and land opposite the fulling mill house, lot where the log house stands (except the house and garden), and woodland on road from Quintons Bridge to Stephen Reeves' mill. To dau. Lydia Platts, land near the graving bank. To son James, remainder of my land, a sorrel horse, a pair of oxen, 2 cows. 6 sheep, plantation wagon, and furniture. To heirs of dau. Clarissa Gibbs: to Richard Gibbs, the bond I hold against Edward B. Gibbs and Jacheus Ray. To son William, all personal estate. Exec. sons William and Oliver. Wit. Phineas Smith, James Campbell and William Brown. Proved April 6, 1833.
D-1

1832, Aug. 27—ABNER PATRICK, Lower Alloways Creek. To wife Hannah, real and personal estate; at her marriage or death, to my children, William, Elizabeth, Mary Ann and Hannah Patrick. Exec. bro Jesse Patrick. Wit. John W. Maskell, Joseph Naylor and Jesse Carll. Proved April 13, 1833. D-3

1833, Jan. 28—JEDIDAH KIRBY, Woodstown. To grandson Charles Costill, $50. To dau, Sarah Kirby, residue of estate. Exec. bro. Samuel Dickson of Woodstown. Wit. Joseph Turner and Joseph L. Risley. Proved April 19, 1833. D-5

1833, May 12—LOT HINCHMAN, Mannington. To wife Catharine, 1/3 of rents, uses and profits of my farm occupied by Albert Layton, and $60 per year. To son Thomas, $600. To son Reuben, the farm I live on until my son Clement is 21 years old, when he shall receive $100 each year from the time of my decease until he is of age. Reuben is to maintain my chhildren, Clement, Margaret and Ruth, while they remain single, until Clement is of age. To dau. Mary Fox, $600. To children, Reuben, Clement, Ann wife of Joseph Robinson, Martha wife of Henry Richman, Margaret and Ruth, remainder of estate. Exec. son Reuben and Henry Richman. Wit. Jonathan Kelty, Joshua Reeves and Thomas Yarrow. Proved June 10, 1833. D-6

1833, Mar. 26—SILAS PEDRICK, Upper Penns Neck. To dau. Martha, furniture. To son Clalkley, bedding. To children Martha, Miles and Chalkley, all real estate. Exec. Jacob Goodwin and Richard Somers. Wit. Arthur H. Green, John M. Springer and Job Bevis. Proved July 6, 1833. D-9

1832, Jan. 19—SARAH VANMETER, Pittsgrove. To dau. Catharine Garnel, $6. To son Isaac VanMeter, $1. To son David Vanmeter, 6 cents. To son Joseph VanMeter, $1. To dau. Sarah Hunter, $6. To dau. Rachel VanMeter, $6. To son Abraham VanMeter, $6 and my large demijohn. To dau. Elizabeth, $2. To dau. Rachel, family Bible. To dau. Rachel and son Abraham, the residue of my estate. Exec. Isaac Johnson, 2nd. Wit. James Coombs and Adam VanMeter. Proved July 23, 1833. D-11

1818, Sept. 8—JAMES KINSEY, Salem. To wife Rebecca, all estate, and she is named as executor. Wit. William Ireland and Paul K. Hubbs. Proved Aug. 31, 1833. D-13

1833, Apr. 25—THOMAS DAVIS, SR.,—Pilesgrove. To my neice, Rebecca, dau. of Elisha Davis, dec'd, all personal estate. (No exec. named; Joseph Coles, acting). Wit. Bevan Flitcraft, Joseph Bishop and Isaiah Flitcraft. Proved Oct. 12, 1833. D-14

1833, May 6—JOSEPH BOLTON, Pilesgrove. To wife Charlotte H., furniture, provisions, and woodland during life; then to son Richard B. if he be living, and if not, to son Samuel H. To dau. Beulah S. Bolton, a gold watch and chain and a cow. To son Joseph L., gold sleeve buttons, silver tankard, the turning lathe that is in the garret of my grist mill, and tools belonging thereto. To daus. Elizabeth I. and Ellen H. Bolton, silverware. To wife and daus. Beulah S., Elizabeth I., and Ellen H. Bolton, each 1/8 of remainder; residue to sons Richard, Samuel and Joseph. Exec. wife and Jacob Howey of Gloucester Co. Wit. J. R. Clawson, Joseph Heritage and Casper Wistar. Proved Oct. 19, 1833.
D-16

1830, May 10—ROBERT WATSON, Lower Alloways Creek. To bros. Thomas Watson of Philadelphia, and Tyler Watson of Cumberland Co., personal estate, after debts are paid. Bushland to Canton Baptist Church, they to erect tombstones similar to deceased wife Hannah's. Exec. David Bowen and Ephraim Turner. Wit. Dalymore Harris, Samuel Fogg and Elizabeth Harris. Proved Nov. 16, 1833. D-19

1833, Mar. 6—GEORGE WISER, Upper Penns Neck. To sisters Elizabeth Shomaker, Hannah Franklin and Susannah Borden, each $50, To bro. James Wiser, remainder of estate, he to provide for my mother, Susannah Wiser. Exec. bro. James Wiser. Wit. John Dickinson, Jonathan Riley and Samuel Linch. Proved Nov. 21, 1833. D-21

1833, Nov. 22—JOHN CARPENTER, Buffalo, N. Y., formerly of Salem Co. To bro. William, my secretary. To bro. Samuel, my watch. To sister Rachel bedding and diamond pin. Apparel to my mother. To the Temperance Society of Salem and the Mannington Township Temperance Society, each $25. To friend William Shelton, Rector of St. Paul's Church, Buffalo, $100, to be applied to the sick and poor of the city. To cousin Thomas Firth, a picture that is in his possession. To mother Mary B. Carpenter, $1000. To sister Rachel Sheppard, $1000 for her comfort and the education of my nephews, William and I. N. C. Sheppard. Remainder of estate to bros. William and Samuel P. Carpenter. Exec. Thomas Firth, Charles Sheppard ond Samuel P. Carpenter. Wit. Jacob R. Elfreth, Aquilla Jones and Eli K. Price. Proved Jan. 6, 1834. D-23

1832, Feb. 11—DAVID DAVIS, Woodstown. To dau. Hannah S., wife of George Hollinshead, use and occupancy of my house and lot and shop in Woodstown, adjoining the Baptist meeting house; during life, and $400. To grandson David E. Hollinshead, the house and shop at her death, land in Bushtown, and $300; he to pay her $12 annually during her life. Exec. son David M. Davis. To granddau. Mary Hollinshead, $1000. Remainder of estate to son David M. Davis. Wit Thomas Davis, Josiah Davis and Thomas W. Davis. Proved Jan. 18, 1834.
D-25

1822, May 15—PATIENCE HILLMAN, Pilesgrove. All estate, after debts are paid, to daus. Ann Gardiner, Patience Flanagin, Margaret Kirby, Rachel Waters, Mary Ann Knight and Rebecca Hammitt. Exec. Thomas Hammitt and Elisha Waters. Wit. Thomas Shull, Silas Tinker and Thomas Pedrick. Proved Mar. 4, 1834. D-29

1834, Feb. 17—MILLER M. FOGG, Mannington. To wife Elizabeth, furniture and provisions and a cow. Children: William, David, Samuel and an expected child. Exec. John G. Mason. Wit. Thomas Yarrow and Thomas I. Yarrow. Proved Mar. 6, 1834. D-30

1834, Mar. 28—JAMES LINDZEY, Salem. To mother Sarah Lindzey, all estate, and she is appointed executor. Wit. Anthony Nelson, George Grier and Mary Lindzey. Proved May 10, 1834. D-32

1833, Dec. 10—ELLIS SIMKINS, Stoe Creek. Exec. Nathan

Sheppard to sell the house and lot where I live. To sons Abraham and Ellis Simkins and daus. Margaret Rann and Hannah Simkins, each $1. Remainder, after debts are paid, to youngest children: Reuben, Richard William and Caroline Simkins. Wit. Sarah Stewart, Joseph C. Sheppard and Isaac M. Sheppard. Proved June 10, 1834. D-34

1832, Jan 8—JOHN ABBIT, Pittsgrove. To son John, my dwelling house and part of plantation and $400. To son David, land. To daus. Elizabeth, wife of Clark Webster, Mary Abbit, Sarah, wife of John Hanby, and Martha, wife of George Hanby, all money arising from sale of woodland. To son Isaac C., $1. Exec. John Abbit and Clark Webster. Wit. Hosea Sethen, Susannah Micksner and Joseph C. Nelson. Proved May 8, 1834. D-35

1834, July 22—BENJAMIN TYLER, Mannington. To son James B., land, mill pond, cripple and swamp called Barrens, in Upper Alloways Creek, live stock, farming utensils and movable property. To wife Ruth, during life, the house and land at Battentown, Gloucester Co.; at her death, to son James. Exec. George Hall. Wit. Caleb Lippincott, James VanMeter and Richard P. Thompson. Proved Aug. 9, 1834. D-39

1827, May 28—THOMAS MANNING, Sharptown. To friend Catharine Riley, $30. To the M. E. Society of Pilesgrove, $10 for repairing the church. To George Dunn, residue of estate. Exec. George Dunn. Wit. Ephraim Barnes, John Cook and Elizabeth Barnes. Proved Aug. 13, 1834. D-42

1834, Aug. 11—DAVID VANMETER, Pittsgrove. To wife Ruth, 1/3 of estate, after debts are paid. To my children, Isaac W., Enoch J., Lewis, Jacob, Hiram, David and Phebe VanMeter, all lands in Salem and Cumberland Cos. Exec. son Isaac. Wit. George Souders, Adam VanMeter and Susannah VanMeter. Proved Aug. 27, 1834. D-43

1831, Sept. 30—SAMUEL AUSTIN, Salem. To grandsons Samuel Austin Allen and Richard Allen, my plantation and meadow in Mannington, and meadow on old crossway leading to Penns Neck, on condition that they pay to my grandson Jedediah Allen $400 when he is of age. To grandson William Austin, the house and part of lot where I live. Remainder of said lot to granddau. Lydia Austin. To granddaus. Lydia rnd Rebecca Allen, each a house and lot in Margaret's Lane and $500. John G. Mason, trustee of grandchildren. Exec. Jedidiah T. Allen and John G. Mason. Wit. John Adams, Enoch S. Reed and John Armstrong, Jr. Proved Sept. 16, 1834. D-45

1834, March 29—JOHN DENN, Mannington. To son John, 4 tracts of land; dau. Elizabeth, 5 tracts; dau. Ann, 4 tracts; dau. Margaret, 4 tracts; dau. Rebecca, 4 tracts; granddaus. Rachel, Mary, Susan and Ann Denn, 4 tracts. Thomas Sinnickson and Jonathan Woodnutt, exec. and grdn. of minors. Wit. F. L Maccallock; E. B. Stoughton and Joseph E. Brown.

Mar. 29, 1834—Codicil. The devise to my granddaus. is voided, as I have sold said tracts and given the proceeds to said granddaus. Wit. F. L. Maccalloch, Isaac Acton and Joseph E. Brown. Proved Oct. 11, 1834. D-47

1827, April 21—JOHN ABBIT, Woolwich, Gloucester Co. To Abbit Atkinson, John, son of John Abbit, and sister Margaret, wife of Aaron Haines, each $50. To Mary, wife of Enos Sithens, $100. To Elizabeth, wife of Daniel Parvin, $50. To Elizabeth, wife of William Charlesworth, and Ruth Shaw. $25 each. To wife Hannah, remainder of estate. Exec. Abbit Atkinson and John Abbit, son of John Abbit, carpenter. Wit. Jacob Mayhew, Abraham Elwell and Eleazar Mayhew. Proved Nov. 5, 1834.
D-61

1833, Dec. 2—GEORGE GOULD, Upper Alloways Creek. To wife Sarah, all estate, and she is named as executor. Wit. John G. Mason, Samuel Ware and Stephen Counsellor. Proved Nov. 27, 1834. D-63

SALEM COUNTY WILLS

1834, Oct. 28—CATHARINE CARNEY, Upper Penns Neck, To son Joseph Katts,$3. To dau Eliza, wife of John Christian Shultz, all movables and real estate; after 10 years, real estate to be divided between daus. Catharine, wife of David Hillman, Martha, wife of Samuel Clark, Eliza. wife of John Christian Shultz, and granddau. Phebe, dau. of my son Peter and Amy Carney, granddau. Phebe to have the house known as the Peter Carney house. Exec. dau. Eliza Shultz. Wit. Neal Curry, Mary Summerill and William Vanneman. Proved Dec. 4, 1834. D-65

1832, May 30—SAMUEL TEEL, Lower Alloways Creek. To wife Isabella, $30 and choice of my houses, except the one I now live in, during life; then to dau. Ruth Mugway. To dau. Elizabeth, wife of Horatio Nail, house and lot; if she dies without issue, then to my dau. Ruth. To grandson Samuel Counsellor, $50 at 21 years of age, and $50 two years later. To grandson James Counsellor, the ground where Rhoda Counsellor's house stands, after death, and $50 when he is 21 years of age. To granddaus. Elizabeth, wife of Joseph Williams, $20. To dau. Ruth. wife of Owen Mugway the house I live in, and remainder of estate, after paying legacies. Exec. son-in-law Owen Mugway. Wit. Morris Hall, Joseph Black and John Hall. Proved Jan. 7, 1835. D-66

Not Dated—RUTH CLEMENT, Salem. Apparel to step-sisters Mary and Elizabeth Clement. Family Bible to neice Elizabeth Clement. Executor to sell house and ground in Salem, where I live. To children of bro. Samuel Clement, dec'd, a small lot of land. 1/2 of proceeds of sale of house to children of bro. Joseph Clement. Remainder of estate to children of Bro Samuel. Exec. Jonathan Freedland and John G. Mason. Wit. Caroline E. Perry, Benjamin Archer and Fenwick Archer. Proved Feb. 3, 1835.
D-68

1835, Mar. 5—JAMES WALKER, Lower Penns Neck. To son Michael, $25, gill net and batteau. To dau. Mary Walker, $25; son Joseph, $75; and son Edward, $50. Residue of estate to wife Mary, dau. Margaret Walker, son Charles Pitman Walker, dau. Rebecca Walker, and son James Walker. Exec. Samuel Dunn. Wit. Neh. Garrison and William Royall. Proved Mar. 18, 1836. D-70

1835, Mar. 30—GEORGE K. PATRICK, Elsinborough. To wife Anna, all estate. Exec. William Darmon. Wit. Elkanah Powell, Jeremiah Russell and Andrew Shields. Proved April 13, 1835. D-71

1835, Mar. 5—EBENEZER FOGG. To dau. Eliza Penton, horse, wagon and harness. To mother Hannah Fogg 6 acres adjoining Jeremiah Powell, during life; then to granddau. Eliza F. Brown. To grandson Ebenezer Brown, house and lot. To grandson Zacheus Brown, land at Logtown. Land adjoining Owen Mugway to grandchildren Eliza. Ebenezer and Zacheas Brown. Remainder of estate to said grandchildren and Rachel Penton. Exec. and gardn. of grandchildren, William Morrison. Wit. Mark Stewart, Dalymore Harris and Benjamin Peterson. Proved Apr. 23, 1835. D-73

1835, Mar. 4—SAMUEL ABBOTT, Mannington. To wife Martha, $1600 and the plantation where I live, and land opposite David Fogg's stone house in Mannington and meadow in Elsinborough Halfway Creek Bank Co., until son Samuel is 21 years of age. To son William G., the farm in Lower Alloways Creek and woodland near head of Gibbs' saw mill pond. Exec. William F. Miller and Caspar Wistar to invest $2700, the interest to be paid to dau. Hannah Allen. To son Samuel the farm where I live, 30 acres opposite David Foggs stone house, woodland in Upper Alloways Creek and meadow in Halfway Creek Bank Co. To son George, a farm in Elsinborough devised to me by my father, William Abbott, except 22 acres devised to my son Samuel, and 40 acres devised to my granddau. Hannah Ann Thompson. To daus. Mary Ann, Lydia and Martha Abbott, $300 each, and residue of estate. William F. Miller and Caspar Wistar grdns. of minor children. Wit. David Fogg, Job Tyler and Asher Buzby. Proved May 4, 1835. D-75

1832, Jan. 16—THOMAS TRUSS, Lower Penns Neck. All estate to wife Mary; at her death to sons Josiah, James and Samuel. Exec. wife Mary. Wit. Richard Sparks, Thomas Reeves and Isaac Snitcher. Proved May 15, 1835. D-79

1835, Jan. 4—BENJAMIN HUGHS, JR, Pittsgrove. To bro. John Hughs, bushland in Pittsgrove and 1/2 of undivided tract bot by John Kandle and myself, and land devised to me by my father John Hughs, and right to undivided share of my bro. Henry Hughs dec'd; also all movable estate. To sisters Rachel and Mary, $10 each; Margaret, $20; and Christiana, $15. Exec. bro. John Hughs. Wit. William VanMeter, Isaac H. Adcock and Andrew Whitaker. Proved July 2, 1835. D-80

1835, Jan. 25—DAVID FOGG. To wife Henrietta, all estate during life; then to bro. Edward Fogg and Eliza, dau. of Zacheus Brown. Exec. wife Henrietta. Wit. Edward Waddington, Jeremiah Powell and Joseph Thompson. Certified July 9, 1835.

An attempt to void the will was made. Testimony relating thereto occupies the following 23 pages. D-83

1830—SAMUEL THOMPSON, Pittsgrove To wife, land bot. of David N. Austin, and all personal estate. To oldest dau. Mary Parvin; $250; dau. Phebe, $300; daus. Elizabeth Shomaker and Harriet Wright, $300 each. To son Newcomb, a note I hold against him. To granddau. Ruth Foster, $50 at 18 years of age, and a note which I hold against her father. To grandchildren, the children of son Samuel, a note held against him. Exec. wife Elizabeth. Wit. Nicholas Olmstead, Isaac Mayhew, Jr., and Sarah Olmstead. Proved Aug. 13, 1835. D-105

1835, Oct. 11—ISAAC WATTSON, Pilesgrove. To wife Rebecca, furniture, 2 cows, a hog and 1/2 of rent of farm until my son is 21 years of age, and my right in house in Woodstown. To sons George and Charles, the farm where I live. To daus. Charlotte, Mary, Ann and Louisa, $500 each when 20 years of age. Exec. Joseph L. Risley. Wit. Thomas Edwares, Empson Haines and Nehemiah Richman. Proved Oct. 29, 1835. D-107

1835, May 23—JAMES W. MULFORD, Salem. To son Richard W., apparel and watch. Daus. Mary and Elizabeth, each a bureau, and if they marry during my wife's lifetime she shall give them as much toward housekeeping as we gave Elizabeth Mayhew when she was married. Remainder, of estate to wife Abigail R.; after her death or marriage, estate to be sold and receipts divided between above named children, except 1/7 part, which I give to my wife's dau. Elizabeth Mayhew. Son Richard W. Mulford and Edward W. Mayhew, executors of the first part of will. Exec. wife Abigail R. Mulford Wit. Solomon H. Nesmith, William Sherron and John P. McCune. Proved Nov. 14, 1835. D-110

1835, Sept. 12—SAMUEL SELBY, Salem. To ister Margaret, Conaroe, a lot on Penn Street, Salem, and $500. Sister Ellener Mecum, residue of estate, she to manumit black boy Lewis White and pay him $30 yearly for 5 years, and pay Rebecca Roberts $50, and the wardens of St. John's Church, Salem, $500. Exec. sister Ellener Mecum. Wit. Job C. Emley, Jacob Curry and Thomas Sinnickson. Proved Nov. 20, 1835. D-112

1835, Nov. 10—JESSE APLEN. To only bro. Joseph Aplen, all real estate that I inherited from my father. To sister Rebecca, wife of Thomas C. Price, $500. To Charles Aplin, son or my dec'd bro Peter. $5. Remainder of estate to sister Elizabeth, wife of John Biddle, and bro. Joseph. Exec. bro. Joseph Aplen. Wit. Thomas C. Holton, Mary Ann Holton and John Summerill, Jr. Proved Dec. 4, 1835. D-114

1835, May 12—JAMES VALENTINE, Lower Alloways Creek. To wife Anna, all estate during life; then to my children, John, Lewis, Samuel, Aaron, Anna, Silas and Asa. Exec. wife Anna. Wit. Dalymore Harris, Parmenas Harris and Lettis Harris. Proved Jan. 13, 1836. D-115

1835, Dec. 13—EDITH GROFF, (widow), Salem. To son

George Groff, bedding. Daus. apparel and bedding. Son William, movables. Personal estate to heirs of son Gzrret, namely, William and Garret, and heirs of son Richard. namely, Sarah Ann and Richard. Dau Sarah Murphy and sons George and Richad Groff, remainder of estate. Exec. son William. Wit. Sarah Hoffman and Thomas W. Cattell. Proved Jan. 19, 1836. D-117

1835, Sept. 16—JEDEDIAH ALLEN, Philadelphia (formerly of Salem Co.). All estate to wife Lettice, who is appointed executrix. Wit. David Whiteman and Samuel Webb. Recorded Jan. 30, 1836. D-119

1836, Jan. 8—ARTIS SEAGRAVE, Mannington. Bro. William Seagrave, exec. and grdn. of my children, namely, Sarah, Charles and Artis. Wit. William Slape, Lott Jaquett and Samuel Seagrave. Proved Mar. 7, 1836. D-122

1833, July 16—JAMES STEWART, Lower Alloways Creek. Estate to be sold and receipts divided among my children, Deborah Stewart, Beulah Bradway, Mary Denn and Samuel Stewart. Exec. Mark Bradway and William Denn. Wit. Edward Waddington, Benjamin Peterson and Richard Waddington. Proved Mar. 22, 1836. D-123

1830, Mar. 24—SARAH SCULL, Upper Penns Neck (relict of Gideon Scull). To daus. Abigail and Sarah Scull, all estate after debts and legacies are paid. To nephew Samuel Bolton, $300; Henry Wallace, $300; nephew Mark Scull, $300; neices Abigail L. Wayman, $200; Ann Scull, Judith Scull, and Sarah Scull James, $100 each To Mary Mattson annd James Stanton, $50 each. Exec. son Gideon and dau. Abigail. Wit Mary White and William White. Proved May 9, 1836. D-125

1830, Jan. 1—MARY SMART, Salem. To neice Mary, dau. of Isaac and Rebecca Smart, a lot and brick house in Salem, where I now live. If she dies without being fully possed thereof, to my nephews and neices, Isaac Smart, Jr., Deborah Brick, Ann Smart, Deborah Smart, Hannah Smart, Jr., William, Rebecca and Ruth Smart. After debts are paid, 1/3 of rents of said property to bro. Isaac Smart and sister Hannah Smart during life. Sister Hannah, looking glass, tablespoons, Bible, trunk marked H & M S, 1675. Neice Mary Smart 1/3 of rent and silverware. Neice Ann Smart, silverware. Neice Catharine Ailen, if she returns to her native place. Neice Deborah Smart, gold buttons given me by my sister, Deborah Smart, and spoons. Neices Hannah, Rebecca and Ruth Smart. spoons. Neices Deborah Brick and Rebecca Hubbs, each $25. Exec. John G. Mason and sister Hannah Smart. Wit. Mary Yorke, Thomas Sinnickson and William T. Mulford. Proved May 14, 1836. D-127

1835, Apr. 3—JACOB GOODEN, Upper Penns Neck. To housekeeper Kitturah Gooden (alias Kitturah Tomlin), residue of movables after debts are paid, and plantion in Upper Penns Neck (except the meadow), for life; after her death, the plantation to my nephew, Jacob Somers. To Lavinia Springer, 6 acres and to John Sharp 4 acres of said meadow. Dau. Catharine S., wife of Edward Pancoast. the plantation called the "Bevis Plantation." George Washington Bevis, woodland. Exec. Hudson A. Springer. Wit. Job Bevis, Richard Somers and Henry Katts. Proved May 30, 1836. D-129

1835, May 28—JOHN SMITH, Pittsgrove. To wife, the homestead during life, and 1/3 of movables; to be sold at her death and receipts divided among my children. Son Hugh D., land where he lives. Grandson Thomas T. Ackley, $20. Sons Hugh, John, Eleazar and Azariah, cedar swamp in Deptford, Gloucester Co. Dau Rachel, a cow. William Lake, money enough to make $50, including a legacy left him by John Dunham. Residue of estate to children, Susan Abbott, Hugh D. Smith, Phebe Ackley, John Smith, Elizabeth Hyers, Eleazar, Azariah and Rachel Smith. Exec. son Eliazar. Wit. John N. Swing, William Butler and Ambrose Whitaker. Proved June 14, 1836. D-131

SALEM COUNTY WILLS

1825, Jan. 22—CORNELIUS BURROUGHS, Pittsgrove. Estate to be bound for support of bro. Joseph Burroughs during life, should he survive me; then to Cornelius Burroughs, Jr., son of my bro. Benjamin. Exec. Cornelius Burroughs, Jr. Wit. Mathew Allen, Jacob Jones and Jacob Wick. Proved Aug. 4, 1836.   D-134

1836, Mar. 23—MARY W. HUNT (widow), Darby Township, Pa. To son John, his father's cane and a clock. Son William, riding chair, harness and a colt. Daus. Mary, Naomi and Hannah. apparel, furniture and $100 each. Lands to sons John and William. Dr. Morris C. Shallcross, grdn. of dau. Hannah. Exec. sons John and William. Wit. Joseph Dodgson, Jesse D. Bunting and Benjamin Pearson. Recorded Aug. 23, 1836.   D-136

1836, Aug. 16—RACHEL MULFORD. To dau. Sarah, bed. Dau. Rachel, high case of drawers. Son Ephraim, red chest. Son William, my watch. Dau. Elizabeth to be brought up by Rebecca Wood. Exec. Ephraim Sayre. Wit David Bowen, Richard DuBois and Jacob DuBois. Proved Sept. 12, 1836.   D-139

1834, Oct. 2—WILLIAM WHITE, Woodstown. To my wife Mary, furniture, a cow, a horse, derburn and harness, the house where I live, during life, all shop or store goods; after her death, to my children. Exec. sons Samuel and Joseph. Wit. Janathan Smith, William Pedrick and John L. Avise. Proved Nov. 4, 1836.   D-140

1836, Oct. 17—VALENTINE BALANGER (signed Valentine Ballenger), Pilesgrove. To son Valentine Balanger and dau. Mary Stretch, estate, with exceptions. Dau. Elizabeth Stretch, all my property that is in her possession, including a cow, and $20 to be paid her in 2 years. To granddaus. Gemima Pirnell and Elizabeth Ballenger, each $5. Grandson Joshua Ballenger to be kept at school until 14 years of age; then put to a trade. Exec. son Valentine Ballenger and dau. Elizabeth Stretch. Wit. Jacob Freas, Joshua Hewitt and John Armstrong. Proved Nov. 8, 1836.   D-143

SALEM COUNTY WILLS 27

1835, Jan. 5—**PAUL JAQUETT**, Pilesgrove. Tombstones to be placed at my grave and that of my deceased wife, Ann. To granddau Elizabeth, dau. of Kitts Jaquett, dec'd, bedding. Residue of personal estate to be sold: proceeds after debts are paid, as follows: To son John, $5; remainder and real estate in Penns Neck to sons and daus., Hance, Peter, and Samuel Jaquett. Jane Neison, Dorcas Amy and Drusilla Jaquett, and granddaus. Elizabeth and Jane Ann, daus. of Kitts Jaquett, dec,d. Exec sons Hance and Peter, and son-in-law Abraham Nelson. Wit. James Keen, John Kidd and Jacob Banks. Proved Dec. 9, 1836. D-145

1831, Sept. 13—**ANN MASON**, Christiana Hundred, Del. To daus. Anna and Mary, spoons. Son Lewis G., $5 and "Clarkson's Works" in 3 volumes. Son Charles C., my double cased watch and gun Son William, silver cased watch. So Delworth Buckman, $25. Remainder of estate to my children. Exec. Ziba Ferris and John Ferris, Wit. Eliza M. Ferris and Benjamin Ferris. Recorded Jan. 20, 1837. D-147

1835, Dec. 27—**SAMUEL DUNN**, Salem Co. To wife Sarah, the house which is about to be erected. Sons Ebenezer and Nehemiah, farm in Lower Penns Neck; they to pay my wife $25 yearly during her life. Sons John and Elijah the farm adjoining above; they to pay my wife $25 yearly. Son Thomas, land on Point Road. Sons Ebenezer and Nehemiah, marsh. Sons John and Elijah, marsh in Finns Point. Farm where I live to be sold. To daus. Eliza, wife of George Snitcher, and Rebecca Powers, $1200 each; daus. Sarah Bilderback, Mary and Ann Dunn, $600 each; son Thackara Dunn, $1000. Daus. Sarah, Mary and Ann shall pay Rebecca, wife of my bro. Elijah Dunn, $100. Remainder of personal estate to sons. Exec. John G. Mason and son Ebenezer Dunn. Wit. W. N. Jeffers, Grant Gibbons and Martin Patterson.

Codicil—Legacies to daus. Eliza and Rebecca shall be $1100 instead of $1200. Wit. William Royall, Grant Gibbon and N. W. Jeffers. Proved Feb. 17, 1837. D-150

1834, May 6—**JAMES JOHNSON**, Lower Penns Neck. To

John, part of farm and marsh on creek called Fishing or Baldridges Creek. Son Wililam, remainder of said farm; sons to pay $3000 incumbrance on the land. Son John, land in Lower Penns Neck bot of sheriff, cedar swamp in Cumberland Co., and 1/2 of cedar swamp in Cape May Co., near Dennis Creek. Son William, timber land near Morrice River, and cedar swamp and cripple in Downe township, Cumberland Co., and Remainder of cedar swamp in Cape May Co. Sons John and William, meadow in Wright's Creek Meadow Co., and all property purchased jointly with sons William and John. Son Alexander, $300. Daus. Rachel Hall, Sarah Lindsey, Ruth Gardner, Mary Dennis, Rebecca Mulford, Ann Mulford and Lydia Challis, and son Abraham Johnson, receive legacies. Exec. sons William and John. Wit. Joseph Kille, Henry H. Elwell and W. N. Jeffers. Proved July 20, 1837.

D-154

1833, Feb. 28—WILLIAM MILLER, Greenwich, Cumberland Co. To sons Lewis and George, apparel. Son George, meadow in Lower Alloways Creek. Wife Mary, residue of estate during life; then to son George and dau. Susan Miller. Exec. bro. Joseph Miller. Wit. Jane H. Bowen, John Miller and Mark Hall. Proved Mar. 11, 1837. D-161

1831, April 12—WILLIAM CARPENTER, Mannington. To wife Mary, $1000 and land bot. of Thomas Clark; sons William and Samuel Preston Carpenter to pay their mother $120 each, yearly. Son William, the farm where he lives, with meadow on Mannington Creek. Son John, after the death of my wife, 1/2 of a stone house in Salem, and 1/2 of the meadows and flats in Mannington, 1/2 of woodland in Upper Alloways Creek, and a note I hold against him. My wife has agreed that at her decease he shall have part of a tract conveyed to her by her sister, Rachel Redman. Son Samuel Preston Carpenter, the farm where I live and a lot bot. of Josiah Miller, he to pay his mother $120 yearly. Dau. Rachel R. Sheppard, $2300, to be held in trust for her; at her death, to her children. Exec. wife, bro. Thomas Clark and sons William and Samuel Preston Carpenter. Wit. Samuel Acton Casper Wistar and Samuel Reeve.

1831, May 31   Codicil—To son William, the silver pitcher which was presented to me as a premium for fattening an extraordinary fat steer. Son Samuel Preston Carpenter, 6 tablespoons marked WEC, made of silver heired from my father, Preston Carpenter. Wit. Caspar Wistar and Samuel Reeve.   Proved Feb. 6, 1837.
                                                                D-163

1829, May 29—SUSANNAH CALEHOPHER, Woodstown. To friend Anna Richman, $50; if she dies, to her son James Richman. Sister Margaret Felty, $50; if she dies, to my nephew Charles Calehopper, who is named as executor.   Wit. Joseph Davis and David Davis.   Proved Mar. 7, 1827.   D-167

1836, June 15—JOSEPH DAVIS, Woodstown.   Executor to sell movables that are not given to my wife and grandsons Joseph D. Folwell and Joseph Pancoast To wife Mary use of house where I live, buildings and lots in Woodstown, a horse, dearborn, harness and a cow. Dau. Martha Folwell, land in Pilesgrove, inherited from my father, David Davis, and woodland in Rutherford's Neck. Dau. Ann H. Pancoast, remainder of land inherited from my father; land bot, of heirs of Thomas and Rhoda Ashburn and bushland in Gloucester County. Samuel Headly, privilege of living in the house where he now lives. Joseph D. Folwell, my watch and shaving box. Grandson Joseph Pancoast, my clock. Wife, $200. Exec. sons-in-law William D. Folwell of Philadelphia and David C Pancoast. Wit. Joseph Winder, Joseph Barnes and George M. Coles.   Proved Mar. 20, 1837.   D-169

1837, Apr. 27—WILLIAM BORTON, Pilesgrove.   To Wife Elizabeth, furniture. Executor to sell personal estate and pay receipts to wife to pay debts. Real estate to be sold; receipts to be placed at interest for her benefit. To Esther Eldridge, who lives with us, $50. Elizabeth Owens, dau. of William Edwards, if living, $100. Abel, son of William Edwards, if living, $50. Nephew William, son of Richard Dorton $100. Nephew Aaron, son of Joel Borton, $100. Sister Hannah, wife of Samuel Moore, the interest from $300, yearly; and the principal when she becomes a widow. If she should not survive her husband, the $300 to be divided between her children. Bro-in-law Thomas Edwards, $100. Half of residue of estate to bro. Thomas Borton, now in Ohio; residue of estate to bro. Joel Borton's children. Exec. bro-in-law Thomas Edwards, Aaron Borton, and wife Elizabeth. Wit. Bevan Flitcraft, Ephraim S. Coles and Amos Peterson Proved Aug. 7, 1837. D-175

1837, July 11—JACOB CLARK, Upper Penns Neck. To wife Elizabeth, cow, a calf, 2 shoats, and furniture. Son Thomas, $5. Grandson Gideon, woodland bot. of my sister Ellenor; if he dies under age, to his bro. Eli. I give Jacob the privilege of building a house on said land. Sons Samuel and Gideon, remainder of estate. Exec. sons Samuel and Gideon. Wit. Jacob Diver, Charles Lanning and Job Bevis. Proved Aug. 19, 1837. D-177

HEZEKIAH WRIGHT, Upper Alloways Creek. John G Mason, exec. and grdn. of sons David and John is to spend $1000 on their education. Estate to said sons when of age. Wit. Oliver Smith, John Sack and Abner Smith. Proved Sept. 11, 1837. D-179

1837, Mar. 8—JOSEPH MOORE, Upper Penns Neck. Exec. to pay debts from sale of movables; surplus to youngest children, Joseph and Mary. Son Joseph, the family bible, to be in care of dau. Rachel. Dau. Mary Ann, silver spoons. Leonard Stanton, my bound boy, my coat. Son Samuel, my Sunday coat. Exec. to put stones at my grave and that of my wife. Exec. James S. Springer. Wit. John K. Louderback, Henry Katts and Job Bevis. Proved Sept. 28, 1837. D-181

1828, Jan. 9—DANIEL RICHMAN, Centerville. Exec. to sell estate. To wife Barcheba, $250, a cow and calf, and furniture. Son Isaac, $5. Dau. Sarah Miller, $5. Residue to sons John W. and David, and daus. Clarissa Smith, Hannah Tice and Eliza Shimp, and grandsons Andrew Jackson Richman and James Lawrence Wick. Exec. bro. Matthias Richman and my son John W. Wit. Jeremiah Stull, Daniel R. Ackley and John L. Clark.

1837, Feb. 6,—Codicil changes bequests to sons Isaac and Andrew Jackson Richman and Sarah Miller and her son, James Lawrence Wick, to equal shares, and appoint wife Bathsheba executrix, replacing bro. Matthias Richman. Wit. Thomas Whitaker, Absalom Newkirk and Mary D. Lake. Proved Oct. 31, 1837. D-184

1835, Feb. 13—REBECCA DAVIS, Pilesgrove. To sisters Esther and Sarah Davis, each $150. Sister Elizabeth Davis, house and lot near Woodstown, and large Bible. Ruth Cassaday, $75. Bro. Elisha Davis, $50, Sarah Grubb's Journal, and book of Wm. Penn's. Movabies to above named sisters. Exec. sisters Esther and Sarah. Wit. Bevan Flitcraft, Hope Haines and Elizabeth Haines. Proved Dec. 2, 1837. D-188

1837, Sept. 2—JANE T. SMITH (widow), Salem. To children Ann T. Garrison and Thomas 'T. Smith, bedding. Son Thomas, $1500. Granddau. Louisa Jane, dau. of George W. Garrison, $500. Son Thomas and dau. Ann, all real estate and residue of personal estate. Exec. son Thomas and son-in-law George W. Garrison. Wit. F. L. Macculloch, Richard M. Acton and Benjamin Archer. Proved Dec. 8, 1837. D-189

1829, Oct. 16, JONATHAN DUBOIS, Pittsgrove. To bro. David and sister Lydia DuBois, all movables. Nephew Jonathan, son of David DuBois, the farm where I live and cedar swamp on Elwells Branch. Exec. nephew Janathan DuBois. Wit. Ambrose Whitaker, Edmund DuBois and Eleanor DuBois. Proved Feb. 6, 1838. D-192

1837, Sept. 9—JOHN LANGLEY, Pittsgrove. To wife Hannah, 1/3 of land and cedar swamp, $500, best horses, 2 wagons, farm impliments, cattle and sheep, and the house I occupy. To wife's dau. Zipporia Jones, $100. Residue of estate to youngest children. Exec. Adam Kandle and son Richard Langley. Wit. Thomas Hill, Michael Potter and Nancy Ackley. Proved Mar. 22, 1838. D-193

SALEM COUNTY WILLS

1835, Jan. 25—SAMUEL GOSLING, Upper Alloways Creek. To dau. Ann Gosling, $10. Son Hiram, residue of estate. John Gosling exec., and grdn. of Ann and Hiram. Wit. William Bowen, John Stutly and William Harris. Proved April 14, 1838.
D-195

1838, Mar. 9—ANDREW CREEMER, Pittsgrove. To wife Mary, real and personal estate; at her death, to dau. Rodah and son Enos. Exec. Thomas Whitaker. Wit. John Clark, Samuel Parvin and Catharine Garrison. Proved April 16, 1838.   D-197

1836, June 25—WILLIAM HALL, Salem. To wife Ann G. furniture, services of colored girl Julian Accoo, profits of homestead in Mannington. Other real estate and woodland near Bushtown to be sold; proceeds to my children. Dau. Mary, wife of William Dickinson, is deceased. Exec. son Josiah Hall and George M. Ward. Wit. Isaac Smart, John G. Mason and James W. Mecum. Proved April 19, 1838.   D-199

1838, Feb. 26—WILCHER GOULD, Mannington. To wife Susannah, movables, and house and lot where I live; at her death, to son Joseph. Exec. Joseph Brown. Wit. Mathias M. Moore Clement Willis and Josiah Read. Proved May 4, 1838.   D-202

1838, Mar. 3—HANCE JAQUETT, Pilesgrove. To sister Dorcas Curry, house and lot on old farm near Sculltown. Real estate to be sold and after debts are paid, residue to dau. Julian Jaquett and Elizabeth, dau. of Kitts Jaquett. Exec. sister Dorcas Curry. Wit. Owen Guest, John Guest and Henry Guest. Proved May 15, 1838.   D-203

1838, May 23—HENRY KANDLE, Pilesgrove. To wife Katharine, her dower. Eldest son John, farm where he lives; he to pay my estate $175. Son Joseph, plantation where I live; he to pay my estate $200. Son Jacob, bush and woodland in Pittsgrove. Son Samuel H., woodland and cedar swamp on Green Branch, in

Pittsgrove. Daus. Lois Feller, Mary Ann. Sarah, Margaret and and Rebecca Kandle, $50 each. Residue to said daus. Exec. sons John and Joseph Kandle. Wit. John Langley, John Gamble and Ambrose Whitaker. Proved June 15, 1838. D-205

1837, Feb. 1—THOMAS BAKER, Pilesgrove. To wife Judah, all estate. She is oppointed exec. Wit. John Elkinton, Joseph Risley and Mark Williams. Proved June 6, 1838. D-207

1838, May 17—JOB WILLIAMS, Pilesgrove. Estate sufficient to pay debts to be sold; balance to wife Mary; after her death, to bro. Samuel Howell. Exec. Joseph Engle. Wit. John Nixon, John Ramsay and Thomas Cooper. Proved July 7, 1838. D-209

1826, May 12—ISAAC McCALLISTER, Pilesgrove. Movables to be sold, except as wife Mary shall chose to keep. Receipts of sale of farm, if title can be cleared, to children, Mary Vanneman, Rachel, Moses, Aaron and Benjamin McCallister. Exec. Thomas McCaliister. Wit. Reuben Robinson, Joseph Nichols and Benj. Nichols. Proved Sept. 3, 1838. D-210

1837, May 18—MARY SMITH, Salem. To nephew James Smith, meadow in Tilberry; Neice Maria Chamblis Ellet, part of brick house where I now live (it having a cellar under it) and 1/2 of my lot on Penn Street, in Salem. Nephew William Smith, 1/2 of said lot. Sarah Chamblis Wilson, dau. of my neice Beulah Wilson, dec'd, part of brick house and frame storehouse occupied by Thompson Tindall, and 1/2 of my woodland in Upper Alloways Creek. Neice Attila Smith, $500; if she should not survive me, to my nephew William Smith. To Chambles, son of William Smith (my nephew on the side of my husband) of Philadelphia, a pair of salt cellars. Hannah Brown, late Smith, the 1/2 yearly rent of the storehouse lately occupied by her. Residue to neices Maria Chamblis Ellet and Sarah Chamblis Wilson. Exec. neice Maria Chamblis Wilson and nephew James Smith. Wit. Joseph Bassett, John G. Mason and Thompson W. Tindall. Proved Sept. 23, 1838.
D-212

1838, June 23—REBECCA RAY, Upper Alloways Creek. To grandson Henry Freas Jarman, son of George Jarman, the plantation where my son George Jarman lives, son George to occupy same during life. Dau. Elizabeth Bright, all movables. Granddau. Elizabeth Jarman, a looking glass. Granddau Sarah Jane Jarman, a watch. Granddau. Hannah Brookfield, all my property in her possession. Exec. son George Jarman. Wit. Henry Fries, George Vanlier and James D. Evans. Proved Oct. 22, 1838.

D-214

1838, Jan. 5—THOMAS DUKEMINEER, Upper Penns Neck. To friend George Barnet, the farm where we live and all property whatsoever. Exec. George Barnet. Wit. Daniel Vanneman, Sarah Hogate and Thomas Whitesall. Proved Jan. 24, 1839.

D-217

1838, Oct. 31—LYDIA FOGG, (widow of Holme Fogg, late of Upper Alloways Creek) of Mannington. To Joseph Robinson with whom I dwell, all right to plantation in Upper Alloways Creek. Exec. Joseph Robinson. Wit. William Shimp, William Lawrence and John Armstrong. Proved Feb. 23, 1839. D-219

1839, Feb. 16—OBADIAH ROBBINS, Pilesgrove. To wife Mary, $500. To wife, Mary and Thomas Robbins, Abigail, wife of David Henley, and Elizabeth, wife of Nathaniel Warner, residue of personal estate. Exec. father-in-law Samuel Humphreys and Thomas Yarrow. Wit. John Smith and Jacob Hunt. Proved Feb. 26, 1839.

D-220

1832, May 5—ROBERT H. VANMETER. To wife Sarah, all my goods and chattels while my widow; then to daus. Emma and Harriet, the house and lot where I live, in Salem. Son Mason, residue of estate. Exec. son Mason. Wit. Henry H. Elwell, John Lawson and W. N. Jeffers. Proved March 25, 1839.

D-222

SALEM COUNTY WILLS 35

1838, Sept. 21—RACHEL VANMETER, Pittsgrove. To heirs of David VanMeter, dec'd., $3. Bros. Joseph and Isaac VanMeter, and sisters Catharine Jarnell and Elizor Thomas, $3 each. Sister Sarah Hunter, $50. Mary, dau. of Abraham and Phebe VanMeter, bedding, carpets and Bible. Abraham VanMeter, land owned jointly with David and Abraham VanMeter. Exec. Thomas Whitaker. Wit. Jacob Hitchner, Matthias Hitchner and Deborah Whitaker. Proved April 2, 1839. D-223

1796, Jan. 4—SAMUEL NELSON, Pittsgrove. To wife Elizabeth, live stock, farming implements, and grain in the ground at the tavern place. Dau. Mary Nelson, land adjoining Samuel Elwell, meadow and woodland. Sons Joseph and John, the place where I formerly lived. Son John land adjoining Judah Foster and land adjoining Joseph VanMeter. Sons Joseph and John, woodland and meadow. Exec. to sell Tavern Place and divide the receipts between my wife and children, Mary, Joseph and John. Exec, wife Mary and Benjamin Champneys. Wit Benjamin Robinson. Rebecca Hughs and Jedediah DuBois. Proved April 10, 1839, by Rebecca Hutchinson, late Rebecca Hughes. D-225

1835, June 5—SARAH ROBBINS, Lower Penns Neck. To sons Obadiah, $170; Thomas, $130; and George, $300. Grandson Alfred Robbins, $20 at 21 years of age. Granddau. Sarah Ann Robbins, bedding and bureau. Granddau. Nancy Robbins, $20 at 18 years Daus. Abigail, wife of David Hurley, and Elizabeth, wife of Nathaniel Warner, each $100. Exec. son George Robbins. Wit. Thomas Yarrow and Jeffery C. Weatherby. Proved May 1, 1839. D-227

1839, Feb. 10—WILLIAM COOK, Pittsgrove. To wife Eliza, furniture, carpet, bedding, spoons. Remainder of estate to dau. Mary. Nephew Joseph Cook, gun and equipment, and land and buildings where my mother and sister Mary live. To sister Mary a bond of $500. Exec. wife and friend Isaac Johnson, 2nd. Isaac Johnson, 2nd, grdn. of dau. Mary. Wit. Jacob Hitchner, Robert Mead and Joseph C. Nelson. Proved May 10, 1839. D-229

1839, April 29—JOSEPH H. WOOD, Mannington. To wife Hannah, 1/3 of all property after debts are paid; residue of estate to children. Exec. wife Hannah. Wit. Henry Wood and John M. Brown. Proved May 25, 1839. D-231

1838, Jan. 5—CONRAD WHITSEL, Upper Penns Neck. Movables to be sold and farm rented. To wife, the farm during life; then to children, Jamima, Jacob, Joseph, Benjamin, Conrad, Matilda, Mary Garrett, David and Thomas. Exec. wife Elizabeth. Wit. Neal Curry, Jacob Clark, Jr., and Daniel Vanneman. Proved Aug. 3, 1839. D-232

1837, Feb. 27—WILLIAM YOUNG, Upper Alloways Creek. To wife Louvisa, 1/3 of personal estate after debts are paid. except my cider works, distillery, casks and fixtures. Martha Jane Young, $1. Neice Elizabeth, dau. of James H. Young, $50 at 21 years of age. Residue to nephew William, son of James H. Young, when 20 years of age. Exec. Stacy Lioyd. Wit. John Sack, Oliver Smith and Gervas Simms. Proved Sept. 2, 1839. D-234

1834, Apr. 28—APACARIUS POWNER, Salem. To grandson Asher Michell $100. Granddaus. Adaline, Mary and Eliza Jane Flemings, each $20. Daus. Mary Michell and Elizabeth Flemings, residue of estate. Exec. John G. Mason. Wit. Thomas D. Bradway and Enos S. Reed. Proved Sept. 5, 1839. D-236

1839, Aug. 6—ASA KIRBY, Upper Penns Neck. Estate, after payment of debts, to wife Maria and daus. Hannah, Priscilla and Elizabeth. Richard Somers grdn. of daus. Exec. Richard Somers and Empson Hains. Wit. William F. Hewitt, John Dickinson and John Dennis. Proved Sept. 16, 1839. D-237

JONATHAN BILDERBACK, Mannington. To daus. Lucy Ann Acton, Mary Jane Acton and Sarah Engle, $1400. Dau. Martha Bilderback, $1500. Sons Alpheus, Joseph and Edward, residue of estate; Alpheus to pay his brothers $100. Exec. sons

Alpheus and Joseph. Wit. Joseph E. Brown, Lott Jaquett and Charles Slape. Proved Sept. 21, 1839. D-239

1835, Aug. 3—ELIZABETH TUFT, Salem. To William and Thompson, sons of my dau. Sarah Tuft, dec'd, each $500. Nehemiah and Ephraim, sons of Nehemiah Garrison, each $50. Residue of estate to Mary G., wife of William K. Seagrave, and Eliza S. Tuft, daus of my dau. Sarah. Exec. William Tuft and William K. Seagrave. Wit. Daniel Garrison and Daniel I. Garrison. Proved Sept. 9, 1839. D-241

1839, Aug. 21—SARAH HALL, Salem. To sister Ann, the lot on which her house is situated and 12 shares of Hazelton stock during life; then to her children; Samuel U., Isaac K. and Sarah Ann Thompson. Nephew Clement H. Thompson, $500. To each of sister Ann's children, $25. Sister Margaret M. Holme, $1000. Children of bro. Morris Hall, dec'd, Margaret W. and James W. Hall. $100. Hannah A. Hall, Salem Bank stock. Rebecca K. Hall, 20 shares Hazleton stock. Sister Prudence Hall, right to house where we now live, and my share of furniture. Sister Deborah K. Ingham, 10 shares Beaver Meadow coal stock and 10 shares Hazelton coal stock. Sister Rebecca K. Sinnickson, a lot in Elsinboro. Nephews John Howard Sinnickson and Clement H. Sinnickson, each $100. Exec. bro.-in-law John Sinnickson and nephew Benjamin S Holme. Wit. Joseph Bassett, John Hall and George M. Ward. Proved Sept. 25, 1839. D-243

1838, Dec. 22—JOHN G. MASON. To Caspar Wistar and Samuel Allen, in trust for an institution near Philadelphia, known by the name of the "contributors of the Assylum for the Relief of Persons Deprived of their Reason," $500. To my executors, $300 in trust to be paid to the trustees of the association for care of colored orphans, called the "Shelter," in Philadelphia. So sister Mary Ware, land, dwelling and store in Salem, and $2500. Bro. William Thompson, salt marsh and woodland in Elsinborough, the house and lot adjoining, and $1500. Neices Susan Pancoast, $800; Ann Fogg a house and lot in Elsinborough, and $500; Hannah

Acton, $500; Ann C. Brown, $500. Nephews Israel E. Brown, a house and lot in Griffith Street, where he now lives, and bushland in Upper Alloways Creek; John W. Brown, house and lot in Salem, land bot. of Henry Brown and a house bot. of William Henry. Step-sister Elizabeth Nicholson, $300; to her dau. Sarah Ann, $100. Cousin Prudence Conrow, $200; to her daus. Mary, Ann, Emily and Sarah Ann, each $100. Rachel, Mary and Sarah Denn, each $100. Mary Paullin of Greenwich $100 in memory of her kindness to my mother. Nephews Job Ware, $100; William G. Beesley, my iron safe. Step-sister Elizabeth Nicholson, cousin Abby Goodwin and Rhoda Denn, each $150, to be applied to the relief of poor people. Sister Mary Ware, $100, in trust for the "Female Benevolent Society of Salem." Residue of estate to sister Mary Ware, bro. William Thompson, neices and nephews Susan Pancoast, Sarah Shourds, Ann Fogg, Ann C. Brown, Israel E. and John W. Brown and Benjamin Beesley. Exec. friend Caspar Wistar, bro. William Thompson and nephew William G. Beesley. Wit. David Bassett, John Powell and Israel B. Smith. Proved Oct. 19, 1839. D-245

1838, Mar. 15—MATTHIAS RICHMAN, Pittsgrove. To wife Hannah, live stock, covered wagon, harness, furniture, $1000 and 2 acres of land. Estate to be sold; proceeds to children, Lidea Ovenbaker, Sophia Ovenbaker, Hannah Kandle, Miranda Ogden and McKendric Richman. Grandson Matthias Richman Ovenbaker, $25. Granddau. Martha Kandle Ford, $25. Exec. son-in-law Michael Ovenbaker and son McKendric Richman. Wit Samuel F. Atkinson, Hannah Atkinson and Isaac Langley. Proved Oct. 23, 1839. D-248

1839, June 5—PETER COX, Lower Alloways Creek. To wife and son Edmund, $40 in trust toward the schooling of the youngest children, Rebecca, David and Ann. To wife Rachel, the residue of estate during widowhood. Exec. wife and son Edmund. Wit. William Kaats and Ellis Ayres. Proved Oct. 29, 1839. D-251

SALEM COUNTY WILLS 39

1839, Sept. 10—ISAAC MILLS, Lower Alloways Creek. To grandson David Mills, land near Canton. Granddau. Mary Mills land adjoining schoolhouse lot, and a wood lot. Son Joseph, apparel. Remainder of estate to my children, Maria, wife of Joseph Baker; Sarah, Rebecca, Andrew and Richard Mills. Exec. and grdn. of minor children, Edward Waddington and Richard Waddington. Proved Oct. 2, 1839. D-252

1839, Nov. 20—RICHARD I. HUGHS, Pittsgrove. To wife Permelia, land bot. of Matthias Hitchner, during widowhood; then to son Oliver. Son Oliver, land bot. of William Coombs. Sons Ira, Hiram and Elam, land. Daus. Almira and Harriet, each $15. Daus. Ann Maria and Eliza each $15 at 21 years of age. Exec. wife Permelia and son Oliver. Wit. George W. Carpenter, John Hanthorn and Joseph Jones. Proved Nov. 9, 1839. D-255

1838, Apr. 18 — MORRIS HALL, Elsinborough. To dau. Sarah, wife of Joseph Bassett, Jr., of Mannington, part of farm in Elsinborough. To son John, remainder of said farm and woodland and marsh: he to pay $1720 to my son David and $2520 to heirs of my son Clement, dec'd. To son Lewis M., $2220 in one year and $1300 heretofore advanced to him. To children of son Clement, dec'd, namely, Mary, Thomas, Emely, Clement, Lydia, Margaretta, Morris and John, $2520 at 21 years of age. The proportionate part due to Mary wife of William Fogg to remain in the hands of son John Hall while she remains the wife of William Fogg. Son John, furniture. Land not disposed of to be sold. Exec. son John. Wit. Joseph Black, Joseph H. Thompson and Joseph E. Brown.

1839, Apr. 14—Codicil Son-in-law Joseph Bassett, Jr., is made co-executor and trustee with son John. Wit. Joseph E. Brown, Joseph Sap and Elizabeth Herson. Proved Nov. 20, 1839.

D-257

1839, Sept. 27, DAVID BACON, Woodstown. Estate to be sold. Sister Rachel Sheppard, bro. Charles Bacon and nephew Moses Sheppard, each $400. Cousin Thomas Bacon, $2000, provided he will pay his father, John Bacon, $120 annually during life.

Cousins John Bacon of Woodstown, $1000; Hannah wife of Samuel Pine, $500; Mark son of Joseph Harmer, dec'd, $1500; Elwood and Richard sons of Joseph Harmer, dec'd, each $500; to daus. of Joseph Harmer, dec'd, Sarah, $500, and Letitia, $300; Mary widow of William White, $300; to four daus. of Martha Pine, dec'd, $200; Charles and John sons of Eleanor Haines dec'd, each $200. Pilesgrove Monthly Meeting, $600. Remainder of estate, after debts and legacies are paid, for the purpose of erecting a building for a school. Exec. Thomas Edwards and Bevan Flitcraft. Wit. William Pedrick, Albertus Somers and Edward R. Bullock. Proved Nov. 25, 1839. D-261

1840, Feb. 6--WLILIAM SEAGRAVE, Mannington. To dau. Rebecca wife of William Lawrence, the woodland on upper part of farm. Son William K. Seagrave remainder of farm, and meadow on Kates Creek: he to pay my dau. Rebecca, $1600. Exec. son William. Wit. Job Wright, Mark Armstrong and John Armstrong. Proved Apr. 4, 1840. D-263

1840, April 3—ANDREW LAWRENCE. To sons Samuel and Gideon, meadow in Boattown Co. Wife, residue of personal estate after debts are paid, and the farm during life; then farm to be sold and receipts divided between my children, Franklin, Andrew Jackson, William, Mary Ann, John, Mary Jane, Richard, Louisa and James. Exec. wife Rebecca. Wit. John Boqua, GabrielDolbow and William C. Mulford. Proved April 17, 1840.
D-265

1840, Feb. 27—JOHN CASPERSON, Lower Penns Neck. To son Samuel, $1. Grandson John P. H. Curriden, $30 at 21 years of age. Sons William and John E., and daus. Catharine and Margaret, residue of estate. Exec. son William. Wit. Benjamin Lloyd, David Fogg and John Peterson. Proved April 17, 1840. D-267

1840, May 15—ISAAC STEELMAN, Lower Penns Neck. To wife, grain and articles she brought at marriage. Dau. Sarah,

Steelman, furniture and $100. Dau. Abigail Steelman, bedding silverware and $85. Son John, a mare and $200. Son Isaac, my watch. Residue to be sold and receipts to sons Isaac, Jonathan and Mark. William A. Dick grdn. of said sons, and exec. Wit. Henry Webber and Ebenezer B. Lott. Proved May 26, 1840.
D-269

1840, June 5—ISRAEL LOCK. To wife Allice, $300 and furniture. Dau. Allice Morgan, $1. Residue to daus. Susannah Peterson, Elizabeth Smith and Martha Bassett, son Samuel and grandchildren Ephraim Barnes and Mary Weatherby, children of my dau. Hannah Barnes, dec'd. Exec. son-in-law Amos Peterson, Wit. Moses Richman, Jr., and Israel Conover, Proved July 27, 1840. D-270

1839, Oct. 26—ANN HALL. To neices Ann, Margaret S. and Susan Darragh, and Eliza Janvier, bedding, silverware and apparel. Granddau. Hetty H. Miller, bedding and furniture. Grandson S. L. I. Miller, my silver watch. Residue of estate to neices and my granddau. Hettie. Exec. William G. Beesley. Wit. Richard M. Acton and Joseph H. Thompson. Proved Aug 29, 1840. D-272

1840, July 15—ENOCH SHEPPARD. To wife Mary, farming implements, stock and furniture. Son John H. (under age), land opposite the house, meadow called "Madison Meadow," and bushland. Dau. Phebe, the Branch Field and bushland. Dau. Elizabeth, the field east of the house. Acting exec. Mary Sheppard. Wit. Joseph Elwell, Johnson Harris and John W. Maskell. Proved Sept. 19, 1840. D-274

1837, Dec. 19—PETER BILDERBACK. To daus. Ann Ridgway and Sarah Bilderback, the plantation called "Kidd Place," the house, storehouse and land in Sharptown. To my exec. the fsrm in Pilesgrove, in trust for said daus. Farm called "Fogg's Landing Place" to be sold. To wife Jane, late Jane Wilson, $500 and $100 yearly during widowhood, and furniture and provisions. Land at Sharptown to Lydia, wife of Albert Layton. Exec. Stacy Lloyd. Wit. James B. Hunt, Samuel Plummer and Thomas Yarrow. Proved Oct. 15, 1840. D-276

1840, May 1—SARAH LINDSEY, Salem. To dau. Mary, house on Griffith Street, apparel and furniture. Son John, $1000. Grandson James, son of John, $400. Granddau. Sarah, dau. of John, bedding and furniture. Exec. son John Lindsey. Wit. F. L. Macculloch, William Sherron and Samuel Prior, Jr. Proved Nov. 16, 1840. D-280

1840, July 11—ABRAHAM HARRIS, Upper Alloways Creek. To grandchildren, Ellis Simkins, Hannah wife of Edmund Griffing, and Margaret wife of Samuel Rain, $5 each. Sons Dalymore and Samuel, remainder of estate. Exec. said sons. Wit. Mark Bradway, Josiah Thompson and David L. Finley. Proved Nov. 11, 1840. D-282

1840, May 8—CLAYTON WISTAR, Mannington. To wife Martha, use of farm until son Richard is 21 years of age; also remainder of personal estate after debts are paid, and an annuity of $150. If Richard dies under age, to my son John, who shall pay her $3000, and annuity shall cease. Son John, house on west side of Market Street, Salem, marsh in Wyatt Marsh Co., and $3000, and $600 to be paid him by his brother Richard. Son Richard, at 21 years of age, the farm where I live, with woodland in Bushtown; also, I give him my watch, and wish him to give the one which he carries to his brother Josiah. Whereas, Catharine Wistar of Philadelphia bequeathed to Richard bank stock, dividends of which have been received by me, I wish him to receive all that shall remain unpaid. If he should not live to inherit, I devise the same to son John, subject to payment of $3000 noted to be paid by Richard. Son Josiah, bushland in Upper Alloways Creek, and an undivided right to cedar swamp on Morris River. Exec. wife Martha. Wit. Richard W. Sheppard, Israel B. Smith and Joseph E. Brown. Proved Nov. 19, 1840. D-284

THOMAS DUNN, Duck Creek Hundred, Kent Co., Del Farm in Duck Creek to be sold. Sons Ebenezer and Jedediah, each $700; son John, $200 and land in Penns Neck. Daus. Hannah wife of John Ferris, $400; Susannah, $600; Elizabeth, $500, and Mary, $500 Wife Ellenor, $1000. Residue to my children. Exec. Michael Offley. Wit. M. W. Bates, Nathaniel Locuson and William F. Smith. Proved Oct. 12, 1840.   D-287

1839, Mar. 22—MARY COOK, Pittsgrove. To daus. Ann Richman and Mary Parker, $1500 each; granddau. Sarah Richman, $200; grandchildren Mary Louisa Cook and Joseph Cook, bushland in Gloucester Co.; sister Beulah Clayton, $300; nephew William Reve, $100; Nancy VanMeter, the girl that lives with me, $25. $1500 to be invested for benefit of grandchildren Mary Louisa and Joseph Cook; $1000 to be invested for benefit of granddau. Mary, dau. of son William Cook. Remainder of estate to said grandchildren. Exec. son-in-law Moses Richman and Charles Elwell. Wit. George Dickinson, Benjamin C. Sithens and Joseph L. Risley. Proved Jan. 7, 1841.   D-293

1841, Jan. 16—SARAH SMITH, Mannington. To son Isaac Smith, 1/2 of the plantation where I live, in tenure of son-in-law John Woodsides, and timber land. Dau. Sarah, wife of John Woodsides, remainder of farm, including the buildings. Exec. son Isaac. Wit. John Armstrong; Elizabeth Haines and Mary Armstrong. Proved Apr. 17, 1841.   D-296

1834, Oct. 5—SARAH NICHOLSON. To dau. Ann N. Ward and granddau. Rachel L. Nicholson, silverware. To widow of my deceased son William, son son Samuel. and daus. Sarah W. Peaslee and Ann N. Ward, each 1/5 of my furniture; and 1/5 to be invested for benefit of my son Daniel Nicholson. Exec. son-in-law George M. Ward. Wit. Joseph Bassett and William Peterson. Proved May 24, 1841.   D-298

1839, Nov. 2—MARGARET WICK, Pittsgrove. To sons Jacob and David Wick, grandson James L. Wick, and dau. Margaret Allen, each $3. To grandchildren, heirs of Elizabeth Johnson, and Margaret Allen, namely, James, William and Margaret Johnson, 1/2 half of residue, and remainder to John W. Allen, Margaret Likins (late Margaret Allen), and Hannah Allen. Exec. son David Wick. Wit. Thomas Whitaker, Daniel Shough and James Peterson. Proved June 8, 1841. D-301

1840, Dec. 28—SAMUEL SEERS, Pilesgrove. To my wife, furniture. Real estate to be sold and 1/3 of receipts invested for benefit of wife. Son William, $150. Remainder, after debts are paid, to my other children, Samuel, Martha, John and Sarah. Exec. Israel Seagrave. Wit. John C. Turner, Richard Stanton and Hannah Vanneman. Proved June 8, 1841. D-303

1841, June 18—JOSHUA SMITH, Salem. To wife Priscilla, support during life. Son James, store goods and debts due the firm, he being accountable for the debts of the firm. Salt marsh to be sold. All real estate to sons James and Joshua B. Smith. Exec. son James. Wit. Daniel Garrison, Quinton Gibbon and William Robinson. Proved June 17, 1841. D-304

1836, Aug. 22—GEORGE STANTON, Upper Penns Neck. To dau. Mary Ann, wife of Benjamin Hampton, bedding and $5. Sons Jacob, Josiah and David, apparel. Son-in-law John Dickinson, $10, and he is to be recompenced for supporting me in my declining years. Exec. to sell real estate; proceeds to my children: Martha Elwell, Ann Dickinson, Mary Ann Stanton, David and Josiah Stanton. Exec. son-in-law John Dickinson. Wit. Job Bevis, William Strimple and Joseph Cammack. Proved July 24, 1841. D-306

1841. June 14—WILLIAM NELSON, Pilesgrove. Movables to be sold. All title to several lots of land to son Jacob. Farm to be sold. Exec. Nephew Jacob Banks and friend Daniel Taylor. Wit. Samuel Bolton, Owen Guest and Susan Louderback. Proved July 31, 1841. D-308

SALEM COUNTY WILLS   45

1838, June 26—LYDIA PAULLING, Pittsgrove. To my children, Henry Ketcham, bedding and $20; Ruth Ketcham, and Caroilne S. Watson, $50 at 21 years of age; and Matilda Paulling at 21 years of age. Exec. Jeremiah Foster. Wit. Gilbert Craig and Elisha Waters. Proved Aug. 3, 1841.   D-309

1828, Sept. 7—SAMUEL TAYLOR, Mannington. To wife Catharine remainder of estate after debts are paid, during life (except son William to have $1); then to my children, Rebecca Bradway, Jonathan Taylor, Mary Fowser, Ann Fowser and Sarah McFarson; son Jonathan to have $100 more than the other children. Exec. Jonathan Taylor. Wit. James Newell, David Hannahs and Lydia Hannahs. Proved 1841.   D-311

1841, Aug. 18—JANE H. M'CALLA, Salem. To be buried in the Presbyterian graveyard at Greenwich, Cumberland Co., next to my husband, William H. M'Calla, and tombstone erected. To trustees of Greenwich Presbyterian Church $400 for the purpose of keeping in order the graveyard and fences. To friend Hagar Hollingshead, $60 yearly; $1000 to be invested during her life; then to my nephews William H., son of Robert P. M'Calla, and Auley M. To Adaline Mills, $50. To neices Margaret, dau. of Robert P. M'Calla, Elizabeth, dau. of Auley M'Calla and Sarah, dau. of Isaac English, furniture. To friend Mrs. Martha Miller, $50. To nephew Joseph M'Calla, $500. To bro. Robert P. M'Calla, my house and lot in Roadstown during his life; then to his dau. Margaret. Exec. Joseph Tatum and William Tatum, of Gloucester Co. Wit. Mary Fithian, Henry Dowdeny and Elias P. Seeley. Proved Sept. 13, 1841.   D-312

1825, Feb. 1—WILLIAM ROYAL, Lower Penns Neck. To wife Sarah, my two farms during life; then to Sarah, dau. of Samuel Dunn, the Cooper farm, and to Mary Ann Dunn, the Philpot farm. Lots at Finns Point marsh to be sold; receipts to Susannah, Mark, Peter and Hannah, children of my bro. Peter Royal, nephew John Robinson, and Ann Vanlewdener, each $100. Remainder of estate to my wife; after her death, to Sarah, Mary and Ann Dunn. Exec. Samuel Dunn. Wit. Samuel Gilman, Jacob Graham and Joseph Holliday. Proved 1841.   D-315

1841, Dec. 5—FRANKLIN MILLER, Mannington. To wife the house and lot in Salem during life; then to dau. Esther C. Miller. Exec. Jonathan Freedland. Wit. Benjamin Sheppard, Samuel Abbott and Joseph G. Mulford. Proved Oct. 30, 1841.
    D-316

1841, Oct. 24—SAMUEL LOCK, Pilesgrove. To wife Abigail, all estate. She is appointed exec. Wit. Moses Richman, Jr., Robert Hewitt and John P. Harris. Proved Nov. 11, 1841.
    D-318

1841, Nov. 16—THOMAS YARROW, Pilesgrove. To son Thomas J., and daus. Eliza B., Clara R., wife of William Sanford, Hannah S. and Sarah Ann Yarrow, my personal estate. Exec. Thomas J. Yarrow. Wit. John Perdue, John Cook and Joseph P. Armstrong. Proved Nov. 25, 1841.   D-319

Not Dated—WILLIAM REEVES. To wife Elizabeth, all my estate. She is appointed exec. Wit. Benjamin Lippincott, William Winner and Margaret M. Taylor. Proved Dec. 20, 1841.
    D-322

1841, Dec. 18—THOMAS McDONNOL, Salem. To wife Catharine, bedding. Son John, my share of the hearse wagon and partnership tools in the shop. Son Samuel, $1. Dau. Hannah Gill, $1. Remainder of estate to be sold; receipts to my children, John, Edward and Thomas Harrison McDonnol. Exec. James Patterson. Wit. Thomas Bacon, James Smith and George Mitchell. Proved Jan. 3, 1842.   D-323

1841, Mar. 26—JAMES GILL, Mannington. To wife Elizabeth, all estate during widowhood; she to support my children until youngest child is 14 years old. Exec. wife Elizabeth and David Ireland. Wit. Clement Acton, Smith Darmon and Robert Guistner. Proved Jan. 22, 1842. D-325

1841, Aug. 24—JAMES REED. To wife Crtharine, furniture. Dau. Mary, wife of Isaac S. Brooks, land where they live, during life of her husband, and as long as she remains his widow; then to her dau. Sarah. Isaac S. Brooks, $50. David Moore, $50. Great-grandchildren, heirs of Isaac S. Brooks, his dau. Sarah excepted, $400. Great-grandchildren, heirs of David R. Moore, $400. Residue of estate to be sold and receipts invested for benefit of my grandchildren and great-grandchildren. Exec. David Madison Bowen. Wit. Stacy Lloyd, Daniel U. Smith and Margaret Lloyd. Proved Mar. 15, 1842. D-327

1839—REBECCA DREW (widow), Salem. All real estate in Lower Penns Neck, and movable estate to dau. Rebecca, wife of Jeremiah Jones. Exec. dau. Rebecca Jones. Wit. Rachel Tindall, John Williams and William Mulford. Proved Feb. 28, 1842.
D-329

1837, Jan. 11—ELIZABETH W. SHEPPARD, Salem. $400 to be invested for benefit of dau. Mary Cooper Son John W. Challis, silver spoons and "Henry's Exposition of the Bible." Son James M. Challis, the family Bible. Rachel Cleaver, my dau. Mary W. Cooper, and dau.-in.law Ann Challis, apparel. Residue of estate to sons John and James Challis, who are appointed exec. Wit. Joshua T. Thompson, Jonathan Belton and James Freas. Proved Apr. 6, 1842. D-330

1841, Feb. 9—JOSEPH NICHOLSON, Lower Penns Neck. To daus. Mary H. Garton and Elizabeth Finley, $5 each. Remainder of estate to the children who have remained at home and taken care of me, Charles, Washington and Louisa Nicholson. Exec. sons Charles and Washington. Wit. William A. Dick and Thomas Rowan. Proved Apr. 7, 1842. D-332

1841, Jan. 1—AARON WADDINGTON, Elsinborough. To sons Joshua and Aaron Bradway Waddington, the farm on which I live, woodlots at Hagerstown and the gum swamp lot; if either dies under age, the survivor shall have the whole. Daus. Sarah Ann Hill, Lydia K. and Jane Waddington, $3000 each. Remainder of estate to said children. Exec. bro. Edward Waddington and my son Joshua. Wit. Joseph Black, Job Black and Robert Waddington. Proved Apr. 18, 1842. D-334

1836, Aug. 7—HUDSON SPRINGER, Upper Penns Neck. wife Christiana, 1/3 of real estate during life, and furniture. Dau. Kitturah, wife of Isaac Lawrence, land at east corner of homestead. Son Richard F., meadow in Woolwich. Son James, the homestead farm, he to pay all my debts. Exec. son James and Job Bevis. Wit. John P. Leap, John S. Baker and John Ridgway. Proved Apr. 27, 1842. D-335

1842, Apr. 1—MARY ROBINS, Pilesgrove. To sister Theodotia Bower $300, to be paid her out of land devised to my sister Ann Mattson. Bro. Nathaniel Robins, a note I hold against him, and a cow. Ann, dau. of bro. Nathaniel Robins, a cow. Neices Achsa Ann R. and Hannah R. Mattson, silverware. Residue of estate to sister Ann Mattson; at her death to her daus Achsa Ann and Hannah. Exec bro.-in-law Elias Mattson. Wit. Jacob Howey, Nathan M. Robins and Jacob C. Davis. Proved Apr. 20, 1842. D-338

1841, Sept. 25—WILLIAM WILLIAMS, Caroline Co., Md. To wife Sarah, $1800 and 1/3 of $500 loaned to James Rogers and William Cheesman of Medford, N. J., 1/3 of a note of $230 against William H. Woster of Burlington Co., 1/3 of judgment against Joshua Woolston of Burlington Co., of $540, 1/3 of 30 shares of Medford Bank stock, 1/3 of farm in Newcastle Co., Del., house and lot in Clarksboro, N. J., a horse, carriage and harness, and furniture. To daus. of my second wife, namely, Elizabeth Haines Williams and Fidelia Williams, each 1/3 of said loans, bank stock, farm house, and part of a house bot. of Jonathan Ogee. To

To daus. Mary Jain, eldest dau. of my first wife, and Sarah H. wife of Henry Bell, eldest dau. of my sscond wife, each property in Salem and Bordentown; they to pay Jain Horn $2 annualy during her life. To wife Sarah, remaining cash on hand at my decease; she to be grdn. of my small children, in conjunction with her bro. Charles Haines. Exec. Charles W. Roberts, Benjamin Davis and James Woolf. Wit Spencer Hitch, William Delahay and Charles H. Morris. Proved Oct. 13, 1841. D-340

1839, May 3—ANN FIRTH (widow), Salem. To daus. Hannah H. Reynolds and Elizabeth Firth, apparel. To dau. Elizabeth, furniture Dau. Hannah, silver cream cup. Residue of silverware to sons. To dau. Hannah, $1200; dau. Elizabeth, $1900; son Thomas, $500 and a promisory note against him for $500; son John, $900 and a note for $100 against him; son Samuel, $1000. Residue of estate to my children. Exec. Dr. Benjamin Archer and my bro.-in-law Thomas Firth. Wit. F. L. Macculloch, Charles Rumsey and Calvin Belden. Proved May 16, 1842. D-346

1838, June 11—CHARLES WINTZELL, Upper Alloways Creek. Exec. to erect stones at grave. $125 due Levi Wintzell to be paid. After debts are paid, 1 2 of remainder to dau. Catharine Fogg; residue to children of my dau. Mary Miller, viz.: Levi, Ann, Catharine and William. Exec. Ellis Ayres. Wit. Andrew Johnson, Henry Hitchner and Sarah Hitchner. Proved June 2, 1842 D-349

1840, Jan. 20—MARY DUNN. After debts are paid, residue of estate to mother Rhoda Dunn; at her death, to sisters Rachel and Susan Dunn and Ann Gibbons. Exec. sisters Rachel and Susan. Wit. Elijah Ware Beulah Ware and Elizabeth Stewart. Proved June 23, 1842. D-350

1842, June 23—WILLIAM G. BEESLEY, Salem. To wife Rachel, $1000 and profits of houses on Griffith Street. To sister Mary Carpenter and Benjamin Beesley, said houses at death of my wife. To sister Mary Carpenter and bro. Benjamin Beesley houses on Griffith and Penn Streets. To bro. Benjamin, land in Illinois, 1/2 of 66 shares of Salem Bank stock, 6 shares of Lehigh Coal, 7 shares of Hazleton Coal stock and 15 shares of Beaver Meadow Coal stock. To sister Mary Carpenter, 33 shares of Salem Bank stock, 8 shares of Hazelton, and 16 shares of Beaver Meadow Coal stock. To bro-in-law William Carpenter, my iron chest. Exec. wife Hannah Beesley and cousin John M. Brown. Wit. Joseph T. Stout, Thomas P. Haines and John M. Brown. Proved July 29, 1842.   D-352

1825, June 14—RACHEL McCALLISTER, Pilesgrove. Real estate, after debts are paid, to grandsons Janeway and Charles McCallister; also my house and lot in Sharptown. Exec. son Charles McCallister. Wit. Thomas Yarrow, Parvin Paullin and Benjamin Nichols. Proved Aug. 2, 1842.   D-353

1839, Feb. 5—JOSEPH PATTERSON, Upper Penns Neck. One half of movables to be sold and debts paid. To wife Mary all estate not sold, during widowhood; then to daus. Rebecca P. and Esther P. To dau. Mary Freed, $450. Son William P. (son by my present wife) the farm where I live. Daus. Rebecca and Esther land on road from Pedricktown to the Cove. Exec. wife Mary. Wit. Jacob C. Stanton, John Justice and Job Bevis. Proved Aug. 10, 1842.   D-355

1842, June 28—JOSIAH GARRISON, Upper Alloways Creek. To wife Charity, personal estate, furniture, a cow and hog. Remainder of estate to be sold and debts paid; residue to be invested for benefit of wife; at her death, exec. to give Harriet, dau. of Mary Ann Stanger, $40 when 18 years of age; residue of estate to Elizabeth, dau. of Eliza Garrison, now living with me. If Harriet and Elizabeth die before reaching 18 years of age, to the heirs of my brothers and sisters, except Jesse, son of my late bro. Thomas Garrison. Exec. Samuel Vanlier. Wit. Jno. H. Lambert, Joseph Camp and William Ferguson. Proved Aug. 20, 1842.   D-357

1840, Feb. 14—MARY ANDREWS, Salem. To dau. Clarissa,

Andrews, $900 and furniture. Exec. dau. Clarissa to invest $700 and, during the lifetime of William Shourds, pay the income to my dau. Martha, wife of said William. If she should not survive William, then to her daus. Rachel and Mary Shourds, $250 each, and her sons Benjamin and William C. Shourds, $100 each. To dau. Martha, silver spoons that were her great-grandmother's. Remainder of estate to dau. Clarissa. Wit. Mark Riley and James W. Mecum. Proved Aug. 30, 1842. D-359

1842, Apr. 13—JOHN HANCE, Maryland. Being on a visit to my friends in Salem, make my will in manner following: To dau. Rebecca Ann Hance, all real estate in Salem, providing she pays to Mary Ann Mulford's child, Millicent; $100 at 18 years of age. Sons Isaac, James and Edward and dau. Rebecca all real estate on condition that they pay some of it to my dau. Mary Ann Mulford, should she be in need. The farm in Maryland where I now live, to sons and dau. Rebecca on condition that they pay Rody Mulford's children, Margaret Millicent and John Edward, $100 between them. Exec. sons Isaac and James. Wit. James Bright, Lewis Green Rachel G. Nicholson and George M. Ward. Proved June 1, 1842. D-361

1841, Oct. 11—JEREMIAH POWELL, Lower Alloways Creek. Executor to retain all personal estate during life of wife Sarah, and pay her the interest; after her death, to grandchildren Beulah Ware and the children of my dau. Ann Griscom. Son John, during life, the plantation in Lower Alloways Creek, where I now live, which descended to me from my father, John Powell, marsh and woodland in said township, and a tract of barrens in Upper Alloways Creek; at his death, to grandson Jeremiah Powell; if he dies under age, to my grandson Samuel Powell. To son William during life, the plantation in Lower Alloways Creek, where he lives, marsh in said township and a tract of barrens; at his death, to his oldest heir. Dau. Elizabeth Thompson, during life, a house and lot in Lower Alloways Creek; at her death to be sold; proceeds to grandchildren, Beulah Ware and children of dau. Ann Griscom. Wife Sarah, house and lot in Lower Alloways Creek occupied by William Morrison, during life; then to dau. Ann Griscom; at her death to grandson Jeremiah Powell. Exec. sons John and Wilham. Wit. F. L. Macculloch, James Smashey and Richard Acton. Proved Sept. 21, 1842. D-364

1842, Sept. 1—JOSEPH APPLIN, Upper Penns Neck. To wife Emma, bedding, furniture and $50. Remaining personal estate to be sold; real estate to be rented and children educated. Exec. Thomas Flanagin. Wit. John B. Dennals, James Lloyd and Joseph C. Summerill. Proved Oct. 8, 1842. D-367

1842, Sept. 17—REBECCA HANCOCK, Upper Penns Neck. To sister Sarah Hancock, movables, and rights in the house and lot in Pedricktown, where we now live. She is appointed exec. Wit Job Bevis, R. C. Pedrick and Charles Pedrick. Proved Nov. 9 1842. D-369

1842, July 14—SARAH HANCOCK, Mannington. To son Chambless, and dau. Elizabeth Smith, each a damask table cloth. Daus. Caroline and Hannah M. Hancock, and sisters Mary Cooper and Elizabeth Thompson, silverware. Remainder of estate to my children. Exec. George M. Ward. Wit. John M. Brown and Hannah Franklin. Proved Dec. 19, 1842. D-380

1841, April—MARY TUFT (widow), Salem. Exec. to rent real estate in Cumberland Co.; rents to son Theophilus E. Beesley. Daus. Mary B. Dayton, Annie E. Tuft and Margaretta C. Cooper, apparel. Granddaus. Mary Beesley and Mary T. Dayton, each $100. Remainder of estate to my children, Theophilus E. Beesley, John B. Tuft, Mary B. Dayton, Anna E. Tuft and Margaretta C. Cooper. Exec. Caspar Wistar. Wit. Benjamin Archer, Rebecca A. Anderson and Rachel T. Archer. Proved Dec. 16, 1842.
D-372

1829, Feb. 4—MARY PIMM, Woolwich. Exec. to sell house in Woodstown and pay debts. To aunt Elizabeth, wife of Samuel Coles, $500; aunt Tracy, wife of Isaac Ridgway, $500; aunt Mary, wife of Thomas Moore, $50; cousin Elizabeth, wife of Peter String, $50; to cousin Elizabeth, wife of Samuel Harker, $100; Benjamin, son of Daniel Harker, $50; Elmer Coles, grandson of Samuel Coles, $50; cousin Samuel Coles Harker, son of Daniel Harker, $50; bro. Jonathan Pimm, residue of estate. Exec. Benjamin P. Lippincott and Thomas Edwards. Wit. William Borton, Samuel Moore and Mary L Somers. Proved Dec. 23, 1842.   D-374

1832, Jan. 4 –JAMES THOMPSON, Pittsgrove. To nephew Joseph Robinson, the farm where I now live; he paying my father, William Thompson. $40 during his life. Sister Elizabeth Robinson, $200, and each of my neices, Emaline and Caroline Robinson, $100. Land bot. of Thomas Ivins to be sold;, and after above legacies are paid, remainder to neices Mary Hinchman add Angelina Robinson and nephew William Robinson. Exec. nephew Joseph Robinson and Thomas Hinchman. Wit. Moses Richman, Jr., Phebe Richman and Hannah M. Wood. Proved Jan. 25, 1843.   D-376

1842, Aug. 30—JOSEPH C. STEWART, Upper Alloways Creek. To mother Sarah B. Stewart, a house and land in Burlington. Exec. father, Thomas G. Stewart. Wit John M. Brown, Ebenezer Dunn, Samuel C. Gilmore. Proved Jan. 28, 1843.   D-377

1836, July 11—SARAH NELSON, Lower Alloways Creek. To dau. Ann, wife of David English, furniture. Residue of estate to William H. Nelson in trust during coverture of my dau. Ann; at her death, to grandson Anthony N. English. Exec Willam H. Nelson. Wit. Dalymore Harris and George Grier. Proved Feb. 2, 1843.   D-379

1841, Oct. 23—SAMUEL GILMORE, Salem. To wife Sarah, furniture, $100, and $85 yearly from rent of farm in Lower Penns Neck. Dau. Ann Gaw and my son Alexander, my home farm in Lower Penns Neck, subject to the payment of $800 each to my grandchildren Elizabeth Finley and Elizabeth Lippincott at 21 years of age. To son Samuel Gilmore and dau. Elizabeth Cattell, farm and meadow in Lower Penns Neck, subject to payment

of $500 to grandson Samuel Lippincott at 21 years of age. Dau. Esther C. Gilmore, farm in Lower Penns Neck during life, then to grandsons Joseph Lippincott and Samuel and John Finley, subject to payment of $30. To grandson Joseph Lippincott, house and lot in Lower Penns Neck, on main Salem road. Dau. Esther $100. Residue of estate to sons Samuel and Alexander. Exec. son Samuel and son-in-law Alexander G. Cattell. Wit. Ebenezer Dunn, John C. Dunn and Michael Powers. Proved Feb. 1, 1843.
D-380

1843, Feb. 20—GEORGE KNOWLES, Salem. To wife Mahalah, personal estate and the property where I now live. To son Thomas Gibson, remaining real estate. Exec. Rev. Edward G. Prescott. Wit. Rebecca Kinsey, Mary Jane Moore and Eliza Handy. Proved Mar. 15, 1843. D-384

1840, Aug. 26—LYDIA HARRIS, Lower Alloways Creek. To sister Elizabeth Harris, all estate. She is appointed exec. Wit. Dalymore Harris and Nathaniel Stretch. Proved Mar. 30, 1843. D-385

1842, Sept. 15—WILLIAM SHIMP. To wife Ann, use of property during widowhood for support and education of my children. Sons Edmund and William, $50 at 22 years of age. Dau. Lydia has had $50, which shall be deducted from her share. Exec. Ann Shimp and Holmes Wright. William Woodnutt declared he was not present at the signing of the will, but on the 20th day of 3d month he heard the testator declare the said instrument to be his last will and testament. Proved Apr. 3, 1843.
D-387

Not Dated—HANNAH WHITE, Pilesgrove. To neice Hannah Clark White, dau. of Isaac White, $100, silverware and all movables. To Benjamin North a note of $32, on condition that he place grave stones for my mother and myself. Residue of estate to Hannah Clark White at 18 years of age. Exec. Stacy Layton.

Wit. Thomas Yarrow and Samuel H. White. Proved Apr. 8, 1843. D-388

1843, Apr. 2—MARY THOMPSON, Salem. To heirs of my late sister Ann Firth, buildings and improvements on lands of the said Ann. Neice Elizabeth C. Firth, gold watch, chain and seal. Neice Mary Thompson, silverware. Neice Rebecca Thompson, bedding. Nephew Joseph H. Thompson, furniture. Neices Han-Reynolds and Elizabeth C. Firth and nephews Thomas, John and Samuel Firth, each $100. Neices Rebecca Ann Anderson, Mary and Rebecca H. Thompson, and to Thompson Reynolds, $50 each. Remainder of estate to heirs of sister Ann Firth. Exec. George M. Ward. Wit. F. L. Macculloch, Joseph Bassett and Rebecca Ware. Proved Apr. 15, 1843. D-390

1842, Nov. 3—JOHN HALL. To Ann, dau. of William Hall, dec'd, $400. Bro.-in-law Thomas Edwards, nephew Samuel Hall and friend Alexander G. Cattell, remaining estate in trust for my son John. To heirs of sister Hannah Nicholson, who was wife of Samuel Nicholson, dec'd, and heirs of bro. William Hall dec'd, Samuel, Josiah, William, Horatio and Ann Hall, Achsah Peterson, Mary Dickinson (late Mary Hall), Mary B. and Elizabeth Nicholson and Ann Smith, children of John Nicholson, Samuel and Josiah Nicholson. Exec. Thomas Edwards and nephew Samuel Hall. Wit. F. L. Maccullough, Christian Brown and William Acton. Proved May 1, 1843. D-392

1843, Feb. 20—GEORGE KNOWLES, Salem. Re-entry of will D-384. D-400

1840, Apr. 6—JANE HALL, Salem. To neices Rebecca, widow of James Kinsey, $7300; Maria Emlen, $2000; and Rebecca, wife of William Strickland, and Mary, wife of Enoch Moore, each $1800. Margaret Smith, $300. Harriet H., wife of Johathan Ingham, $300. Elizabeth Jones, whom I brought up, $100. Neice Maria Blondeau, dau. of my bro. James Trenchard, $100 yearly during life. Ann Vallance, dau. of my bro. Curtis Trenchard, dec'd, $120 yearly during life. Frances, widow of my nephew William Thackara, $150 yearly for 5 years. Hannah, James, Frances, William H. and George T., children of William Thackara, dec'd, each $480. Remainder of estate to neice Rebecca Kinsey, who is appointed exec. Wit. Thomas Sinnickson, Edward Q. Keasbey and T. Jones Yorke. Proved Aug. 31, 1843 D-401

1842, Nov. 12—CLARISSA PARRETT BURROUGHS, Salem. To mother Clarissa Burroughs, all estate. She is appointed exec. Wit. Thomas Sinnickson, Matthew Keasbey and T. Jones Yorke.

1843, July 15—Codicil. As I survive my mother, all my estate is devised to my two relations, Thomas, Jr., and William Sinnickson, and they are appointed exec. Wit. James VanMeter, Thomas S. Smith and Thomas Sinnickson. Proved Oct. 6, 1843. D-405

1842, Apr. 27—EZEKIEL SIMPKINS. To son Alfred, the occupancy of the farm until next 25th of March after my death. Real estate to be sold; proceeds to sons Joseph, Samuel, Alfred, Zaruh Maris, wife of William Peterson, and children of Elizabeth, late wife of Philip Curden. Exec. son Alfred. Wit. Joseph Summerill, John Summerill, Jr., and John Summerill. Proved Oct. 12, 1843. D-407

1842, June 27—JOHN GOSLING, Upper Alloways Creek. To wife Sarah, furniture, 1/2 of residue of personal estate, and $40 yearly during life. Residue of personal estate, after debts are paid, to Hiram Gosling at 21 years of age. To Boston Gosling, who has children John Fenwick, Hannah and William, the farm where he now lives; at his death, to his son John F. To William, son of Boston Gosling, bushland. If Boston Gosling brings an account against my estate it shall be deducted from the residue of my personal estate which would fall to him, and given to my sister Martha Mower. Exec. Boston Gosling. Wit. John H. Lambert, Richard M. Stretch and Joseph K. Riley. Proved Oct. 30, 1843.
D-407

1840, Jan. 7—JACOB HOFFMAN, Pilesgrove. Son Jonathan and dau. Mary, wife of John Carter, proceeds of sale of personal estate after debts are paid. Real estate to dau. Mary; she to pay son Jonathan $400. Exec. son-in-law John Carter. Wit. Bevan Flitcraft, Edward Hanes and Aaron W. Wood. Proved Nov. 20, 1843. D-411

1843, Oct. 20—JOHN POWELL, Elsinborough. To son Jeremiah, part of the James Denn farm, in Lower Alloways Creek. Son Joseph, my right in a mortgage given me by my bro. William Powell. To wife, right to lease on John Craven farm in Elsinborough, to enable her to support and educate my children, Samuel, John, Elizabeth, Elias H., Anna and Rebecca Powell. Residue of estate at the end of 10 years from March 25, 1844, to my children, Sarah Griscomb, Samuel, John M., Elizabeth, Ann and Rebecca Powell. Exec. son Jeremiah and cousin William Carpenter. Wit. Edward Waddington, Thomas Fogg and James Friant. Proved Dec. 2, 1843. D-413

1843, July 1—CATHARINE READ, Salem. To neice Mary Kemp, apparel. Stepdau. Mary Ann Fogg, bedding. Stepdau. Pheoby Brooks family Bible and "Baptist Codfession of Faith." David Ewing, son of Margaret Lloyd, residue of personal estate. Exec. Stacy Lloyd. Wit. Valentine Ballenger and Mary S. Rudolph. Proved Dec. 16, 1843. D-417

1842, July 4—JOHN GILL, Woolwich. To son David, $200; son Joseph, $600; dau. Ann, $500. If there be any other articles about the house belonging to me, I order them to be divided between my daus. Hannah Borton and Sarah Ann Gill. Son-in-law William Borton a cow, a wagon, and all interest on an obligation I hold against him. Exec. Thomas Edwards. Wit. Samuel E. French and Aaron Edwards. Proved Dec. 23, 1843. D-418

1843, May 17—GERRARD SPARKS, Upper Penns Neck. To son Robert, the house in which he lives. Granddau. Elizabeth Biddle, $25. Granddau. Anna Margaret Tidmarsh, $50, in lieu of the articles I took of her mother's of Joseph Tidmarsh at her mother's death, and $100 to be invested; the interest to be paid her at 18 years of age, and the principal at 21 years. If she dies without issue, all money that has not been paid her is to be divided between Edith Pedrick and Catharine Hartnock. Grandson Gerrard, son of Thomas Peterson, $50 at 21 years of age; if he dies, to Ebenezer Pedrick. Real estate to be sold; receipts to my children, Elizabeth Peterson, Robert, Ebenezer and Edward Sparks, Edith Pedrick and Catharine Hartnock, and the children of my deceased son Samuel. Exec. and grdn. of Samuel's children, son-in-law George Peterson and son Ebenezer. Wit. John Dickinson, Sarah Bevis and Job Bevis. Proved Dec. 23, 1843. D-420

1842, July 18—STEPHEN REEVES, Upper Alloways Creek. To sons Enos P., Jacob P. and Josiah H. Reeves, my mill tract, tavern house and lot in Allowaystown, glasshouse tract and other land. Son William, land in Beesleys Neck the Stone House farm and bushland; in case of his death, to his bros. Charles and Stephen. To son Charles my farm bot. of Joseph Sheppard and land called String Land. To daus. Hannah Ann Barker, Sarah Ann Ballenger and Mary Jane Smith, my mill and mill tract bot. of Samuel Kean, called "Newkirk Property," my stock in the Salem Bank, my sloop "John A. Watson," and all money due me by Reeves & Bros. Dau. Hannah Ann Barker, woodland. Sons Enos P., Jacob P, Josiah H., William, Charles A. and Stephen, all personal estate and residue of real estate. To son-in-law James B. Barker; all debts due me. Enos P. Reeves, grdn. of Jacob, Josiah, William and Charles. Wife Sarah, grdn. of Stephen. Exec. son Stephen and son-in-law James Barker to erect stones at the graves of my father, mother and myself. Wit. B. R. Shimp, Samuel Shimp and Ellis Ayres. Proved Jan. 1, 1844. D-422

1843, Dec. 21—GEORGE FRIES, Allowaystown. To German Lutheran Church at Friesburg, $600. Neice Elizabeth Fries, $300. Margaret, dau. of James Reeves, $300. Residue of personal estate to sister Margaret Fries, and all undivided right of a tract of land given us by grandfather Jacob Fries; and my house and lot in Allowaystown where I now live, and other lots nearby; after her death to be sold and proceeds distributed as follaws: to neice Elizabeth Fries, $500; Margaret Reeves, 1/2 of residue. Daniel Fries, my farm bot. at sheriff's sale, he to pay legacies to John, son of Thomas Fries, $390; Margaret, dau. Thomas Fries, $200 when they are 21 years of age. Johnson Ray, bushland. Elizabeth Fries, land bot. of John Fries. Exec. cousin Henry J. Fries. Wit Ellis Ayres, David Nicel and David Bowen. Proved Feb. 2, 1844. D-426

1843, June 21—SARAH PETIT, Salem. To son Jonathan, my half eagles. Dau. Mary Hogbin, apparel and interest on a note against my grandson David Petit during widowhood; if she marries or dies, to my son Woodnutt Petit during life; at his death, to his children, Rachel Beesley, David, Joseph, Samuel C., Ann Roberts, James I. and Sarah B. Petit. Granddau. Rachel Beesley, silver cup and half-eagles. Grandson David Petit, my silver watch and musketo curtains Grandson Joseph Petit, "Sewell's History," and my down cover. Grandson Samuel C. Petit, the largest of my worked pocked books. Granddau. Ann Roberts, sugar tongs. James J. Petit, a chest. Granddau. Ruth J. Petit silver cushion band. Granddau. Sarah B. Petit, silver spoons. Son Woodnutt Petit, high drawers; at his death, to his son David. Remainder of estate to my son Woodnutt. Exec. grandson David Petit Wit. Ephraim Haines and William Barber. Proved Feb. 5, 1844. D-428

1841, May 22—JOHN BOQUA, Upper Penns Neck. To wife Martha, all estate; after her death, to grandson John Wesley Stiles, $200; residue to my children, Hannah, Ann, Margaret, Catharine and Hannah Ann Boqua. Exec. wife and Daniel Vanneman. Wit. William Summerill, Jr., Hannah Ann Summerill and David Peterson. Proved Feb. 6, 1844. D-430

1844, Jan. 30—MARY ANN ABBOTT, Mannington. Noncupative will made in the house of her brother Samuel Abbott. To neice Hannah, dau. of sister Hannah Allen, $500, to be invested by my bros. Samuel and George Abbott, until she is 21 years of age. Nephew Samuel Abbott Willits, son of sister Martha A. Willits, my watch. Neices Mary and Amy Abbott, small articles. Neice Hannah Ann Bassett, $200. Remainder of estate to sisters Lydia Abbott and Martha Willits, after bros. Samuel and George have taken out what they deem proper. Wit. Rebecca Wistar, Susan Denn and Martha Abbott. Proved Feb. 20, 1844. D-432

1844, Feb. 7—PAUL SCULL, Pilesgrove. Exec. to sell personal estate. To wife $1000, $500 part to be paid her annually by son Isaac; $250 to be paid annually by each, dau. Sarah, wife of Biddle Reeves, and dau. Deborah Scull, during her life. Son Isaac, the homestead farm, except that part devised to dau. Deborah. Dau. Sarah Reeves, the farm in Upper Penns Neck. Dau. Deborah, land on northwest side of road from Swedesboro to Sharptown, and $1000. Exec. to finish a house he contemplates building. To Thomas Munyan, Jr., and Jonathan Layton, Jr., each $100. Exec. son Isaac and cousin Samuel Bolton. Wit. William Morris, Charles Swing and Gervas Simms. Proved Feb. 29, 1844. D-433

1843, Dec. 25—PETER WRIGHT, Mannington To wife, 1/3 of rents and furniture to the amount of $75; at her death, furniture to dau Elizabeth. To wife, during life, the house I live in. Real estate to my children, Harrison, Job, Stephen and Elizabeth Wright. To children of my son Thomas, each $100. To his widow, $100. Granddau. Anna Lippincott, $100. Granddau. Lydia Rogers, $150. Exec. sons Harrison and Job and George M. Ward. Wit. Nathan Wright, Benjamin Patterson and Ruth W. Appleton. Proved Mar. 9, 1844. D-437

1844, Jan. 29—EDWARD WADDINGTON, Elsinborough. Sons Richard and Joseph, the farm on which I live, subject to payment of a mortgage of $4000. Daus. Sarah Smith, Prudence Barratt, Elizabeth Welch, Lydia and Rebecca Waddington my farm in Lower Alloways Creek. Exec. sons Richard and Joseph. Wit. William Thompson, John H. Patrick and Ephraim C. Patrick. Proved Mar. 14, 1844. D-439

SALEM COUNTY WILLS 61

1843, Aug. 2—MARIA R. WOOD, Pittsgrove. Estate to my sisters Sarah and Elizabeth Wood, who are named exec. Wit. Harman Richman, John Burt and William Richman. Proved Mar. 14, 1844. D-441

1836, Oct. 28—JOEL VANMETER, Northern Liberties, Philadelphia. To wife Anna, my plantation in Pittsgrove during life; then to bro. James VanMeter. Wife, a lot on Apple Street, Northern Liberties; at her death to bros. John and James and sister Elizabeth Cathrall's children. Wife, all personal estate. Anna Stratton, dau. of my wife, a two-story brick house on Delaware Fourth Street, near Poplar Lane and a two-story brick house in West Kensington. Isaiah Stratton, son of my wife, two two-story houses in West Kensington. Two houses on Second Street, Northern Liberties, to be sold. Exec. wife and Joseph C. Nelson. Wit. George Dickinson, Benjamin Van Ieter and William C. Mulford. Proved Mar. 21, 1844. D-443

1839, June 10—LYDIA PERRY, Pilesgrove. To son George W. Davis, a clock and 1/2 of money due me from my father's estate. Son Horatio G. Davis, remainder of said money. Dau. Eliza, wife of Dudley B. Tinker. apparel. Dr. William Bacon, $10. Remainder of money on hand to sons George and Horatio. Exec. son-in-law Dudley Tinker. Wit. Joseph Cook and Joseph L. Risley. Proved Apr. 3, 1844. D-445

1844, Feb. 21—PETER JAQUETT, Lower Penns Neck. To son Robert, a colt, furniture, and 1/2 of produce of peach trees. Dau. Eliza Jaquett, furniture. Real estate to remain subject to a lease between me and my son Paul, except the rght to 1/2 of said peach orchard; after three years the real estate to be divided among my children, dau. Anna Jane, wife of Thomas I Batten, to have a share. Son Hance, $50 to be invested for benefit of grandson Peter (son of Hance), and paid to him at 21 years of age. Exec. sons Robert and Paul. Wit. Japhet J. Somers, Josiah S. Newcom and William A. Dick. Proved May 16, 1844. D-447

1841, Feb. 24—REBECCA KINSEY, Salem. Exec. cousin Thomas Sinnickson. To Thomas Sinnickson, my farm in Upper Penns Neck and meadow in trust for benefit of Margaret Johnson Prescott, wife of Rev. Edward G. Prescott, and dau. of my cousin Mary Smith, during life; at her death the trustee shall pay Rev. Edward G. Prescott annually $300 out of rents of my farms in Lower Alloways Creek and Upper Penns Neck. If Margaret dies without issue, I devise the farm in Lower Alloways Creek to Mary Smith, sister of said Margaret; if she dies without issue, to my cousin Mary, wife of Enoch Moore of Bridgeton. I also give Margaret woodland in Upper Alloways Creek that was bot by my uncle Thomas Sinnickson, dec'd. Harriet Howell Ingham (whom I adopted), wife of Jonathan Ingham, and dau. of cousin John Sinnickson, the farm and woodland that descended from my father George Trenchard, dec'd, in Lower Penns Neck, and the house where I live, the store house and land laid off to me in the division of lands of my uncle Thomas Sinnickson; also the lot devised to me by my aunt Sarah Sinnickson and the building called Masonic Hall; exec. to pay Jonathan Ingham $300 annually from profits arising from same. If Harriet should die without issue, I give the land that descended to me from my father, to the daus. of my cousin Rachel, wife of William Strickland, and children of my cousin William Thackara. Cousin John Sinnickson, meadow in Tilbury. Sarah, widow of Archibald Little, of Bridgeton, $500. Cousins Sarah Dick, Ann Kille, Margaret Conarroe and Ellen Mecum, each $100. Cousin Maria Dick, $300. Cousin Mary Smith, my gold watch and $50. Wit. William Bassett, John M. Brown and Edward Q. Keasbey. Proved June 20, 1844. D-449

1839, Nov. 4—SAMUEL NICHOLSON. Exec. to sell all real estate in Mannington. Son Samuel, 3 cents. Residue of estate to the children of my dau. Sarah Davis, dec'd. Exec. bro.-in-law George M. Ward. Wit. John Hall, John Bassett and Rachel G. Nicholson. Proved June 7, 1844. D-459

1844, June 3—HANNAH WADDINGTON, Lower Alloways Creek. Bro. Jesse Waddington, furniture. Sisters Anna Hildreth, Sarah Tracy and Martha Hancock, apparel. Bros. Wllliam and Jesse Waddington, all real estate. Residue of estate in trust by bro Jesse, 1/2 to be paid the Missionary Society of the M. E. Church, the remainder to the superanuated preachers of said church. Residue of estate to brothers and sisters. Exec. William Waddington. Wit. Daniel Stretch, Benjamin Peterson and Dalymore Harris. Proved July 13, 1844.   D-461

1844, July 10—DRUSILLIA HAINES, Upper Penns Neck. To dau. Rachel Haines, all real estate; if she dies without issue, to my children, Hannah Clifton and Samuel Linch. Exec. son-in-law Joseph B. Clifton. Wit. Alfred Simpkins, Owen Guest and Samuel Bolton. Proved July 24, 1844.   D-463

1839, Jan. 17—JOHN SOMERS, Upper Penns Neck. To wife Edith, furniture, house and land during life. Dau. Mary L. Lippincott, bedding and silverware. Receipts from sale of real estate to my children, Sarah, dec'd, (her children to take her share), Tolitha, Deborah, John, William, Elwood, Chalkley, Eli and Mary. Exec. sons William and Chalkley. Wit. Joseph White, Daniel Taylor and Jacob Pedrick. Proved Aug. 26, 1844.
D-465

1844, Aug. 16—CLAYTON LOCUSON, Upper Penns Neck. To wife Rachel, $200 yearly during life; also bedding and furniture. Son George, $120 yearly during life. Heirs of Harriet Robbins, dec'd., $400 each at 18 years of 'age. Marian, wife of Charles Haines, $500, subject to deduction of a note held against Charles. Rachel, wife of Samuel Hurley, $500, subject to deduction of an obligation. Clayton Locuson, Jr., $500 Beulah, wife of Joseph Stout, Jr., $600. Son Joseph T., remainder of personal and real estate, he to pay bequests to my wife, sons George and Clayton, Jr., and Beulah Stout. Exec. son Joseph T. Wit. Samuel Bolton, Christian Clifton and Daniel Taylor. Proved Aug. 30, 1844.
D-469

1837, Aug. 12—THOMAS DAVIS, Woodstown. To wife Esther, the privilege of living in either of my houses in Woodstown, goods to the value of $300, and $1000 to be invested and divided between my children, Richard, Mary Ann, Esther and Sarah Davis. Son Jacob, the farm he now occupies. Son Josiah, the brick house he now occupies, in Woodstown, on the Philadelphia road. near the Friends' meeting house and corner of land of my nephew David M., son of my bro. David Davis, dec'd. Son Thomas W., the house I now live in. Son Richard and daus. Mary Ann, Esther and Sarah, each $1000. Sons Jacob, Josiah and Thomas, bushland left me by my father Jacob Davis; they to provide a comfortable home for my son Samuel, and each pay their mother $30, and Josiah to pay my estate $1500. Exec. sons Josiah and Thomas. Wit. George M. Cole, David M. Davis and Samuel Coles. Proved Sept. 28, 1844. D-471

1842, Aug. 8--MARTHA REEVE, Salem. To dau. Millicent Reeve, all except furniture devised to son Joseph Reeve. Wit. William H. Doran and Francis Doran. Proved Aug. 29, 1844. Letters of administration granted to Millicent Reeve. D-476

1842, Dec. 27—LYDIA MAYHEW, Pittsgrove. To daus. Charlotte Sparks and Phebe Sparks, apparel. James Mayhew, bedding. Granddau. Clarence Mayhew. $1. Granddau. Lydia Mayhew, furniture. Grandson John Mayhew, remainder of estate. Exec. Mark A. Mayhew. Wit. John M. Sparks and Isaiah Mayhew. Proved Sept. 6, 1844. D-477

1844, Mar. 4—DAVID BASSETT, Salem. To wife Anna C., $600 and land in Mannington during life; then to be sold and receipts to my children, William, Hannah D., Davis and Samuel Bassett. Land in Lower Penns Neck to be sold. Exec. Benjamin Bassett. Wit. Maurice Welch, William M. Baker, Joseph C. Sheppard. Proved Oct. 7, 1844. D-479

1844, Aug. 14—ISAAC SHUTE, Upper Penns Neck. To son Thomas C., all real estate; he paying his sisters Sarah C. and Lydia, $500 each. To wife Rebecca Ann, $50 yearly, furniture, a hog, grain and poultry. Exec. Thomas Flanagin, $50 to be spent for improvements yearly. John Shoemaker to have the place for 5 years. Wit. William D. Burden, John B. Daniels and John K. Louderback. Proved Oct. 23, 1844. D-481

1844, Dec. 27—THOMAS CORCORAN, Salem. To mother Susannah Corcoran, all estate. She is appointed exec. Wit. Daniel Garrison, Ebenezer Smith and Ellen Mecum. Proved Jan. 13, 1845, D-483

1844, July 31—JOB BEVIS, Upper Penns Neck. To wife Ann, use of estate during life. Dau. Ann, wife of Nathaniel Lloyd, the house where Nathan Sivil lives and all my land on west side of road from Perkintown to Pedricktown, and 2 shares in the litterary school house. Dau. Sarah Bevis, land on said road, and the house where Thomas Munion lives. Son George W., residue of real estate and 2 shares in said school house after the death of my wife, and my library. After the death of my wife, all personal estate to be sold and stones erected at our graves. To trustees of the M. E. Church at Perkintown, $20 to help build a stone fence along the front of the grave yard. Henry Katts and Nathan Loyd, apparel. Exec. Hudson A. Springer. Wit. Hudson A. Springer, Jacob. S. Pedrick and William Somers. Proved Jan. 27, 1845. D-485

1844, Mar. 1—MARK WILLIAMS, Pilesgrove. Exec. to sell all estate; receipts to wife; after her death, to cousin Freeman Collins. Exec. wife Atlantic Williams and Joseph Harker. Wit. John A. Carman, Joseph Rich and Jeremiah B. Fox. Proved Feb. 13, 1845. D-487

1844, Dec. 2—ANTHONY WATERS, Philadelphia. Estate to wife Hannah during life; then to dau. Rachel Waters, the house and lot on Seventh Street between Spruce and Pine, furniture, and a debt of $500 due me from Ann Eliza Harback. To grandson Anthony Reeves. bushland in Salem Co. Residue of estate to sons Clement, John, Moses and Job, and daus. Rebecca Belden and Sarah Smith. Exec. wife Hannah and Michael Null of

Salem Co. Wit. Joseph C. Clay and George Spackman. Proved Dec. 4, 1844. D-489.

1844, Mar. 7—SARAH EARLEY, Upper Alloways Creek. Exec. to erect grave stones at my grave and that of my husband, James Earley. Money in the house to sons Robert and John Earley and dau. Keziah McCain. Remainder of estate to my sons, Robert, John, Jesse, William and Caleb Earley and daus. Keziah McCain, Sarah Heritage, Ann Hews and Catharine Heritage. Exec. son John. Wit. Daniel Vanneman, Zaccheus Ray and Henry D. S. Mart. Proved Feb. 24, 1845. D-494

1845, Dec. 11—HENRY WOOD, Mannington. To wife, $200, to be invested. Granddau. Sarah Elizabeth Githens, $100 at 21 years of age. Residue of estate to son William, the children of son Joseph, dec'd, and son William in trust for dau. Ann, wife of William A. Baker. If son William dies, Richard P. Thompson shall act as trustee in his stead. Exec. William W. Wood of Philadelphia, and my wife Bathsheba. Wit. Anna Maria Thompson, Joseph H. Thompson and R. P. Thompson. Proved Mar. 21, 1845. D-496

1841, Sept. 8—SAMUEL S. JAMES, Salem Co. Exec. to sell real estate in Mannington and pay debts. To wife Mary Hall James, the house and lot where we live. Dau. Mary H. James, said house after her mother's death, as long as she remains unmarried, and use of $1000, and income of my real estate. Exec. to sell all real estate except said house and lot and divide receipts among my children, Clarissa Reeve, Esther Miller, James S., Caroline Buck, Samuel S., Edward H, and Sarah L. Pierson. Exec. son-in law David Reeves of Philadelphia and Robert S. Buck of Bridgeton. Wit. William J. Shinn, Robert Guestner and George Fox. Proved Apr. 1, 1845. D-498

1844, June 24—POMPEY TYLER, Upper Alloways Creek. To Mary Cuff, dau. of John Murrey and wife of John Cuff, all estate. Wit. Daniel Vanneman Smith Ware and Benjamin T. Ware.

Proved Mar. 24, 1845. Letters of administration with testament annexed granted to Jonathan Cuff. D-500

1842, Dec. 12—ELIZABETH NICHOLSON Lower Alloways Creek. Exec. to sell personal estate. To exec., one undivided fourth part of estate, after debts are paid, in trust for dau. Rachel, wife of Thomas Y. Hancock; if she survives her husband, to be paid to her; if she dies, to her children. Remaining estate to my children, William, Joshua T. and Sarah Ann Nicholson. Exec. William Nicholson and George M. Ward. Wit. Joseph Bassett, James Bright and Christian Brown. Proved Apr. 14, 1845.
D-501

1843, Oct. 2—PATIENCE GARDINER, Salem. To Sarah, wife of John Quicksall of Burlington, and dau. of John Gardiner, dec'd. my silver watch, and the family Bible which belonged to her father. Christiana Lippincott, dau. of my sister Mary Black, a mahogany wash stand. To Christiana Lippincott and Elizabeth, wife of Lewis Green, and dau. of sister Mary Black, all household goods. To neices Christiana Lippincott and Elizabeth Green and nephew Job Black, who are appointed exec., my house being built, in Salem. Wit. John M. Brown, Isaac Acton and Ann C. Brown. Proved June 7, 1845. D-503

1842, Feb. 28—GEORGE HITCHNER, Upper Alloways Creek. Exec. to pay debts and place grave stones. To wife Hannah, personal estate, and use of land during life; then estate to friend Alpheus Lawrence. Exec. Ellis Ayres. Wit. John M. Gill, Isaac S. Ayres and Eli Davis. Proved July 14, 1845.
D-505

1845, June 12—LYDIA ABBOTT, Mannington. To mother Martha Abbott, $100 and bedding. Bro. Samuel Abbott, my watch and $400. Bro. George Abbott, my purse and silver clasps. Apparel to sisters Martha A. Willits and Hannah Allen. To exec. $1000, in trust, for benefit of neices Mary A. and Amy G. Abbott, at 21 years of age. Neice Hannah G. Allen, cream spoons. Exec.

to furnish my nephew Samuel A. Willits, son of my sister Martha, a Bible at 21 years of age. Remainder of estate to my mother and brothers Samuel and George Abbott. Exec. said bros. Wit. John M. Brown and Samuel Mulford. Proved July 31, 1845.
D-506

1845, May 21—JAMES SMITH, Salem. Exec. to settle my father's estate, of which I was exec. Exec. to sell of my estate as is necessary to pay debts. Cousin Edith, wife of Thomas C. Sterling of Trenton, $500. Bro. Joshua, residue of estate. He is appointed exec. Wit. Elias Phillips, B. Rush Plumley and William E. Vannist. Proved Nov. 11, 1845. D-508

1845, Apr. 19—SAMUEL W. PALMER. Exec. to sell movables. To wife Sarah S., two houses, and land, where I live and where John Palmer lives, in Pennsville, during life; then to my children. She is appointed exec. Wit. William McNichols, Edmund Lumley and William A. Dick. Proved Dec. 9, 1845.
D-510

1840, Feb. 1—BENJAMIN ARCHER, Salem. To son Fenwick H. Archer, who is appointed exec., $800 in addition to about $1600 which I have heretofore given him, and all real estate. Personal estate to wife Rachel and son Fenwick. Wit F. L. Macculloch, Benjamin Acton and John B. Tuft. Proved Jan. 12, 1846. D-511

1846, July 10—SARAH CURRIE, widow, Pilesgrove. To sons Stacy F. Deacon and James Currie, all land in Pilesgrove. To dau. Martha Boots, apparel, bedding, carpet and silverware. To granddau. Sarah, dau. of Stacy F. Deacon, a quilt. Residue to dau. Hannah's children, Edward, David, Gilbert and Charles. Exec. bro. Charles French. Wit. William Stratton, Joseph Bell and Joseph L. Risley. Proved Mar. 25 1846. E-513

1845, Dec. 30, RHODA DENN, Salem. To dau. Rachel J.

Griscom, $593. Dau. Susan Denn, $674. After debts are paid, remainder to daus. Rachel J. Griscom, Susan Denn and Anne Gibbons. Jonathan Freedland and Richard M. Acton, trustees; or if they die, daus. Rachel and Susan shall appoint trustees to carry out my will. Dau. Susan to have the occupancy of the house I now live in, she paying each of her sisters $20 yearly rent. Exec. dau. Susan; if she is married at the time of my death, I appoint Jonathan Freedland and Thomas Sinnickson, exec. Wit. Elijah Ware, Beulah Dare and T. B. Stow. Proved Mar. 16, 1846.
D-514

1846, Apr. 4. WELLS PERRY, Upper Alloways Creek. After debts are paid, residue to sisters Mary Kline, Julian Hunter, Susan and Elizabeth Perry. Exec. John W. Maskell. Wit. John W. Maskell, Philip Shimp and Richard G. Shimp. Proved Apr. 17, 1846. D-517

1846, Apr. 3—EDMOND WILLIT, Lower Penns Neck. To wife Sarah, bedding, pork, grain and $50. Exec. to sell residue of estate and pay debts; residue to my children, Hope Dunn, Edmond, David, Matilda, George, Francis, Tamar and Leah Willitt; to be invested until daus. Matilda, Tamar and Leah are 18 years of age. Exec. William A. Dick. Wit. Samuel Powers, Sarah Wilson and William A. Dick. Proved Apr. 27, 1846. D-518

1845, Nov. 24—MARGARET CONARROE, Salem. To dau. Sarah Little, tee house in Salem in which I live. Dau. Rebecca Laurence, the house occupied by Jacob Mankins. Granddau. Ellen M. Little, $600. Residue after debts are paid, to daus. Mary, wife of Abraham Johnson, Margaret, wife of George C. Rumsey and Rebecca Lawrence, and sons William M. and George W. Conarroe; Rebecca to receive $400 less than the other children. Exec. son George Conarroe and George C. Rumsey. Wit. Daniel Garrison, Mary Garrison and Daniel I. Garrison. Proved May 12, 1846. D-520

1846, Feb. 28—JOHN RISNER, Upper Penns Neck. To wife

Elizabeth, household goods. Dau. Hannah, wife of Jacob Justice, meadow in Amicable Meadow Co., and in Sevil Meadow; at her death, to her dau. Ann Elizabeth Harbison. Grandson John R. Justice, land at Perkintown and meadow; at his death, to his bro. Wilson Lee Justice. providing he pays his grandmother $65 yearly during her life, and $200 to his sister Mary Ann Justice. Grandson Jacob Kreamer Justice, the Beaver Creek farm; he to pay his grandmother $35 yearly; at his death, to his brother Wilson Lee Justice and his sister Emeline E. Justice. Grandchildren Wilson Lee Justice and Hannah J. Justice, woodland. $100 for the purpose of building a schoolhouse at Perkintown on land belonging to the M. E. Church. To John, son of Thomas Risner, $25. Exec. Hudson A. Springer. Wit. John Denris, Thomas J. Batten and William H. Pedrick. Proved June 23, 1846. D-521

1845, Sept. 29—RICHARD HILES, Mannington. To wife Priscilla, $35 yearly. Children Richard, George, Elizabeth, Sarah and Mary Ann, all my lands and movables. Exec. to pay the children of my son William, dec'd, Abigail $30; Joseph $30; Catharine, $40; and son John's children, Ann Eliza, Samuel K. and Sarah Elizabeth, $100, to be divided between them. Exec. dau. Elizabeth Hiles Wit. Lott Jaquett, Edward Bilderback and Joseph Lippincott. Proved June 29, 1846. D-526

1846, Feb. 2—SAMUEL ALLEN, Mannington, To wife, $100 and furniture; sons David, Samuel and Edward each to pay her $66.66 yearly during life. Son David, 1/2 of farm land and meadow and 1/3 of cleared land and timber in Upper Alloways Creek, the horsepower and threshing machine. Son Samuel remainder of the farm where I now live, next my bro. Jeremiah's land, and 1/3 of said cleared land and timber. Son Jeremiah, land in Upper Alloways Creek, bot. of estate of Sheppard Blackwood, and land and timber in Mannington and 2 shares of Salem Bank stock, he to pay the same price charged to his brothers for similar ones furnished them at the time of their marriage, and $1500 to be paid him by his brothers. Dau. Hannah, wife of Francis Bacon, land and cedar swamp in Morris River township, and $1200 to be paid her three brothers. Residue of personal estate to my wife and children. Exec. son David and Jonathan Freedland. Wit. Richard S. Sheppard, Clement A. Ware and Sarah Remington. Proved July 22, 1846. D-528

1840, Mar. 30—HULDAH GOODWIN, Elsinborough. To son Lewis M. a cow and a clock. Son William T., bedding, desk and bookcase. Daus. Hannah T. and Mary M., bedding. Residue of estate to said children. Exec. dau. Hannah and George M. Ward. Wit. Elizabeth Nicholson, Joseph Bassett and John Hall. Proved July 20, 1846. D-530

1846, Aug. 17—JOHN KANDLE, Pittsgrove. To wife Christeen, the farm where I now live, and timberland adjoining it, during widowhood; if she marries, exec. to sell said farm and timberland and divide proceeds among my children. To wife, a horse, cow, farming implements and cedar swamp. Son Henry, $700. Daus. Catharine, wife of Jesse Downs, Mary, wife of Uriah DuBois and Christeen, wife of Samuel Jones, each $100. Son John, $600 and two horses. Dau. Elizabeth, wife of Joseph Miller, $180. Daus Sarah and Lydia, each $180. Exec. wife and sons Henry and John. Wit. Adam Kandle, John Hughes and Jacob W. Ludlam. Proved Sept. 22, 1846. D-532

1845, Sept. 12—JAIL SMITH, Salem. Exec. to sell sufficient real estate to pay debts, the farm on Alloways Creek to be sold first. So Caspar Hall Nicholson, the house where I now live, and land remaining after payment of debts. To friend Ann Smith, remainder of lot where I now live. To Daniel N. Smith and Emily N. Smith, silverware. Hannah, dau. of sister Ruth Wilson, a dressing glass. To Ruth's dau. Jane, sugar tongs. Remainder after debts are paid, to nephew James Nicholson. Exec. John Hall of Elsinborough and George M. Ward of Salem. Wit. Samuel H. Clement, Elijah Ware and H. B. Ivins. Proved Oct. 19, 1846. D-534

1846, Sept. 21 — WILLIAM PLUMMER, Lower Alloways Creek. Exec. to sell real estate. To wife Rachel, $500. Daus.

Emley, $50; Janetta, $100; and Amy, $150. Remainder of estate to my children, William, Edward K. P., Elizabeth wife of Isaac Allen, Charles H., Sarah L., Emley, Janetta and Amy. Exec. bro. John Plummer. Wit. James Butcher, Eli Wood and Samuel Reeves. Proved Dec. 26, 1846. D-537

1847, Jan. 10—JAMES KEEN, Sculltown. To Mary, dau. of Jacob Curry, dec'd, $200. Cousin Sarah Mattson, $5. Elijah and William, sons of bro. Moses Keen, $100 each. Exec. Mark A. Mayhew. Wit. Mark. A. Mayhew, Harrison Strang and Jacob Leap. Proved Jan. 22, 1847. D-539

1846, May 16—WILLIAM HALL, Salem. To wife, the house and lot where I now live, and all my estate, except the amount I am required to pay annually toward the maintenance of my sister, now boarding with Rebecca Ware. Exec. nephew Joseph D. Test. Wit. William Bassett, Thomas Mullica and George M. Ward. Proved Feb. 6, 1847. D-540

1846, Apr. 20—STEPHEN MULFORD, Salem. Personal estate to be sold, book accounts collected, and debts paid. Remainder to daus. Sarah F. Willis and Tamson Smart. To dau. Prudence M. Rose, a house and lot on Broadway, Salem. Exec. dau. Prudence. Wit. Henry Freas, William D. McDaniel, and John M. Cooper. Proved Feb. 26, 1847. D-543

1845, May 10—HANNAH FOGG, Lower Alloways Creek. Sons Samuel and Edward Fogg, and granddau. Eliza Penton, each 1/3 of my personal estate after debts are paid, and 1/3 of my undivided real estate. Nephew William Carpenter of Elsinborough, trustee of granddau. Eliza Penton while she remains the wife of Abner Penton. Exec. sons Samuel and Edward. Wit. Mark Bradway, William Pierpoint and William Powell. Proved Feb. 24, 1847. D-543

1846, Oct. 20—PETER TOWNSEND, of advanced age. To sister Milliscent Garrison, $5000. To friend Thomas S. Bacon, in consideration of the kind care he and his wife have extended to me in my declining years, $300. To their daughters, Elizabeth and Mary Bacon, bedding and silverware, To friend Jonathan Freedland, my books. Residue of estate to Elizabeth and Mary Bacon. Exec. Jonathan Freedland. Wit. Charles Howard and Asbury Howard. Proved Feb. 27, 1847. D-545

Not Dated—GEORGE FOX, SR., Pittsgrove. To grandson George Clark, title to land bot. of Daniel and John Woodruff; if he dies, to grandson George Fox. To grandsons George Clark, the house known as my residence; also cedar swamp on Green Branch, and 1-2 of my cedar swamp on Little Ease and all movables, notes and debts. Dau. Hannah Ogden, during life, remainder of tract bot. of Benjamin Sweaton; then to her son Nathaniel Ogden. Son Job Fox and daus. Anne Clark and Hannah Ogden, each $5. Exec. grandson George Clark. Wit. Uriah Ackley, Samuel Hann and Richard Hanthorn. Proved Mar. 3, 1847. D-547

1847, Jan. 1—EDWARD A. REEVES, Lower Alloways Creek. To bro. Josiah, apparel, watch, breast pin, Bible, gunning skiff and surplus money; if he dies before estate is settled, surplus money to Jeremiah and Elizabeth Reeves when of age. Exec. bro. Josiah Reeves and William Morrison. Wit. George Grier, Clayton Denn and Samuel H. Thompson, Proved Mar. 3, 1847. D-549

1847, Feb. 15—STEVEN WRIGHT, Mannington. Estate, after debts are paid, to wife Ann. She is appointed exec. Wit. Job Hoffman and George M. Ward. Proved Mar. 6, 1847. D-550

1836, Mar. 20—JEDEDIAH GARRISON, Lower Penns Neck. To wife Ann, the house and lot in Lower Penns Neck, during life; then to son Jedediah. Son Gamaliel, land in said township. Son Samuel, woodland. Grandchildren George and Ann, children of Thomas Gibbon, each $25. Residue of estate to sons Gamaliel, Samuel, Jedediah and John. Exec. sons Gamaliel and Samuel.

Wit. John Powers, Samuel Dunn, Jr., and Josiah Tuft. Proved Mar. 26, 1847. D-552

1846, June 1—JAMES FISH, Upper Pittsgrove. To dau. Clarissa Davis, bedding and a share of remainder of estate after debts are paid. Dau. Harriet Rodan, $20 and a share of estate. Dau. Emily Ann, wife of Silas Green, a share of estate, the principal to be invested; if her husband dies, she shall receive the principal. Sons William, James and Richman, each a share. Residue to dau. Sarah Avis' children, William, Ruth and Rebecca. Exec. Charles Elwell, Michael Hurse, John Harding and James Hurse. Proved Mar. 29, 1847. D-553

1846, Feb. 9—SARAH POWELL, Lower Alloways Creek. To daus. Elizabeth Thompson and Ann Griscom, all estate. Exec. son-in-law Samuel Griscom and dau. Elizabeth Thompson. Wit. Thomas Shourds and William Powell. Proved Mar. 31, 1847.
D-556

1846, Dec. 17—THOMAS S. BOWEN, Lower Alloways Creek. To wife Keziah, all household goods, except silver spoons marked TSB, which she may use until son David is 21 years of age, and 1/3 of remainder of personal estate and interest until David is 14 years of age; wife to pay all encumberances that I have to pay my mother and aunt Rachel. David to have remainder of personal estate. Real estate in Indiana to be sold; proceeds, 1/3 to wife, remainder to son David. Exec. bro. David M. Bowen, and wife Keziah. Wit. William Hancock, Richard DuBois and Ephraim Turner. Proved Apr. 9, 1847. D-557

1847, Apr. 13—HARVEY S. DEHART, Upper Alloways Creek. To Christopher M. Campbell, $35. William Dehart, apparel. Amarila Vaneman, blankets. Mary E. Vaneman, watch and coverlid. Frederick Stokely, all goods he now has in his posession. Abigail Vaneman, bedding and silverware. Exec. Daniel Vaneman. Wit. Benjamin T. Ware, Smith M. Ware and Richard W. Vaneman. Proved Apr. 24, 1847. E-559

SALEM COUNTY WILLS 75

Not Dated—JOSEPH TREDWAY. To wife Sarah, $100 and bedding. Son Samuel and dau. Edith. wife of Johnson Crow, a mortgage of Kimsey Morgan for $200. Daus. Sarah Ann, wife of Samuel Peterson, and Hannah, wife of Samuel Cobb, a $200 mortgage. Son Aaron Wood Tredway, meadow on road from Elsinborough to Salem. Dau. Lavinia, wife of Richard Applegate, $100. Residue of estate to above named children. Exec. son Aaron Wood Tredway and son-in-law Richard Applegate. Wit. John Hall, William B. Fogg and Samuel Sheppard. **Proved** Apr. 26, 1847. D-561

1847, Jan. 6—**THOMAS P. HAINES**, Salem. To wife Adelia, all estate after debts are paid. She is appointed exec. Wit. A. D. Keasbey, Charles P. Smith and A. N. DuBois. **Proved** Apr. 26, 1847. D-563

1846, Jan. 29—**ELIZABETH E. BORTON**, Pilesgrove. Personal estate to be sold. To bro William Edwards, $100; if not living, to his dau. Elizabeth Owen. Sister Mary Ballenger, $50 and silverware. To bro. Thomas Edwards $50. To Samuel Miller, $50, in trust for his son William B., at 21 years of age. Rebecca Hanna, $50. Esther Eldridge, $50. Bro. Samuel Edwards' children, Joseph, Charles, Mary Clement and Rachel Edwards, $50, to be divided betweed them. To Amelia Applegate, $150 at 21 years of age. Remainder of bedding to Elizabeth Miller and Reuben Hanna. Aaron Borton, $25. Sarah, dau. of my bro. Thomas Doughton, my case of drawers. Residue of estate to sister Mary Ballenger. Exec. bro. Thomas Edwards. Wit. Bevan Flitcraft, Sarah Flitcraft and Richard Matlack. Proved May 6, 1847.
D-564

1847, June 24—**ASA SMITH.** To wife Abigail and dau Sarah, all estate during their lives; then to be sold; proceeds to my children, John W., Charles W., William F. Thomas L. and Martha Smith. and grandsons Samuel Asa and Charles Henry McClintock. Exec. son Charles and son-in-law David Smith. Wit. James Flanagan and Gerrard Sparks. Proved May 13, 1847. D-566

1845, Oct. 22—JAMES NEALEY, Lower Alloways Creek. To wife Sarah, what she took away, or what is now in her possession, and $10. Grandson James Nealey, my chest. Grandson William Nealey, my gun. Granddau. Sarah Hancock, my beaureau. Grandson James Hancock, high draws and $5. Grandson Casper G. Simkins, $10. Son David, apparel. My children, David Nealey, Elizabeth Simkins and Mary Ann Hancock, residue of estate. Exec. son-in-law Aaron Hancock. Wit. Jesse Carll, Ephraim Carll, Jr., and William Carll. Proved May 15, 1847.
D-568

1843, Jan. 5—JOSEPH BASSETT, Salem. To wife Mary, furniture and the house and lot now occupied by me, during life; then to daus. Rebecca Wistar and Mary Craft. To said daus., land in Tilbury. Granddau. Amy (late Amy Cawley), $2000. Granddaus. Rebecca and Amanda, daus of my son Samuel, dec'd, each $1000. Son William, $4000, to be paid him when he shall pay the bonds executed by him. To exec. in trust, $2000, the interest to be paid my wife; at her death to Rebecca Wistar and Mary Craft. I have deeded land to sons Elisha, David and Benjamin, which is considered equal to their share of my estate. Residue of estate, after debts are paid, to daus. Rebecca and Mary. Exec. sons Elisha, Joseph and David. Wit. William Hall, George M. Ward and F. L. Macculloch. Proved May 15, 1847. D-570

1847, Mar. 30—ANNA M. BOWEN, Lower Alloways Creek. To son David M. Bowen, the house and land where he lives; he to pay my grandson David, son of Thomas S. Bowen, $350 at 21 years of age; if he dies, said sum goes to son David and daus. Rachel Butcher and Mary Ann Waddington. Granddau. Anna B. Waddington, case of high drawers and gold ring. Grandson David B. Waddington silver spoons. Daus. Rachel and Mary Ann, apparel. Exec. son David to procure tombstones. Residue of estate to son David and daus. Rachel and Mary Ann and grandson David Bowen. Wit. John W. Maskell, John Finlaw and Isaac Finlaw. Proved June 11, 1847. D-577

1847, May 7—GEORGE COLE, Upper Penns Neck. To sister

Elizabeth Cole, all estate after debts are paid. Exec. Hudson A. Springer. Wit. William H. Pedrick, Jacob S. Pedrick and Isaiah Barber. Proved June 23, 1847. D-579

1847, May 21—MARIAH KIRBY, Upper Penns Neck. Personal estate to be sold and debts paid. Residue of estate to my sister Lydia Hains, my step-dau. Hannah Kirby, and my daus. Priscilla and Elizabeth Kirby. Exec. Richard Somers. Wit. Hudson A. Springer and Samuel Salesbury. Proved July 7, 1847.
D-580

1847, June 6—ELIJAH GRIFFITHS, Salem, formerly of Philadelphia. Exec. to sell my two brick houses, Nos. 37 and 39 N. Fifth Street, Philadelphia, and part of farm called the "Retreat," in Pilesgrove, and pay receipts to my heirs, Elijah S. Griffiths, Rebecca Ann Griffiths, Margaret S. Foster, Thomas S. Griffiths, Joseph M. Griffiths, Henry H. Griffiths, Mary Ann Griffiths and Eugenia Holly Griffiths. The Park farm, in Pilesgrove and Mannington, shall remain unsold; rents to my single daus, Rebecca Ann, Mary Ann and Eugenia Holly Griffiths, as long as they remain unmarried. Residue of estate to my children. Exec. David Weatherby of Philadelphia and my son Henry Griffiths. Wit. Thomas W. Cattell, Joseph H. Thompson and Thomas V. F. Rushing. Proved July 28, 1847. D-582

1847, Mar. 5—JOHN DUNLAP, Pencater Hundred, Del. Exec. to inter me in the grounds of the Presbyterian Church in Salem, near the grave of my late wife. To sister Amy Carel (or Carrol), usually called Amy Dunlap, $50 annually during life. Friend Nathan T. Underwood, use of money he owes me free of interest until my dau. Elizabeth Harriet is 14 years of age. Sister-in-law Sarah Underwood and her daus. Emily C., Mary Ann and Elizabeth H., each $20. Exec. to release bro.-in-law Isaac Hackett from all claims of my estate. Thomas Sinnickson, grdn. of dau. Elizabeth Harriet, who shall remain in the family of her aunt Sarah and cousin Emily, where she is now. Residue of estate after debts are paid, to dau. Elizabeth Harriet Dunlap. Exec

Thomas Sinnickson. Wit. E. J. Janvier and Jacob Harris. Proved Aug. 6, 1847. D-586

1846, May 28—ANN G. HALL, Mannington. To Mary Groff Dyer, my gold watch. John G. and Reeves S. Dyer, each a silver cup. Anna J., dau. of Charles F. Groff, Elizabeth G. James and Anna J. Groff, silver ware. Exec. to sell my house and lot in Salem, and pay 1/4 of proceeds to Charles H. Groff. Maria Steward, $100. Remainder to Reeves S., John G. and Mary Groff Dyer. Charles H. Groff, gold spectacles. Exec. nephew, Reeves S. Dyer and Stacy M. Steward. Wit. John Elkinton, Edward Clark and W. S. Clarkson. Proved Aug. 18, 1847. D-588

1845, Jan. 8—DANIEL ASHTON. Lower Alloways Creek. To granddau. Hannah Steel Ashton, $5. Remainder of personal estate, after payment of debts, to wife and daus. Hannah wife of Eliakim Smith and Mary Ayars. Exec. to rent real estate during life of my wife; at her death, part to dau. Hannah and after her death, to her son Daniel Ashton Smith. Residue to dau. Mary, during her life; then to her sons Samuel Ashton Ayars and Joseph Ashton Ayers Exec. son-in-law Eliakim Smith and James Butcher, Jr. Wit. James Butcher, Jr., Robert Butcher and Absalom Sembes. Proved Aug. 21, 1847. D-591

1834, Dec. 13—THOMAS JONES, storekeeper, Salem, To sister all my property which my father bot of William Parret in Salem. corner of Broadway and Market street, opposit the jail, occupied by myself and John W. Maskell, the land which my father bot. of Joseph Hall, in Salem, and woodland at Turnip Hill, in Upper Alloways Creek, and in Elsinborough, and all my furniture. To nephew Thomas Jones, a farm and woodland in Beesleys Neck, land in Maddentown, and bushland near Morris schoolhouse, in Upper Alloways Creek. Land in Gloucester and Burlington counties to sister Mary Yorke and nephews Thomas J. and Lewis S. Yorke. Exec. nephew Thomas Jones Yorke. Wit. John G. Mason, Thomas Sinnickson and John Sinnickson. Proved Aug. 23, 1847. D-593

1847, Sept. 17—MARK STRETCH, Lower Penns Neck. To wife Tamson, $100, and $2000 in one year. Son Joseph H., meadow upland, bushland and woodland in Upper Alloways Creek, 1/2 of meadow in Elsinborough, and a house and lot in Lower Penns Neck. Daus Joanna N. Stretch and Mary H. Morris, a farm in Mannington, subject to the payment of $2000 by Joanna and $1000 by Mary. As I am bound to pay Elizabeth Jones, late Fox, a sum for dower in the Fox farm, I order Joanna and Mary to pay same. Daus. Elizabeth and Deborah, the house in which I live, and woodland in Upper Alloways Creek, and residue of estate. Grandson William Morris, Woodland in Upper Alloways Creek. Son Joseph H. Stretch and son-in-law John H. Moore, exec. and grdn. of Elizabeth and Deborah. Wit. F. L. Macculloch, John N. Madara and William H. Elwell. Proved Oct. 16, 1847. D-596

1847, Sept. 20.—ISAAC WHITE, Upper Penns Neck. To children of my first wife, land in Pilesgrove. Daus. Rebecca Elizabeth and Sarah, proceeds of sale of land in Pilesgrove. Wife Margaret P., the farm where I now live, during her lifetime; then to her children; also bushland in Upper Penns Neck. Personal estate to wife and her children. Exec. sons Samuel and Isaac White. Wit. W. S. Vanneman, Joseph B. Wily and Michael Allen. Proved Oct. 28, 1847. D-601

1840, Mar. 12—ELIZA MORRIS, Pilesgrove. To dau.-in-law Rachel Humphreys, $200. Children of Samuel Humphries, viz: Charles, John, Josiah, Mark and Hannah, the house and barn in Sharptown, to be at the disposal of son Samuel until his youngest child is of age. Grandson Furman Robins, $200. Remainder of real estate to be sold; proceeds to my children, Samuel, Isaac, John, Elizabeth wife of William Morris and Rebecca wife of Smith Hewitt. Exec. son-in-law William Morris and son Isaac Humphrey. Wit. Thomas Yarrow, John Stalcup and Elijah S. Barber. Proved Nov. 2, 1847. D-603

1845, Jan. 3—MOSES LAMBSON, Lower Penns Neck. To daus. Rebecca wife of Philip Hitchner, and Sarah wife of Isaac

Lippincott, each $200. Son-in-law John Williams, $200. Son Merrick and Thomas Dickinson, in trust, all my lands during the lifetime of my wife Clarissa, and out of rent pay her $150 yearly in lieu of dower; after her death, real estate to be sold and receipts distributed 1/6 to each son Merrick, and daus. Sarah and Rebecca; 1/6 to Michael, William and Caroline, children of son John Lambson, dec'd; 1/6 to William L. Williams, Sarah N. Williams and Moses L. Williams, children of dau. Elizabeth Williams, dec'd. Exec. Thomas Dickinson, Jr. Wit. Hudson A. Springer, A. Q. Keasbey and F. L. Macculloch. Proved Dec. 1, 1847. D-605

1844, Mar. 2—WILLIAM F. MILLER, Salem. To wife Hannan, 12 shares of Camden & Amboy R. R stock and 30 shares of Mine Hill & Schuylkill Haven R. R. stock and 2 shares of Delaware & Chesapeake Canal stock, furniture and library. Thomas Lippincott of Pilesgrove, apparel. My watch and all the silver plate that belonged to me before marriage with my present wife, to my granddau. Esther C. Miller, my nephew, Clarkson Sheppard to keep possession of said watch and plate until Esther is of age. Real estate to wife Hannah during her life; then to granddau. Esther C. Miller. Personal estate, after debts are paid, to Samuel Abbot and Clarkson Sheppard, in trust for wife Hannae, and pay her $200 yearly; after her death, trustees to transfer a bond and mortgage of $1000 to Thomas S. Bacon of Mannington, and residue of bond and mortgage to Priscilla, wife of John N. Reeve of Evesham, Burlington County. Exec. William Carpenter of Mannington and Joseph Tatem of Gloucester County. Wit. F. L. Macculloch, Clement Acton and A. Q. Keasbey. Proved Dec. 29, 1847.
D-608

Not Dated—JOB BLACK, Salem. To bro.-in-law Lewis Green, apparel. Remainder of estate, after debts are paid, to sisters Christiana Lippincott and Elizabeth Green, to be invested and interest paid them; at their death, principal to sons of my bro. Thomas Black, $3000 to Job Black and the residue to his bro. Edward. Exec. George M. Ward. Wit. Elisha Bassett, Holiday Jackson and Henry D. Hall. Proved Jan. 10, 1848. D-612

SALEM COUNTY WILLS 81

1842, July 22—ELIZABETH BLACK, Salem. To sister Sarah Atkinson, bedding, furniture, and all real estate. Residue to be sold and debts paid. Exec. Samuel C. Atkinson and John M. Brown. Wit. Daniel Tracy, Jedediah T. Allen and Francis Sickler. Proved Jan. 18, 1848. D-614

1838, May 10—HENRY BUCK, Upper Alloways Creek, To wife Mary, 1/2 of personal estate after debts are paid. Son Dayton, remainder of personal estate. Granddau. Mary Jane, dau. of son Henry Buck, dec'd, $100 at 18 years of age. Sons James, Robert and Dayton, all my lands. Exec. son James. Wit. James Coombs, Henrietta Coombs and Henry Rammel. Proved Mar. 31, 1848. D-615

1847, Oct. 18—JONATHAN DALLAS. To daus. Elizabeth Stanger, Ann D. Sinnickson and Mary B. Reeve, certain obligations amounting to $1450, and the house at the end of Fenwick street, in Salem adjoining the African meeting house. Son Holmes Dallas, all live stock and farming utensils on the farm where I now live; he to pay his sisters each $100. To above named dhildren, all the ready money I have at the time of my death. Exec. son-in-law John M. Sinnickson. Wit. William H. Thompson, John Foster and John A. Cooper. Proved May 16, 1848. D-617

1848, May 1—MARTHA ABBOTT, Mannington. Apparel to daus. Hannah Allen, Sarah W. Abbott and Ruth S. Abbott, sister Hannah Townsend and neice Mary Ann Davis. Son Samuel Abbott, silverware. Son George Abbott, silverware and $25. Dau. Hannah, wife of Jedediah Allen, $30 per year during life. Grandson Samuel Abbott Willetts, $100 at 21 years of age. Children of William G. Abbott, dec'd, John Abbott and Mary, wife of John Somers, $150 each. Remainder of estate to sons Samuel and George, who are appointed exec. Wit. James Robinson and Hannah V. Wood. Proved May 27, 1848. D-619

1848, Apr. 28—MARTHA HOFFMAN, Pilesgrove. To neice Mary Guestner, $12. Remainder of estate to sister Abigail Hoffman. Exec. Thomas Edwards. Wit. James M. Reed, William B. Kirby and John Thompson. Proved June 24, 1848. D-621

1848, June 13—MARTHA JARMAN, Salem. To mother Isabella Teel, land on Union Street, Salem, during her lifetime; then to dau. Catherine Jarman. Personal estate to be sold and debts paid. Residue to Josiah Thompson, in trust, for benefit of my mother during her life; then to my dau. Catherine. Exec. Josiah Thompson. Wit. William Fisher, John Williams and John R. Powell. Proved July 21, 1848. D-623

1842, Jan. 17—STRETCH HARRIS, Lower Alloways Creek. To wife Rebecca, $1000. Sons Hiram and Amos, all real estate. Residue of personal estate to sons, provided Hiram pays $1000 to granddau. Hannah, dau. of dau. Ann Fogg, dec'd, at 20 years of age and that Amos pays $1000 to grandson John H. Fogg, son of dau. Ann at 21 years of age. Exec. sons Hiram and Amos. Wit. David Stretch, James M. Woodnutt and Dalymore Harris. Proved Aug. 21, 1848. D-624

1848, Aug. 25—ELENOR MECUM. To neice Sarah, dau. of sister Margaret Conaroe, dec'd, $1800. Neice Rebecca Lawrence, dau. of said Margaret, $1400. Great neice Ellen Little, apparel furniture, and $1000. George, Ellen and Maria, children of nephew George Conaroe, $500 each. Nephew James W. Mecum, $600; he to pay Ann Lawrence, dau. of my dec'd bro. William Mecum, the interest during her life; then pay the sum to her children. Grand nephew Henry, son of George C. Rumsey, $500. Grand neice Ellen, dau. of James W. Mecum, my gold watch. Friend Maria Ewan of Philadelphia, $300. Rebecca Roberts $9 yearly during her life. Nephew James W. Mecum, all my real estate, and he is appointed exec. Wit. Mary Smith, Susan Corcoran and Thomas Sinnickson. Proved Sept. 7, 1848. E-1

SALEM COUNTY WILLS 83

1848, Aug. 13—SAMUEL LOW, Salem. To wife Harriet, all estate. Exec. John McDonnol and Thomas Stow. Wit. Joel Simkins, Jonathan Belton and I. T. Nicholson. Proved Sept. 8, 1848. E-3

1845, July 12—JACOB NEWKIRK, Pittsgrove. To son William Mills Newkirk, the plantation where he now lives. Son Joast, the plantation where he now lives. Personal estate and the plantation on which I live to be sold, Granddau. Mary Ann N., dau. of my dau. Mary Sithen, dec'd, $200 at 18 years of age. Grandson Sedgwick R. son of my dau. Sarah Sithens, dec'd, $500. Granddau. Lucy V. Sithens, dau. of dau. Sarah, $200 at 18 years of age. Grandson Jacob, son of my son Jacob, dec'd, $600. To my housekeeper, Ann Abbott, $50. Exec. William and Joast. Wit. Jonathan Cawley, Isaac Johnson, 2nd, and Moses Richman, Jr. Proved Sept. 27, 1848. E-5

1845, Dec. 10—WILLIAM B. SMITH, Philadelphia. To wife Sarah, apparel, furniture, bonds, interest and mortgages. Residue of money to be invested. To wife, $3 per week or $100 per year during life. To sisters Hannah B., wife of Robert Goforth, Sarah R. Smith, and Ruth, wife of Peter Martin, remainder of interest. After wife's death, to the Baptist Church of Woodstown, of which I am a member, $500, and to the Baptist Association of New Jersey, $500. To be buried in the Baptist graveyard at Woodstown, and gravestones to be erected where my mother and sister Mary Ann were laid. Exec. bro.-in-law Jonathan Belton and my wife. Wit. Caleb Wood, Elisha Casseday and M. R. Allen. Proved July 10, 1748. E-9

1848, Sept. 9—LEVEN HARMER, Penns Neck. Exec. to sell estate sufficient to pay debts. Residue to exec. Benjamin Griscom, Sr., William Bassett and George M. Ward, in trust for benefit of the Friends at Salem worshiping in the meeting house in Margaret's Lane. Wit. Johnson Freas, Samuel Wallen and John Murphey. Proved Nov. 18, 1848. E-18

1838, Oct. 10—JOHN EMMEL, Upper Alloways Creek. To son John, the land whereon he has built a house. To my children, William, John, Emanuel and Philip Emmel and Rosanna Clark and Sarah Horner, all real estate. Exec. bro. Philip Emmel. Wit. George A Davis, Lydia Ann Emmel and Rosanna Emmel. Proved Dec. 21, 1848.
E-19

1839, Dec. 9—JAMES SIMS, Upper Alloways Creek. To Ann Sims, furniture which she brought at marriage, all personal estate $70, and the house and land where I now live during widowhood, she paying to Hedge Sims $5 yearly, for repairs on said house. Son John land on road from Quintons Bridge to Wood's mill, excepting a room in the house on said land, which dau. Mary is to have. Son John to pay son Hedge $300. Son Smith, land on said road. Son Mason, land in tenure of William D. Simkins. Dau. Silva Davis, house and lot occupied by said Simkins, woodland and $150; at her death to be paid to her dau. Hannah Ann Sims. Sons Gervas and Hedge, residue of woodland. Son Gervas an obligation for $200, and $500 in cash. Son Hedge, $700 at death or marriage of my widow. Exec. Benjamin Archer. Wit. Oliver Smith, Stephen Smith and Ephraim Harris. Proved Jan. 27, 1849.
E-22

1844, Mar. 14—SAMUEL JAQUETT, Pilesgrove. To wife Hannah, all personal estate after debts are paid. Sons David and Jacob, the house where I live. Remainder of land to sons John and Abraham and dau. Hannah Elizabeth. Wife Hannah to have use of estate while she remains my widow. Exec. wife and son David. Wit. James Keen, John Jordan and Jacob Banks. Proved Feb. 17, 1849.
E-26

1848, July 12—GEORGE GRIER, Lower Alloways Creek. To wife Ruth, an annuity of $120 to be paid by my son Robert, the house and lot in Hancock Town, furniture and $500. To son Jonathan Butcher Grier, $7500. Dau. Rachel, wife of John Patrick, bushland in Upper Alloways creek, a house in Hancock Town and

$1500. $400 to be invested by my exec.; interest to be paid her during her life. To son Robert, the homestead, including two houses and bushland in Beesleys Neck. Son Charles bushland in Upper Alloways Creek: after death of my wife, the house in Hancock Town. Exec. sons Jonathan and Robert. Wit. Thomas S. Smith, Thomas W. Cattell and William Morrison. Proved Mar. 7, 1849. E-28

1847, Dec. 27—DANIEL VANNEMAN, Upper Penns Neck. To wife Hannah, furniture, $100, and the house and lot at the Cove, during life. Son John, a farm in Pilesgrove and a house and lot in Penns Grove, he to pay his mother $100 yearly. Dau. Rebecca C., wife of Rev. Anthony Atwood, the farm bot of William Holliday, property in Pilesgrove and a house at the Cove; she to pay her mother $50 yearly. Son William S., my share in the house and ground at the northeast corner of Twentieth and South Streets Philadelphia, and the house at the Cove, where he lives, meadow and bushland; he to pay his mother $100 yearly. Dau. Hannah Ann, wife of William Summerill, Jr., the farm on Salem Creek, that I heired from my father and uncle, and a house at the Cove, after the death of her mother, and $150; she to pay her mother $25 yearly. Dau. Sarah Jane Vanneman, property by the Salem Creek and a house and lot at Penns Grove Pier Cross Roads; she to pay her mother $50 yearly. Exec. wife Hannah and son William. Wit. David Holton, John Summerill and James D. Simkins. Proved Mar. 8, 1849. E-32

1849, Jan. 18 — JESSE WADDINGTON, Lower Alloways Creek. To wife Rachel, $500, furniture and the house and land conveyed to me by Martha Waddington, during life, then to dau. Sarah. Dau Rachel $1000. My interest in the homestead of my father, William Waddington, after the death of my mother, Martha Waddington, to my bro. William; he to pay my dau. Sarah $1000 after my mother's death. Residue of estate to wife and dau. Sarah. Exec. bro-in-law William Scudder. Wit. Andrew Smith, Joseph A. Hancock and Alphonso S. Eakins. Proved Mar. 14, 1849. E-35

1849, Mar. 2—JOEL SIMKINS, Elsinborough. To wife Rebecca, furniture, and occupation of the house where I live and the ground adjoining, during life; then to my dau. Mary. Land to be sold to pay debts. In case of Mary's death, above is to go to my nephew William Simkins. Exec. Charles Mulford and Isaac English. Wit. Jonathan Belton John Hires and John Miller. Proved Mar 19, 1849. E-37

1847, Jan. 12—HENRY MARTIN, Upper Pittsgrove. To granddau. Matilda Smith, furniture. Son Jacob, $1000; he to pay debts from money due me. Sons John, Henry, Peter and George and dau. Barbara Foster, $1000 each. Dau. Elizabeth Mench, $2. Grandsons Henry and Mark Mench and granddaus. Jane and Harriet Foster and Elizabeth Mench, $333 each. Granddau. Matilda Smith, $100. Dau. Catharine Deal, rents of all my houses and ground on northeast side of Marlborough Street, Kensington, during life; at her death, exec to sell same and pay receipts to sons and daus. Exec. son John. Wit. Nathaniel Swing, Ebenezer Harris and Ambrose Whitaker. Proved Mar. 20, 1849. E-39

1846, May 8—ELIZABETH GROFF, Woodstown. To Exec. William Borden, husband of my granddau. Emily S. Cawley, the house and lot where William M. Cawley lives, during life; then to my granddau. To son Amasa Groff, a note I hold against him for $50. Son Joseph, $50 (to his son Benjamin my silver watch), and to each of his children, Hannah, Benjamin, Stephen, Sarah Ann, Arrabella and Joseph, $9. Bequests to Mary C. Mecum, Joseph, Parthenia and William, children of my son Amasa Groff. Dau. Elizabeth, wife of Samuel E. French, residue of estate; at her death, to her children, Hewlings, Joseph and Mary Elizabeth French. Wit. Jacob Howey, Robert C. Pedrick and Henry Richman. Proved Apr. 3, 1849. E-43

1845, Aug. 11—ANDREW HIGH, Upper Alloways Creek. To wife Elizabeth, 1/3 of personal estate after debts are paid. Dau. Susanna Ayres, a case of drawers and a lookingglass. Grandson David Gagers, $50. Residue of estate to sons Lot,

Joseph and Cilas High and dau. Susanna Ayres. Exec. John Burroughs. Wit. James Buck, Robert Buck and Levis W. Austin. Proved Apr. 5, 1849.   E-46

1849, Mar. 31—JOHN HOLTON, UpperPenns Neck. To son John, the house and land where he lives. Son Thomas, the house and land where I live. Son Andrew, the house and land now occupied by son Thomas. Sons Jesse and Philip, land. Heirs of son William, dec'd, Mary Eakin and Louisa Holton, each $25. Heirs son Samuel, dec'd $25. Exec. to sell meadow in Biddle Meadow Co. and pay bequests. Residue of proceeds to children of sons Thomas, John and Andrew, and my grandchildren, John and Jesse, sons of my son Jesse. Exec. son Thomas. Wit. Agustus Cann, Jr. William Harker, Benjamin D. McCollister. Proved Apr. 16, 1849.   E-49

Not Dated—SARAH WESTCOTT, Canton. Sons Elikum Smith and Job Smith, each $125. Dau. Hannah Ayres, silverware. Remainder of personal estate and woodland to be sold; receipts to sons, and daus., Sarah Hewart and Hannah Ayres. Exec. son Elikum. Wit. John S. Wood, Sarah Ann Wood and Robert D. Loper. Proved May 26, 1849.   E-51

1847, Jan. 1—REBECCA ROBERTS, Salem. To John M. Brown, the house in which I live. Ann C. Brown, Bible, workstand and apparel. Israel E. Brown, $10. Elgar Brown, silver watch, trunk and bed. Mary Brown, silverware, apparel and books Elizabeth Brown, spectacles and silver sisor hook. Nancy Brown, silver knitting sheath and thimble. Residue of estate to be sold and debts paid. Exec. John M. Brown. Wit. Isaac Hackett and Ann W. Hand. Proved June 4, 1849.   E-53

1849, May 29—WILLIAM K. SEAGRAVE. To wife Mary G., all estate during widowhood; then to my children, Sarah T., William, Robert, James M., George W., Joseph S. and Clement S. Exec. wife. Wit. James Newell, Charles Mulford and Isaac English. Proved June 12, 1849.   E-55

Not Dated—CATHARINE MONCREEF, Pittsgrove. To son Hugh, the place where I reside, he to live on the farm and furnish a home for his sisters Margaret and Catharine; if he marries, or leaves the farm, it is to be sold; proceeds to said children Daus. Margaret and Catharine. bedding and live stock. Personal estate and timber to be sold. $60 is to be deducted from son Edward's share, and $15 from son Robert's share To son Henry, $15 more than his equal share. Exec. son Hugh. Wit. Adam Kandle, John Hughes and J. S. Whitaker. Proved June 16, 1849   E-57

1849, Mar. 21—WILLIAM FISHER, Salem. To wife Elizabeth, all estate. She is appointed exec. Wit. Josiah Thompson, John P. McCune and Jeremiah Tracy. Proved June 23, 1849.
E-59

1849, May 1—JONATHAN TOWNSEND, Salem. To wife Sarah F., furniture, store house, and ground on south side of Broadway. Sons Jonathan, Charles and Adam, each bedding. All personal and real estate, except as devised, to be sold and debts paid; residue of receipts to wife, granddau. Ellen Townsend, dau. of son Jeremiah, dec'd, son Jonathan, grandchildren William F. and Emma Ireland, daus. Ellen Hutchens and Caroline, wife of Samuel B Dumont, sons Charles and Adam F. Exec. George M. Ward. Wit. George T. Boon, Smith Darmon and Joseph H. Cooper. Proved Aug. 18, 1849.   E-60

1849, June 19—CHRISTIANA FIELDS, Pilesgrove, widow of Patrick Fields. To son Benjamin, furniture, silverware, and $630. Mary, wife of Samuel Cock, $210. Samuel Fields, $210. Residue of estate to sons Benjamin, Joseph, James and Samuel. Exec. son Benjamin. Wit. Dan Ware, Samuel D. Brogan and Joseph L. Risley. Proved Aug. 29, 1849.   E-64

1849, July 11—MARY CARPENTER, Philadelphia. To my sister, Rachel Clark, and my daus. Rachel R. Sheppard and Hannah A. Carpenter, apparel. Son William, meadow in Mannington Marsh Co., granted to me by my late husband, William Carpenter, dec'd, on condition that he shall convey all his title to a house and land on Market Street, Salem, meadow at foot of Salem Bridge in Mannington, and woodland in Upper Alloways Creek in such manner that same may be held for use of my dau. Rachel R. Sheppard and her children. I also devise to him $1000 on same conditions. Son Samuel P., land adjoining his farm and two meadow lots, and $400, on condition that he shall convey all his right in the house and lot, meadow and bushland as above. To sons William and Samuel, all my title to aforesaid property; also $1000 in trust during the lifetime of dau. Rachel, for her benefit. Remainder of estate to my three children. Exec. sons William and Samuel. Wit. James G. Clark, Charles Bullock and Thomas Williamson. Proved Sept. 1, 1849. E-66

1849, July 28—ANDREW MINTERS, Pilesgrove. To wife Abigail the house and lot where I live, during her lifetime, and $660. Remainder of estate to be sold; receipts to sister Kesiah Miller and children of my deceased bro. Barzillai Minters. To my nephew, Andrew Minters, my gold watch. Exec. Thomas Edwards. Wit. Ephraim S. Coles, Aaron Edwards and Barclay Edwards. Proved Sept. 11, 1849. E-70

1849, June 17—JOSIAH NEWCOMB. All title to land in Salem County, left by my mother Keziah Newcomb, dec'd, and in which my father, Reuben Newcomb has a life interest, to be divided between my wife, Sarah, and my bro. John R. Newcomb. Exec. bro. William Newcomb. Wit. William B. Taylor, P. Altemus and R. Williams. Proved Aug. 12, 1849. E-73

1849, July 3—EBENEZER HARMER, Lower Alloways Creek. Real estate in Cumberland County to be sold. To wife Hannah B., $350. Neice Mary B. Harmer, dau. of bro. William, a house and land on Beesleys Neck Road, adjoining the Friends' graveyard. To wife, the farm where I now live, except the above named house and lot; also my right to the farm where Charles B. Ayars lives, during life; then to Elwood Harmer, son of my bro. Joseph, Mary B. Harmer, dau. of bro. William, Mary Ann, Lydia

Hannah Ann and Rebecca Harmer, daus. of my nephew, Mark Harmer. After sale of remaining estate and debts are paid, residue to Mary B., dau. of bro. William Harmer, Ann Elizabeth, dau. of Seeley Shute, and Elizabeth H., dau. Samuel Richmond. Exec. wife, and bro. Waddington Bradway. Wit. Jesse Carll, Archer Stackhouse and Joseph Bowen, Jr. Proved Oct. 13, 1849. E-76

1849, Aug. 29— SAMUEL DICKESON, Pilesgrove. To son Dr. Thomas Dickeson, my grist mill property, 2 houses in Woodstown, land occupied by Richard Allen and Grace Dickeson, bushland and woodland in Rutherfords Neck. Daus. Sarah and Mary H. Dickeson, my farm and woodland on road from Woodstown to Daretown, my Bushtown farm and my houses and land where I now live in Woodstown, and the house and lot adjoining the Friends' old graveyard, land in upper part of Woodstown, on the road to Eldridges Hill, and woodland. Granddau. Anna F. Dickeson a house and lot on the street from Woodstown to Salem. The brick storehouse and my tavern house in Woodstown to my grandsons David and Samuel Dickeson, in trust by my son Thomas, until they are of age. Son Thomas P., large brass kettle, dsk. bookcase and bedding. Daus. Sarah and Mary to pay grandson David Dickeson $500 at 21 years of age. Residue of estate to my children. Exec. son Dr. Thomas P. Dickeson. Wit. John Cook, William H. Reed and Joseph Risley. Proved Oct. 27, 1849. E-80

Not Dated—SARAH BRADWAY, Salem. To granddau Sarah, dau. of Johnson Crow, my bureau. Daus. Edith Crow, Sarah Ann Peterson, Lavinia Applegate and Hannah Cobb, apparel. Residue to my son and daus. Exec. T. V. F. Rusling. Wit. Mason VanMeter and DeWitt Clinton Clement. Proved Oct. 27, 1849. E-83

1848, June 12—WILLIAM WALKER, Upper Alloways Creek. To son William S., the westerly part of my plantation during his life; then to his children, William S., David S., Charles H., Thomas S., Sarah, Anna and Emma Jane. Son William, marsh in Elsinborough. Grandsons Sheppard H. and Robert Flannagan, t he easterly part of my plantation and a house and land in Allowaystown. Granddau. Sarah S. Bilderback, the southeast part of my plantation. Residue and personal estate to son William, and he is appointed exec. Wit. Joseph C. Nelson, Dan Nichols and Ruth Ann Nelson. Proved Dec. 27, 1849. E-85

1843, Oct. 9—SARAH PRESS, Lower Alloways Creek. To dau. Clarissa Sayre, apparel. Dau. Mariah, wife of John Corliss $1. Son William Press, $1. Grandson James Sayre, $2. Grandson William Sayre, and granddaus. Sarah D. and Ann Sayre, each $10. Remainder of estate, after debts are paid, so son-in-law Reuben Sayre, who is appointed exec. Wit. George Githens, John Mills and John Williams. Proved Jan. 5, 1850. E-88

1849, Mar. 10—ANDREW NEWKIRK, Pittsgrove. Exec. to sell timber on back lot. To my children, William, Enoch, John, Edmond and Rebecca Newkirk, all real estate. Grandson Andrew, 3d, son of Israel Newkirk, dec'd, $1000. Dau. Rebecca, furniture. Residue of estate to my children. Exec. sons William and John. Wit. Judah Foster, Jonathan Burroughs and Andrew Surran. Proved Jan. 19, 1850. E-90

1849, May 26—ELIZABETH DAVIS, Pilesgrove. To sister Ann, wife of Nicholas Pidgeon, $25 and apparel. Residue of estate to John Carter son of Elizabeth, widow of Francis Davis. Exec. John Carter. Wit. Edward Hanes and George Flitcraft. Proved Jan. 19, 1850. E-92

1842, July 15—JOHN COUNSELLOR, Salem. To dau Rachel Jones all estate She is appointed exec. Wit. Daniel Garrison and John McChalliff. Proved Jan. 24, 1850. E-93

Not Dated—SAMUEL SOMERS, Pilesgrove. To son Albertus, $1. Son Joshua, $100. Son Richard, $1. Dau. Serena A., wife of John Robinson, a bureau. Dau. Mary, wife of Thomas Long, a chest. Daus. Serena, Mary and Abigail, wife of John McAltioner, remainder of estate. Exec. sons-in-law John Robinson and Thomas Long. Wit. William Cawley, Ephraim Waters and John Bacon. Proved Feb. 5, 1850. E-94

1850, Jan. 8—ABIGAIL MINTERS, Pilesgrove. To Amy Grice, bedding and apparel. Elizabeth Mathews, furniture, $50 and apparel. William Borton, $100. Hannah and Rachel, daus. of William Borton, each $14. Sarah Edwards, $100. Henrietta and Isabella Howey, each $50. Franklin Howey, $100. Residue to Elizabeth Mathews. Exec. William Borton. Wit. Thomas Edwards and Elizabeth T. Anderson. Proved Feb. 8, 1850. E-96

1840, Sept. 23—MARY DAVIS, widow of Joseph Davis, of Woodstown. Grandsons Joseph D. Folwell, and Joseph D. Pancoast, each $150 and furniture. Granddaus. Mary E, Martha and Ann Elizabeth Pancoast, each $150, to be invested, and furniture. Mary Clark (nee Pierson), Lydia Wiley (nee Pierson), and Elizabeth Hyle (nee Pierson), each $20. Remainder of estate to daus. Martha and Ann Exec. William Folwell. Wit. Edward Hanes and Andrew Armstrong.

Codicil—Whereas, since making my will, my dau. Ann H. Pancoast, has had three sons, David, William Henry and Charles F., I devise each of them $150. Wit. Albertus Somers. Proved Feb. 15, 1850. E-98

1849, June 2—THOMAS BIDDLE, Lower Penns Neck. To wife Maria, $200 annnally during her life. Son George, my Hawks Bridge farm. Son Thomas, my homestead farm, two young horses and farming utensils. Son Aaron, land where Thomas Tuft lives, a house and land near Penns Grove, and woodland. Daus. Beulah and Susannah Biddle, my farm on the Hook. Residue of estate to son Thomas, in trust for support of my wife, Maria. Exec. sons Thomas and George, and my wife, Maria. Wit. Alphonso L. Eaken, John M. Brown and Isaac Hackett. Proved Feb. 15, 1850. E-101

(Note at bottom of page says, see Book R of wills, page 757 for correct reading of the will.)

1850, Feb. 2—SARAH D. PEDRICK, Lower Penns Neck. The house in Pedricktown to my children, John, Hannah and Joseph. Exec. son Joseph D. Pedrick. Wit. Joseph Diver, Thomas Jones and Hudson A. Springer. Proved Mar. 13, 1850.
E-104

1848, Aug. 3—HANNAH SMART, Salem. To neices Deborah Smart, Rebecca Branson and Ruth Smart, silverware and furniture. Neice Deborah Brick, $200. Nephew John Smart, $100. Residue of estate to be placed in trust, the interest for maintenance of my brother, Isaac Smart; at his decease, residue to neices Deborah Smart and Rebecca Branson. Jonathan Freedland, trustee of above. Exec. William T. Smart and Jonathan Freedland. Wit. Richard M. Acton and Sarah W. Acton, Jr. Proved Apr. 26, 1850.
E-105

1850, Mar. 28—JOHN BURCH, Mannington. To wife Ann, estate during widowhood; then to daus. Maria Mullica and Lydia Frost. Exec. Richard Woodnutt. Wit. F. L. Macculloch, John M. Brown and David Petit. Proved May 24, 1850.
E-107

1850, Mar. 22—JEDEDIAH ALLEN, Salem. Personal estate to be sold. To wife Hannah, silverware, interest on $3000 yearly, and the house and lot where I now live, on Yorke Street, Salem. Remainder of personal estate to my children, only one, Chambles, is mentioned by name. Exec. William Carpenter and Richard M. Acton. Wit. John N. Cooper, Andrew Sinnickson and William Patterson. Proved June 25, 1850.
E-109

1850, Jan. 16—ELIZABETH GIBSON, widow of Hezekiah Gibson, Upper Alloways Creek, now of Northern Liberties, Philadelpiha. To son Hezekiah, $5, as he has had his share. Children of John Rose, dec'd, late of Millville, $20. Dau. Hannah R. Camplett, residue of estate. She is appointed exec. Wit. Amos W. Griffith, Lewis D. Belair and Jacob Stearly. Proved June 3, 1850.
E-111

1850, June 26—ELKANAH POWELL, Alloways Creek. To wife Anna, the house, garden and barn where I live, in Quintons Bridge, during widowhood; then to be sold; reciepts to my children, Daniel, John R., and heirs of Ruth McCune and Mary Anne Elliot. Exec. son Daniel. Wit. Oliver Harris, Ephraim C. Harris and Stephen Smith. Proved July 13, 1850. E-115

1850, Apr. 17—DAVID ENGLISH, Elsinborough. Estate to be sold and proceeds to my children. Son Enos P. English, grdn of son Southard Quinton English, and son Anthony English, grdn. of son Timothy Craft English, and my daus. Sarah and Jael English Exec. sons Enos and Anthony. Wit. Thomas S. Smith, Benjamin F. Pine and Jacob P. Nicholson. Proved July 15, 1850.
E-117

1847, Jan. 25—MARY CHASE, Salem. To dau. Lucy, wife of Josiah Cline, and my sons Samuel, Stephen and Daniel Chase, $250 to be divided between them. To dau. Lucy, all household goods. Exec. son Samuel. Wit. Daniel Garrison. Proved Aug. 2, 1850.
E-119

1848, Dec. 2—JOHN MURPHEY, Pilesgrove. To wife household goods, cow, and rent of homestead. Remainder of estate to be sold; receipts to daus. Rachel and Phebe, son John, dau. Mary Holdshorn, William C. Nichols and David Nichols. Exec. Ambrose Whitaker. Wit. Benjamin Dare, Enoch VanMeter and George C. Sithen. Proved Sept. 12, 1850. E-121

1850, Feb. 12—WILLIAM THOMPSON, Salem. To wife Elizabeth, $100. Estate to be sold; receipts, 1/3 to wife; residue to my children, Susan G. Hancock, Sarah Grier, Joshua, William, Abigail Dunn, Lewis, Thomas, and Ann Elizabeth Thompson. Exec. wife, and son Joshua. Job Tyler, James Fogg and Josiah Thompson. Proved Sept. 24, 1850. E-123

1850, Apr. 20—ROBERT G. JOHNSON, Salem. To dau

Anna G. Hubbell, during life, the Netherland Farm, subject to payment of $600 to my wife, Juliana E., annually. To said dau. the house in which I live, during life, my wife to occupy said premises. To wife, 2 cows. My books and papers to remain in my mansion, for use of my wife and dau. and her children. To said dau., the Spring House Farm, the Guilford Hall Farm, and all buildings opposite where I live, during life. Grandsons Johnson Hubbels, after the death of my wife and his mother, the mansion house and all buildings; and the plantation on Grant Street and road to Quinton, together with the cottages at the sand hill, and three lots on Guilford Hall Farm, the brick house called the office, and the old house over the alley, with 1/2 the garden and the stable and shed, with a lane between garden and barn, to be fenced between him and his sister Anne; also woodland called Thunderbolt Marsh, in Tillbury. To granddau Anne Law Hubbell, the Netherland Farm, after the death of my wife and her mother, part of the family house, 1/2 of the garden and the barn. Granddaus. Helen Hubbell, after the death of her mother, the Guilford Hall Farm the house, garden and stable adjoining that given her sister Anne. Nephews Thomas and Andrew Sinnickson, cedar swamp on Manumuscin Branch of Morris River. Exec. Thomas Sinnickson and John S. Wood to sell all live stock and farming utensils. Wit. William Bassett, I. Ingham and Charles W. Roberts. Proved Oct. 14, 1850. E-125

1849, Sept. 25—HANNAH HERITAGE. To son Jonathan, $150. Son William, $130. Dau. Esther Cauley, interest on $150; at her death, principal to her dau. Esther H. Cauley. Dau. Elizabeth H. Atkinson interest on $150; at her death, principal to her son Benjamin H. Son Benjamin F., $150. Dau. Emma Ballinger, interest on $150; at her death, principal to her son and dau. Joseph and Priscilla Ballinger. To son Joseph, $5, and aquit him from a note of $195. Granddau. Priscilla M. Wright, $120. Granddau. Priscilla M. Heritage, bedding. Granddau. Hannah Atkinson, case of drawers. Granddau. Esther Cauley, bedding. To my children, Jonathan Heritage, Esther Cauley, Elizabeth H. Atkinson, Benjamin W. Heritage and Anna Ballenger, remainder of estate. Exec. son Jonathan. Wit. Richard Wright, William Haines and Rachel Haines. Proved Oct. 14, 1850. E-130

1849, Oct. 13—POWELL CARPENTER. Real estate to be sold. Wife Mary. Exec. father William Carpenter. Wit. A. D. Keasbey, Edward Keasbey and Eli Adams. Proved Oct. 29, 1850.
E-132

Not Dated—JAMES DARE, Upper Pittsgrove. To wife Hannah A., all estate, after debts are paid, for life; then to daus. Rebecca Hughes, Hannah Jones and Rachel Harris, each $5. To sons Samuel A., James A. and Josiah A., residue of estate. Exec. sons James and Josiah. Wit. Judah Foster and John Johnson, 3d. Proved Oct. 29, 1350.
E-134

1846, July 22—ANN THOMPSON. To son Samuel Thompson, 1/2 of house in Salem, during life; then to his children; if he dies without issue, to John Sinnickson, in trust for my dau. Sallie Ann Robinson, with remainder of the house, during life; then to her children. Letters administration cum testo annexo granted to Joseph Robinson. Wit. S. D. Ingham, D. K. Ingham and R. T. Ingham. Proved Feb. 21, 1848.
E-136

1850, Nov. …—AULEY B. WOOD. To William Simpkins, $100. Mary Mitchell, $50. Remainder of estate to Joseph Henry Wood; if he dies a minor, to the M. E. Church at Sharptown. Exec Oliver Risley. Wit. Joseph L. Risley and Elmer Biddle. Proved Dec. 10, 1850.
E-137

1850, Sept. 27—JOEL S. PRICKITT, Upper Pittsgrove. To sister Ruth Ann Newkirk, my cloak. Neice Elizabeth, dau. of William M. and Ruth Ann Newkirk, bedding, Pictorial Bible, and $5 to have the book bound. Nephew Joseph, son of William and Ruth Ann Newkirk, a trunk and silver watch. Bro. Job Prickitt, my secretary, watch, apparel and my share of land in Burlington County. Neice Hannah, dau. of Job Prickitt, my Book of Marters. Neice Hannah, dau. of Garrett Prickitt, washstand, looking glass and $10. Nephew Lorenzo, son of Clement Newkirk, $10. Residue of estate to be sold; proceeds to bros. and sisters, Garret,

SALEM COUNTY WILLS 97

Job, and Thomas Prickitt and Ann Newkirk and Mariah Newkirk. Exec. bro.-in-law William M. Newkirk. Wit. Judah Foster and Daniel F. Fisler (?or Foster). Proved Dec. 12, 1850.   E-139

1850, Dec. 11—JOESPH TEST, Mannington. To wife Hannah, furniture and 1/2 of remainder of estate. Residue to my children. My son Thomas's children to have their father's share. Nephew John Test, my watch. Exec. wife and Champion Atkinson. Wit. Isaac Hoffman and Anderson Welch. Proved Dec. 14, 1850.   E-141

1849, July 22—LEVI ENGLE, Pilesgrove. To bro. Josiah Engle, $100. Sister Martha Petitt, $100. Neice Elizabeth Davis, my watch Sarah Urion, $5. Pilesgrove Preparatory Meeting, $100, to be invested, interest to be paid annually. Remainder of estate to my bros. and sisters. Exec. bros. Joseph and Josiah. Wit. Thomas Edwards, John G. Ballenger and Aaron Borton. Proved Jan. 20, 1851.   E-143

1829, Sept. 2—JOSEPH ELWELL, Lower Alloways Creek. To dau. Hannah Britton, $1. Son John Elwell, $1. Dau. Mary Harris, $1. Residue of estate to wife Mary during life; then to sons Enoch, Thomas, Abraham, Isaac and Jacob. Exec. wife and son Abraham. Wit. John W. Maskell, Enoch Shepherd and Asa Barratt. Proved Jan. 25, 1851.   E-245

1856, Sept. 10—JAMES BUTCHER, Lower Alloways Creek, To wife Mary during life, the house and land in Lower Alloways Creek and land in Stoe Creek; then to dau. Mary Butcher; if she dies under age, to daus. Elizabeth Lambert, Hannah Lindzey and Lydia Ann Butcher. Woodland to son Robert, and the farm now in his occupation, he to pay my dau. Lydia Ann $833.34, and granddaus. Hannah and Isabella I. Butcher each $333.33. Daus. Elizabeth Lambert and Hannah Lindzey, land in Upper Alloways Creek. Remainder of estate to said daus. Exec. son Robert and sons-in-law John H. Lambert and John Lindzey. Wit. Thomas S. Smith, J. T. Sharp and F. L. Macculloch. Proved Feb. 4, 1851.   E-147

1849 Apr. 3—BENJAMIN FARNKLIN, Mannington. Exec. to sell real estate. Receipts to granddau. Mary Emma Robinson. $1000 to be invested by my son-in-law, James Robinson. Grandson Benjamin Franklin Stocks, son of Luella Stocks, my silver watch. Residue of estate to daus. Hannah Robinson, Esther Moore, Mary Stokes, Sarah Foster and the heirs of my dau. Ann. George M. Ward grdn. of children of dau. Ann. Exec. sons-in-law James Robinson and Joseph Foster, Jr. Wit. Joseph R. Chew, Lydia A. Thomas and John M. Conover. Proved Feb. 13, 1851. E-151

1850, Oct. 5—DANIEL GARRISON, Salem. To wife Mary, land in Pilesgrove and Lower Penns Neck, the house and lot on Penny Hill, in Salem, called the "Smith House." Dau. Ann C., wife of Lewis Brinton, my homestead farm on the Delaware River, in Lower Penns Neck, at Church Landing, and land and swamp east of Hook Road. To son-in-law Lewis Brinton, land in Scull-town, in trust for grandson Daniel Garrison Brinton; if he dies before the lot is sold, then to my dau. Anna C. Brinton. Son-in-law Lewis Brinton, remainder of homestead farm, he to pay my son Daniel J. Garrison $2800, and to trustees of my dau. Juliana Stull, $2000. If he does not accept the land with these conditions, I give 1/2 to son Daniel J. Garrison, and the remainder to Lewis Brinton, in trust for said Juliana. Son Daniel J. Garrison, the Church Landing Farm, part of the tract called "Twelve Rod Road," and part of the "Day Farm." To son Daniel J., and son-in-law Lewis Brinton, the "Murphy Farm," in Lower Penns Neck and all my houses and lots in Salem, called "Simpson Lot," and after my wife's death, the house on Penny Hill, in trust for benefit of my dau. Juliana, wife of John Stull. Grandchildren Artemesia, wife of Charles Newell, Lurina, Edmond and Grant Gibbons, the remainder of the "Day Farm," after the death of my wife. Granddau. Lurina Gibbons, after the death of my wife, the house in Upper Penns Neck. Exec. wife Mary, son Daniel and son-in-law Lewis Brinton. Wit. Isabel P. Thompson, Joseph H. Thompson and R. P. Thompson. Proved Feb. 24, 2851. E-154

1851, Feb. 26—JAMES THOMPSON, Upper Penns Neck. To wife Edith, furniture. As dau. Eliza Ann in her lifetime has had much of my property, I leave her nothing. Son James, my 8-day clock. Personal estate to my children, Mary Jane Baker, Andrew, Samuel and Daniel B., except John W. Thompson, to whom I give $100 more than the rest. Exec. sons Samuel and John W. Wit. James S. Springer, John Simkins and David Peterson. Proved Mar. 13, 1851. E-161

1851, Mar. 2—JOHN DICKINSON, Pilesgrove. To wife Sarah, furniture, and interest on a bond and mortgage held against Deannis Peterson. Son Richman, land in Woodstown. Dau. Sarah Tomlinson, house and lot on Main Street, Woodstown. Dau. Hannah Ann Somers, land conveyed to me by the Friends' Society of Woodstown. Son Mahlon D., a farm near Woodstown, he to pay $200 to my son Richman and $300 to my grandson Charles son of my dau. Maria Groff. $1200 to be invested for benefit of the children of my dau. Eliza Brooks, dec'd. Son Richman, $100, in trust for my son John J.; at his death, to his children. To wife, $50. Exec. sons Richman and Mahlon. Wit. James M. Reed and F. S. Clawson. E-163

1851, Mar. 13—WILLIAM HOLETON, Upper Penns Neck. To wife Matilda, furniture and live stock during life; then to my children. Wit. Samuel Tussey, Joseph Tussey and Samuel C. Ireland. Letters administration granted to William Summerill. Proved Apr. 11, 1851. E-167

1846, Apr. 1—JOHN BLACKWOOD, Upper Alloways Creek. To daus. Clarissa, Fannie, Rosanna, Miranda, Roxanna and Saloma, my fulling mill, factory house, waterworks and land adjoining Henry Freas, Stephen Reeves, Stacy Lloyd and Lauren Boon. If either dies without issue, their share to my son John. Son John, the farm where I now live. Exec. son John. Wit. Ellis Ayres, John M. Davis and Job Ayres. Proved May 1, 1851. E-168

1851, Apr. 14—GABRIEL DOLBOW, Upper Penns Neck. To sons Eli and George, the farm where William Holeton lives. Dau. Amy, wife of Joseph P. Davis and grandsons Gabriel Vanburen

Dolbow and John Bennet Dolbow, remainder of estate. Exec. son-in-law Joseph H. Clark. Wit. Garrett Summerill, John H. Louderback and William S. Vaneman. Proved May 10, 1851.
E-171

1851, Feb. 6—DAVID STRING, Pilesgrove. Receipts of sale of personal estate, after debts are paid, to wife Rachel. She is appointed exec. Wit. Thomas Edwards and Sarah Ballenger. Proved June 10, 1851. E-173

1847, Aug 6—JOHN STEVENSON, Pittsgrove. To wife Elizabeth, all estate. Exec. wife and James H. Trenchard. Wit. John Gamble, John Johnson and William Ackley. Proved June 18, 1851. E-174

1851, Feb. 12—JONAS HORTMAN. To wife Sarah and children Sarah Ann, Samuel Gustavus and Peter Andrew, use of estate. Exec. William Summerill. Wit. Walker Lounsbury, Samuel Justice and Jonathan White. Proved July 23, 1851.
E-176

1851, Mar. ...—THOMAS HARDING, SR., Upper Pittsgrove, To dau. Ann Fisler, $100. Son Benjamin, graveyard lot. Granddau. Lydia Prickitt, $100. To my children, Benjamin, John, Catharine Abbott, Ann Fisler, Rachel Ayres, Elizabeth Burroughs, Thomas, Henry and Eli, remainder of estate. Exec. son Benjamin. Wit. William Mayhew, George B. Martin and Thomas R. Clement. Proved Sept. 3, 1851. E-178

1849, July 26—CHRISTIANA LIPPINCOTT. To grandson Samuel F. Lippincott, my silver watch. Granddau. Christiana B., dau. of dau. Amy Lippincott, silverware. Christiana B. Kitchen, silverware. Sisters Elizabeth Green and Margaret Dolbo, apparel. Sister Elizabeth Green, use of household goods during life; then to neice Sarah B. Kitchen. Neice Margaret Dolbo, $200. Residue of estate to neice Sarah B. Butcher. Exec. bro. Joseph Black and George M. Ward. Wit. John Fowler and Thomas F. Lambson. Proved Sept. 6, 1851. E-180

1846, May 17—SAMUEL HACKETT, Upper Alloways Creek. To wife Elizabeth, house and lot in Allowaystown, where I live, furniture, and $100 per year during widowhood. Personal estate to my children, Joseph R., Samuel, Rebecca wife of John Mower, Jr., Rachel wife of Benjamin Ware, and Elizabeth wife of Samuel Bell. Exec. sons Joseph and Samuel. Wit. Jno. H. Lambert, Charles Hogbin and Henry Powell.

1850, July 24.—Codicil. Exec. to pay $100 to the M.E. Church in Allowaystown toward the building of a parsonage. Wit. William House, Henry Powell and William I. White. Proved Sept. 6, 1851. E-181

1851, July 11—MATHEW MORRISON, Woodstown. To wife Sarah, furniture, silverware, and interest on $1200 yearly. Nephew Jacob Freas, my 8-day clock. Nephew David Freas, my secretary. Friend Elizabeth James, after the death of my wife, workbox and silverware. Elizabeth Ann Newbern, silverware. Elizabeth Ann and Jane, daus. of my sister Jane Penton, dec'd, chinaware. House and lot where I live to be sold; proceeds to the children of my sisters Jane Penton and Mary Freas, including James Mayhew as one of said Mary's children. Share of Elizabeth Ann Newbern to be placed in the hands of her brother John Freas, in trust during the life of her present husband. Exec. Michael Mills. Wit. William Cauley, John M. Clintock and Israel Applegate. Proved Oct. 2, 1857. E-185

1851, Sept. 11—RACHEL RICHMAN. Timber to be sold. Tombstones to be erected at my grave. Residue of estate to my sisters Hannah Richmond and Amanda Richman. Movable estate to sister Amanda. Exec. uncle John Hughes. Wit. Ann T. Johnson, John H. Hitchner and Jacob S. Ludlam. Proved Oct. 18, 1851. E-187

1851, June 5—JOHN BACON, Woodstown. Land on road from Woodstown to Alloway to be sold and debts paid. Wife Sarah, during widowhood, residue of estate; If she remarries, to my children, John, William C. and Hannah Bacon. Allen Wallace grdn. of children. Exec. bro-in-law Isaiah Conklyn. Wit. Paul Cobb, Howell B. Hoffman and William Cauley. Proved Oct. 23, 1851. E-189

1851, Jan. 15—JAMES SHERRON, Salem. All real estate in Lower Alloways Creek to be sold. Granddau. Ann Catharine, a bureau. Grandson Samuel H. Sherron, my desk and watch. The following legacies to be paid: Son James and dau. Elisa Eakin, each $600; grandson James S. McCall, $300; granddau. Hannah Manes, $400; grandson Samuel H. Sherron, $500; grandsons Albert W. Sherron, Charles B. Sherron, George Sherron and Gervas Sherron, each $200; granddaus. Eliza Jane Sherron and Mary Sherron, each $200; granddau. Ann Catharine Sherron, $600; Josephine, widow of Frederick Restine, dec'd who was a grandson of my late wife, $100; Sarah, widow of my late son William Sherron, $200; Mary Brown, who lived with me many years, $100; John C. Cann, $100; Mrs. Elizabeth Cray Raft, $100; Hannah Cann, $50; Mary, wife of Joseph Mankin, $50. Exec. Edward VanMeter. Wit. F. L. Maccullough, Samuel Copner and Joshua Jeffers. Proved Dec. 9, 1851. E-191

1833, Apr. 5—RACHEL GIBBON, Salem. To sons Mason Seeley Gibbon, Edward Keasbey Gibbon, Anthony Keasbey Gibbon, Leonard Gibbon and Quinton Gibbon and dau. Elisa Parvin, each $5. Dau. Sarah Ann Gibbon, remainder of personal estate and the property where I dwell. Exec. Dr. Edward Q. Keasbey and my son Quinton. Wit. Delzil Keasbey, Kezia Keasbey and Ann Mecum.

1846, Mar. 30—Codicil. As the house and lot devised to dau. Sarah Ann has been sold, I order that the proceeds of the sale be paid to her. Wit. Prudence Q. Keasbey. Proved Jan. 2, 1852.
E-194

1851, Dec. 27—GEORGE HALL, Salem. To wife Matilda Stiles Hall, household goods and the house in which we live, and an annuity of $150 from my farm. Son George W., my plantation in Quaker Neck, Mannington, timber on Turnip Hill, in Upper Alloways Creek, and meadow on Nathans Creek; if he dies, to my children Hannah B. Test and Caroline Thompson, subject to payment of the annuity to my wife. Daus. Hannah and Caroline, the dwelling where I live, when my wife ceases to be my widow, also each $100. Remainder of estate to my wife and daus. Exec. Joseph D. Test and Joshua Thompson. Wit. Joshua H. Reeves, Anna M. Riley and Josiah Thompson. Proved Jan. 9, 1852.
E-196

1848, Mar. 7—ANN WALLACE, Pilesgrove. Exec. Peter String and Samuel Garwood. To Peter String and Sarah his wife, and grandsons Samuel and Ephraim Garwood, each $100. To Peter String and Samuel Garwood, $200 during the life of Elmer K. Coles, husband of my granddau. Elizabeth Garwood; after her death, to grandsons Samuel and Ephraim Garwood. Residue of estate to grandchildren Samuel, Ephraim and Elizabeth Coles. Wit. Hugh Grimshaw, Thomas Elwell and Samuel Pimm. Proved Jan. 26, 1852.
E-198

1851, May 22—DAVIS NELSON, Elsinborough. To son William H., 1/2 of estate, and remainder in trust during life of son-in-law William Waddington; if my dau. Eliza M. Waddington shall survive her husband, pay her 1/2 the estate; if the husband survives her, to their children, Frances A. and William R. Waddington. Exec. son William H. Nelson. Wit. Jacob W. Mulford, Charles H. Plummer and Edward VanMeter. Proved Jan. 31, 1852.
E-201.

1851, Dec. 30—JOHN CASPAR, Pilesgrove. To wife Sarah, furniture, and house and lot in Sharptown, during widowhood. Son Thomas J., the house and lot where I live. land on road leading to Penns Grove, land on Swedesboro road, land in Bushtown, and residue of my real estate. Son John, 100 Spanish dollars, bequeathed to me by my father. Grandson Joseph Caspar a note which I hold against Auley B. Wood. Grandsons Charles, Clement and Thomas, a note held against Elijah Horner. William Caspar, a note hled against William Armstrong, and my desk. Granddaus. Hannah, Mary and Anna, a mortgage held against Lorenzo Dow Keen. Exec. son Thomas. Wit. Thomas Elwell, Nathan Kiger and W. T. Clauson. Proved Feb. 7, 1852. E-203

1852, Jan. 3—RUHAMA SHUTE, widow, Upper Penns Neck. To dau. Mary Ann, wife of John Shoemaker, all my money and real estate. Son Atley Shute, the family Bible. Exec. son Samuel C. Shute. Wit. William S. Vaneman, Joseph Diver and Thomas Myles. Proved Mar. 14, 1852. E-206

1852, Feb. 16—ENOS P. REEVES, Upper Alloways Creek. To wife Hannah, use of personal estate during widowhood, excepting $3000, which I order her to hold as grdn. of my children, Sarah Jane, William Henry, Hannah, Anna and Jefferson. Exec. wife and David Bowen. Wit. Jno. H. Lambert, James Husted and William Reeves. Proved Mar. 1, 1852. E-207

1852, Feb. 5 — BENJAMIN FIELD, Pilesgrove. Personal estate to be sold. Receipts, after debts are paid, to be invested for benefit of my wife, during widowhood; then to my children. Exec. Henry Richman. Wit. Charles McCollister, A. H. Foster and William Cauley. Proved Mar. 4, 1852. E-209

1852, Feb. 21—ISAAC REEVES, Upper Alloways Creek. To wife Sarah, the house and lot in Pittsgrove and partly in Upper Alloways Creek; after her death to be sold, and interest on $500 to Township Committee of Upper Alloways Creek for benefit of Nazareth M. E. Church, or trustees of said church, for keeping in repair the meetinghouse, graveyard and fence; balance arising from sale to my heirs, Samuel Reeves, Charles P. Reeves, Elmira Collier and Sarah Reeves. Wife, interest on $500, a horse, wagon and harness. At her death, $200 to above mentioned children; $50 to bro. Caleb Reeves, and $25 to friend Andrew Haun. To son

Samuel, $1000; he to liquidate all claims against my estate, and he is to have $500 out of my real and personal estate. Son Charles, $2000. Exec. Joseph C. Nelson and David D. Dare. Wit. Providence Sheppard, Andrew Haun and George Avis, Jr. Proved Mar. 5, 1852.   E-211

1850, June 24 — NORTON NICHOLS, Upper Pittsgrove. $1000 to be invested and I devise the interest to wife Abigail Ann, during life; then to Achsah Ann Richman, dau. of said wife. To wife, income from bushland and the house and lot where I now live; at her death to Achsah Ann Richman. Exec. Ambrose Whitaker. Wit. Gilbert H. Craig, John M. Swing and Harriet Craig. Proved Mar. 15, 1852.   E-215

1851, Sept. 9—REBECCA MILES, Salem. To dau. Adaline Miles, during life, the house where I now live; at her death to dau. Elizabeth Henry during life. If Adaline survives Elizabeth, then to Elizabeth's daus., Elizabeth, Maria and Amelia Henry. Exec. dau. Elizabeth Henry. Wit. Edw. S. Singley and N. Leeds. Proved Mar. 15, 1852.   E-217

1849, May 23—GEORGE BOWEN, Salem. To sons Clinton and George, each a bureau. Son Thomas H., my watch and apparel. Residue of furniture to wife, who is made grdn. of the children. Exec. wife and William Carpenter. Wit. F. L. Macculloch, Isaac English and Charles Mulford. Proved Mar. 18, 1852.   E-218

1852, May 14 — ANN LADOW, Upper Alloways Creek. Estate to grandchildren, Charlotty and Isaac Moore. They are appointed exec. Wit. Daniel Vaneman, Mason Simms and Lewis M. James. Proved June 2, 1852.   E-222

1851, July 14—PRUDENCE KEASBEY. To sister Hannah VanMeter, land in Elsinborough. To trustees of First Presbyterian Church of Salem, $1000 to be expended for the erection of a new edifice. To the several boards of the (old school) Presbyterian Church in the U. S. A., viz: to the trustees of the Board of Missions, $200; Church Extension, $400; Board of Education, $200; Board of Publication, $200. $1000 to be invested for benefit of my sister Hannah VanMeter. Sisters Rebecca A. Hannah and Annah K. Hannah, each $100. Neices and nephews, children of deceased bro. Mathew Keasbey, Caroline and Elizabeth, each $500; Charles, Anthony, Quinton and John, their father's note for $150, to be divided between them. Children of bro. Edward P. Keasbey, Anthony Q, Edward, Helen and Anne A. Keasbey, each $100. Children of Anna K. Hancock, Charles Gilbert and Percival Araby, each $300; Cornelia Artemesia, $500. To Rev. James G. Ware, $300. Rev. John Burtt, $200. Mrs. Rebecca Ware, $200. Sarah A. Gibbons, $100. Garret Parvin, $200. Ann, dau. of Edward Keasbey, $100. Bro.-in-law James M. Hannah, exec., $100. Wit. George C. Rumsey, John Wistar and H. B. Ware. Proved June 3, 1852. E-223

1852, Apr, 8—WILLIAM N. ANTRIM, Pilesgrove. To wife Tabitha, my watch; at her death, to stepson Benjamin Fish of Philadelphia. wife remainder of personal estate. Exec. stepson Benjamin Fish. To wife during widowhood, the house and lot in Newtown, Pilesgrove, said Benjamin Fish to have the house and lot in his care while my wife remains my widow; then to said Benjamin. Wit. William Cauley, Samuel B. Bradway and Asher Lecroy. Proved June 22, 1852. E-226

——, Dec. 27—ISAAC ADCOCK,. To son Isaac P., land in Pittsgrove and in Woolwich and Harrison Townships, Gloucester Co., subject to incumberances. To Elizabeth, wife of son Isaac, two shares in the steamboat "Cohansey," of Bridgeton. Dau. Martha O., wife of Jonathan DuBois, land in Fairfield Township, Cumberland Co., and two shares in said steamboat. Dau. Amy, wife of Jeremiah DuBois, land called Pamphylia Farm, in Deerfield Township, and also land in Pittsgrove, and two shares in said steamboat. Residue of estate to daus. Martha and Amy and son Isaac. Exec. son Isaac. Wit. Jacob Howey, Elizabeth Howey and Thomas Riley. Proved July 3, 1852. E-228

1845, Mar. 20—SARAH MORRISON, Pilesgrove. To son Matthew, silverware, gold pencil and rings. $1500 to be invested for benefit of my husband during life; then to son Matthew. Exec. John L. Risley. Wit. Joseph Cook, David F. Turner and Ebenezer S. Reeves. Proved July 7, 1852. E-231

1851, Dec. 2—NOAH LEEDS. Real and personal estate and five shares in the Salem B. & L. Ass'n to dau. Ann L. Singley. Exec. Edward Singley. Wit. George M. Ward and Elijah Ware. Proved July 29, 1852. E-232

1849, June 29—JOSEPH NEWKIRK, Upper Pittsgrove. To wife Susannah, during widowhood, $600 to be invested. The farm to Friendship M. E. Church, providing that if said Church ceases to be in connection or under control of the New Jersey M. E. Conference, I give the farm to Clement, Cornelius Isaac, Joseph and William Newkirk. To wife, horse, wagon, cow, furniture and $100. Neices Mary V. Robinson and Sarah DuBois, each $100. Residue of estate after debts are paid, to nephews, Clement, Cornelius D., Isaac, Joseph, William M. and Joast Newkirk. Exec. nephew Clement Newkirk. Wit. Moses Richman, Jr., Henry Harding and Robert Patterson. Proved Nov. 11, 1852. E-234

1851, May 16 — REBECCA HUBBS, Pilesgrove. Estate to be sold and debts paid. Remainder to son John and dau. Beulah Hubbs. Exec. Caspar Wistar. Wit. Jonathan Freedland, Thomas B. Cooper and Hannah A. Warner. Proved Oct. 19, 1852.
E-236

1852, Aug. 27 — DORCAS CURREY, Upper Penns Neck. Real estate to be sold. To dau. Ann M. Mayhew. Granddau. Margaret Mayhew, silverware. Remainder to children, Ann M. Mayhew, Elizabeth Guest, Abraham A. Currey, Sarah Cosens, John Currey, Harriet Kirby and Ann Cosens. Exec. Mark A. Mayhew. Wit. Joseph L. Horner, Anthony A. Jorden and Jacob Banks. Proved Nov. 29, 1852. E-237

108   SALEM COUNTY WILLS

1847, Aug. 4—MARY N. THOMPSON, Salem. Land on south side of Broadway, Salem, to my mother, Esther Thompson, during life; then to sister Esther Thompson. Residue or estate to sister Elizabeth Thompson. Exec. sisters Esther and Elizabeth. Wit. F. L. Macculloch, O. B. Stoughton and Richard M. Acton. Proved Dec. 13, 1852.   E-238

1849, July 24—THOMAS M'CALLISTER, Pilesgrove. Exec. sons James and Thomas. To wife Deborah, furniture and an annuity of $200 during life. Son James, privilege of occupying the farm; he to keep the buildings in repair and pay the taxes, and pay $200 to my wife, and $300 to be divided among my children, Sarah Nichols, Jane M'Callister, Thomas M'Callister, Charlotte Jenkins, Harriet M'Callister, Rebecca Harker, William M'Callister, Isaac M'Callister and Mary Isabella M'Callister. Wit. William M. Cauley, John H. Lippincott and Isaac Lewis. Proved Jan. 15, 1853.   E-240

1847, June 5—GEORGE SHIMP, Upper Alloways Creek. To wife Margaret, furniture and $50. Daus. Elizabeth Reeve and Mary Remster, each $50. Son Simon, woodland. Son Archibald, residue of farm. Heirs of sons Daniel and George, each $1. Granddau. Sarah, dau. of Benjamin Remster, $1. Tombstones to be placed at grave, and if wife Margaret is buried in the same graveyard as my first two wives, my sons to put suitable stones at her grave. Exec. sons Simon and Archibald. Wit Jno. H. Lambert, John Shimp and David Shimp. Proved Jan. 29, 1853.
    E-243

1852, June 1—JOSEPH BOWEN, Mannington. To dau. dau. Elizabeth Madkiff, $100. To her son Dansel Madkiff, $50. To Joseph Henry Bell, son of my grandson Benjamin Bell, $150. Son Robert Bowen, $100. Rachel, wife of my grandson Benjamin Bell, bedding and $50. Dau. Hannah Bell, $100. Exec. grandson Samuel Bell. Wit. Lot F. Miller, William House and Thomas I. Yarrow. Proved Mar. 1, 1853.   E-245

1848, Apr. 7—MARY CAMP (widow). To grandchildren Thomas Lippincott of Philadelphia and Mary Ann wife of Ebenezer P. Dunn, children of my dau. Elizabeth wife of Samuel Cole, by her first husband, furniture, the house I occupy and all real estate. Exec. Andrew Sinnickson. Wit. Thomas Sinnickson. Samuel L. Cooper and Thomas Dickinson. Proved Mar. 2, 1853.   E-247

Not Dated—MARK SEEDS, Pittsgrove. To wife Catharine I., all furniture and land during life. To children Benjamin, Mark, Ann, Jeremiah, and Alexander, $1 each. Son John and Fithian, each $1 and 1/2 of real estate after the death of my wife. To Mary Ann Whitaker, $1. Exec. wife. Wit. J. Sheppard Whitaher, Isaac Langley and William Langley. Proved Mar. 17, 1853.
E-251

1852, Feb. 27—BACON WARE, Salem. Estate to wife Anna Jane, and she is appointed exec. Wit. William M. Roberts, John E. Preston and Thomas Sinnickson. Proved Apr. 4, 1853. E-252

1852, Aug. 29—JOHN ROBBINS, Upper Alloways Creek. Exec. to sell all estate. To neice Deborah Somers, $30. To the Seventh Day Baptist Missionary Society $10. David Clawson, $10. Remainder, after debts are paid, to Dickason Moore, Levi Keen, John R Moore, Sr, Mary Fursman, all of Philadelphia; John R. Moore, Jr., Elizabeth Bivins, Elizabeth Danzenbaker, Daniel Moore, John Loper, Richard Burt, Sarah wife of Isaac Davis, Keziah wife of William Reeves, Susan wife of Joseph Robinson, Keziah wife of Caleb Davis, Hezekiah Gibson, John Keren and Robbins Ayres. Exec. Belford E. Davis. Wit. Horace B. Davis, Charles G. Frazer and George H. Davis. Proved Apr. 5, 1853.
E-254

1852, Nov. 1—CLARISSA ANDREWS. To neice Mary W. Matson, bedding, silverware, and interest on a mortgage during the life of her husband. If she dies without issue, to her sisters, Martha C. Andrews, Rachel Shourds and Mary A. Shourds. To

Clary A. Shourds, silverware and $10. Residue of estate to neices Rachel and Mary A. Shourds, who are appointed exec. Wit. John M. Brown and George B. Robertson. Proved Apr. 18, 1853.　　　　　　　　　　　　　　　　　　　　　　　　E-255

1853, Mar. 18—THOMAS BACON, Salem. To wife Elizabeth, furniture, and the dwelling in which we live, during life; then to son John S. Remainder of personal estate to be sold, and receipts invested for benefit of my wife; at her death, to son John S. Bacon and stepson Joshua B. Stretch. Exec. son-in-law Waddington Bradway. Wit. Moses Richman, Jr., Job Tyler and Josiah Thompson. Proved Apr. 18, 1853.　　　　　　E-258

1833, Mar. 8—WILLIAM D. BAKER. To wife Susannah, personal estate, after debts are paid. Bros. Jacob, John and Joseph Baker, each $18.33. All real estate to wife, who is appointed exec. Wit. Jno. H. Lambert and F. T. Calehopper. Proved Apr. 26, 1853.　　　　　　　　　　　　　　　　　E-259

1853, Apr. 7—DAVID HILLMAN, Upper Penns Neck. Exec. to sell farm, and the rest of real estate after the death of my wife. To wife Catharine, the farm bot. of her bro. and sister. After her death, estate to youngest daus., Hannah N. and Martha C., who are to have $20 more than the other children. Exec. Hudson A. Springer. Wit. Neal Curry and Josiah DuBois. Proved Apr. 26, 1853.　　　　　　　　　　　　　　　　E-261

1849, Aug. 21—SAMUEL BOND, Upper Penns Neck. To wife Elizabeth, the share she would have received had I died intestate. $1500 to be divided between daus. Mary Jane, Rebecca Ann and Harriet. Remainder of estate to sons William, Asa and John. Exec. Hudson A. Springer. Wit. Samuel M. Hunt, Griffith Owen and Richard P. Sparks. Proved Apr. 26, 1853. E-263

1851, Jan. 25—JOSEPH L. F. ENGLISH, Lower Alloways Creek. To bro. Anthony English, $1. Theodore English, child of

Rebecca Cline, wife of Joseph Fox, $100 at 21 years of age. If he dies before becoming of age, to my sisters, Mary, wife of George W. Stretch, Sarah and Jael English. Bro. Samuel L. Southard English, $100 at 21 years of age. Remainder of estate to my sisters. Exec. William H. Nelson. Wit. R. P. Thompson and Israel Smith. Proved May 14, 1853. E-264

1853, Apr. 7—SUSAN D. AYRES, Upper Alloways Creek. To son Winfield S. Ayres, my silver watch. Daus Rebecca Jane and Lucetta M. Ayres, silverware. Personal estate to be sold; receipts to my children, John B., Rebecca J., Winfield S. and Lucetta M. Mordecai Davis, grdn. of youngest children, Winfield and Lucetta. Exec. John B. Ayres. Wit. Jeremy Davis, Mary B. Davis and Belford E. Davis. Proved May 23, 1853.
E-266

1853, Apr. 8—ELISHA MAYHEW, Elsinborough. To wife Maria, all real estate during life; then to my children, David, Mary and Mark Mayhew. Exec. William Powell. Wit. Thomas Shourds, John Councillor and John D. Stewart. Proved May 18, 1853. E-268

1853, May 18—ANTHONY M. ENGLISH. To wife Hannah S., a cow, hog, furniture, wheat and potatoes. Residue of estate to be sold; receipts to wife and children, William S., Mary S., and David S. Wife and Samuel Patrick, grdn. of children. Exec. bro. Enos P. English and Robert Grier. Wit. William S. Cleaver, James H. Patterson and Benjamin N. Smith. Proved July 5, 1853. E-270

1853, Mar. 21--SARAH LITTLE, Salem. To Henrietta, wife of L. P. Smith, $25. Neices Mary and Margaret Johnson, daus. of my sister Mary, $25 each. Residue of estate to my children, Margaretta, wife of Isaac A. Sheppard, Ellen M., wife of Thomas Griffith, Robert E., Sarah Jane, wife of Joseph Griffith, and Benjamin Franklin Little. Exec. dau. Margaret C. Sheppard. Wit. Margaret Rumsey and Jane Mecum. Proved July 28, 1853.
E-273

SALEM COUNTY WILLS

1853, July 16—HANNAH REEVES, Upper Alloways Creek. To children, Sarah Jane, William H., Enos P., Hannah, Anna and Jefferson Reeves, real and personal estate at 21 years of age. Exec., and grdn. of children, William Sickler and bro-in-law John P. McCune. Wit. William House and David Shimp. Proved July 30, 1853.   E-275

1852, Aug. 12—ELIZABETH MARTIN, wife of Jacob Martin. All estate to friend Isaac Johnson, in trust, my husband to manage during his life and pay the taxes; after death of husband, to son Henry, 1/3 of estate; 1/3 to said Isaac Johnson in trust, my son George to occupy same during life, and then to grandson Jacob, his son; 1/3 to Isaac Johnson, in trust. son Samuel to occupy same during life, then to his children. Residue of estate to dau. Mary Martin. Exec. husband Jacob Martin. Wit. Peter Martin, John Fox and D. M. Fox. Proved Aug. 4, 1853.   E-277

1853, July 14—JOHN EMLEY, Allowaystown. To sister Keziah McIlvain, all estate. She is appointed exec. Wit. James Reeves, George E. Bee and William W. Foster. Proved Aug. 15, 1853.   E-281

1853, July 25—DAVID STANTON. To bro. Richard Stanton, $250. Interest on remaining estate to the Baptist Home Missionary Society of the U. S., until the death of my bro. Richard; then estate to his children. Exec. bro. Richard Stanton and George Kelton. Wit. Daniel J. Freas, Thompson Tuft and William Lawrence. Proved Aug 6, 1853.   E-283

1853, Apr. 25—DAVID FRAZER. To wife Elizabeth, $100. Sons Joseph K., Charles P. and Caleb N., each $100. Hester, wife of John Frazer, $25. Remainder of estate to my children, Isaac N., David S., Adam N., Jacob M., John, Samuel M. and Lydia. Exec. son Joseph. Wit. William House and John R. Tice. Proved Aug. 8, 1853.   E-284

SALEM COUNTY WILLS 113

1847, Apr. 2—BATHSHEBA WOOD, Pittsgrove. To Bathsheba and Henry W. Hanthorn, each $50. Rachel J. Bell (nee Young) and Mary Young, each $25. Estate to be sold; proceeds to Mary D. Hanthorn (nee Lake), Rachel J. Bell, Mary L. Young, Henry W. Hanthorn, Moses Thomas and John D. Thomas. Exec. to pay devises given to Bathsheba and Henry Hanthorn to their father, Simon Hanthorn. Exec. Moses Thomas. Wit. Jonathan Hogate Mark Garton and John H. Trenchard. Proved Aug. 29, 1853. E-287

1853, July 23—EDWARD BRADWAY, Salem. To wife Mary, the dwelling occupied by Isabella Teel, and the goods she brought at marriage. Grandsons Edward B. Fennemore, my silver watch. Real and personal estate to be sold; receipts, $300 to my wife; remainder to son William W. and daus. Elizabeth Bradway and Ann Fennemore. Exec. Waddington Bradway. Wit. John Williams, Joseph Sanderlin and Daniel Jarman. Proved Sept. 9, 1853. E-289

1851, Aug. 30—ASA GROFF, Upper Pittsgrove. Real estate to heirs of sister Sarah Ivins, dec'd, heirs of sister Letitia Holdcraft, dec'd, heirs of sister Martha Sweetman, dec'd, children of bro. John Groff, bro. William M. Groff, sister Deborah Harker, and heirs of bro. Benjamin A. Groff, dec'd. Exec. bro. William M. Groff. Wit. Thomas R. Clement, Charles Bacon, William C. Elwell. Proved Sept. 27, 1853. E-291

1853, Sept. 20—MATTHEW McBRIDE, Salem, Exec to sell saw mill property on Chop Tank River, in Maryland. Exec. to retain property for five years and pay dau. Mary $50; then residue of estate to son John and dau. Mary. Exec. wife Ann and son John. Wit. Edward VanMeter, John Comminskey and William Ough. Proved Oct. 3, 1853. E-293

1852, May 28—ISAAC ENGLISH, Upper Alloways Creek. To son Aulay, silver watch. Dau. Sarah D., the gold watch that belonged to her mother. Daus. Mary Jane and Hannah silverware. Estate to be sold; receipts to my children, William McCalla English to have $200 less than the others, he having had more than that amount Exec. sons Charles H. and James and bro.-in-law Aulay McCalla. Wit. Robert F. Young, Charles Mulford and John W. Mulford. Proved Sept. 24, 1853. E-296

1853, Oct. 18—REMMERS WESTERBECK, late of Ost, Freesland, in the Kingdom of Hanover, now a resident of Woodstown. Having left a mother and three sisters in my native country, and having no near relatives in the U. S., I feel that my property should not pass out of my family. Exec. to sell estate and pay debts; residue to my mother and sisters. Exec. Mahlon D. Dickinson and George T. Groff. Wit. Theophilus H. Hillman, Charles C. Loudenslager and Martha D. Dickinson. Proved Oct. 31, 1853. E-298

1853, Sept. 5—JAMES D. CRAIG, Upper Pittsgrove. To wife Pamela, use of new house, bedding bureau, and $36 to be paid by son Samuel, yearly. Dau. Sarah Brown, during life, the saw mill tract, lot bot. of Nathan Lawrence, adjoining saw mill tract, a small lot on south side of road adjoining Providence Sheppard and a lot on west side of house where she now lives; at her death, to son Samuel, execpt lot on west side is to be divided between son Samuel and dau. Mary Ann C. Boon. To son Samuel, the old farm on which I now reside, and woodland laid out in the division of my father's estate to my brother Samuel and myself, after taking off the saw mill tract; also wood lot opposite James Peacock's house, To dau. Mary Ann C. Boon, the farm where they now live and woodland and swamp. To Albert S., son of dau. Elizabeth Emmel, woodland in Alloways Creek; if he dies, to son Samuel and dau. Mary Ann C. Boon. Exec. Nathaniel G. Swing. Wit. Andrew Hann, John Dickinson and Mary Dickinson. Proved Nov. 6, 1853. E-300

1853, Oct. 21—JOSEPH BARNES, Pilesgrove. To wife Phebe Ann, the house and lot where I live during life, and $200 worth of furniture. Daus. Rebecca Hall and Mary Jane Barnes, the farm in Woodstown on the Sculltown road. The farm and woodland where Ebenezer Kirby lives, to daus. Phebe Ann and Arrabella. Residue of estate to be sold. Exec. Joseph N. Riley, James Woolman and Samuel Bolton. Wit. Thomas Brick, Richard Gosling and Joseph L. Risley. Proved Nov. 7, 1853. E-304

1853, Oct. 18—ISAAC HUMPHREYS. Exec. William Austin and Robert P. Robinson. To wife Lydia, furniture. $200 to be invested for benefit of Ann, wid. of Samuel Johnson. To wife, out of my estate, $300, and $350 yearly. Children mentioned, but not by name. Wit. Israel Applegate, George W. Willis and W. S. Clawson. Proved Nov. 7, 1853. E-306

1853, May 3—JOSEPH TUSSEY, Upper Penns Neck. To wife Sarah, all estate during widowhood; then to my children, Samuel, William, David and John. Exec. son Samuel. Wit. Clement A. Borden, Joseph Paulson and John K. Louderback. Proved Nov. 9, 1853. E-308

1853, Apr. 28—ADAM HARBESON, Upper Penns Neck. To wife Margaret, $60 annually during life. Son Elijah to pay her $40, and dau. Margaret, wife of John Peterson, to pay $20. Dau. Margaret, the plantation occupied by John Peterson, during life; then to her dau. Mary Jane Peterson, during life; if she dies without issue, to my children, David, Isaac, Hannah Pedrick, and George, subject to the payment of $20 annually to my wife. Dau. Prudence Lawrence $30 annually during life. Heirs of sons Samuel and John, $5. Sons Robert, David, Isaac, George and dau. Hannah, $5 each. Son Elijah remainder of estate. Exec. son Elijah. Wit. John K. Louderback, David Sheets and William Holeton. Proved Dec. 2, 1853. E-310

1851, Nov. 3—DANIEL PENTON, Upper Alloways Creek. To dau. Hannah Hitchner, all land on north side of the road from Salem to Allowaystown by way of Guineatown. Dau. Elizabeth

Ann, house and land in Guineatown during life; then to her children. Residue of estate to be sold. receipts to daus. and my granddau. Sarah Penton. Exec. John H. Lambert. Wit. William House and John Laurence. Proved Dec. 24, 1853. E-313

Not Dated—WILLIAM BENSON, Upper Alloways Creek. To sons Samuel and Morris and dau. Mary Jane, wife of John George, each $1. Grandson Josiah, son of son Samuel, the house and land in Maddentown. To Elmer Benson, son of dau. Mary Jane George, land in Maddentown. Son Lewis, residue of estate. Exec. Thomas S. Smith. Wit. Thomas Dickinson, S. A. Allen and Henry Fox. Proved Mar. 4, 1854. E-316

1852, Nov. 24—JOAST NEWKIRK, Upper Pittsgrove. To wife Mary, real and personal estate where I now live, and my farm on the road from Pole Tavern to Little Ease Mill, until my children are 21 years of age; then 1/3 of real estate to wife during life; then to my children. After the death of my wife, the farm occupied by William Curry to be sold; receipts to sister Sarah Sithens' children, Mary Ann, Sedgwick R. and Lucy V. Sithens. Exec. Cornelius D. Newkirk. Wit. Joseph C. Nelson, John Delks and Moses Thomas, Jr. Proved Apr. 11, 1854. E-318

1850, Oct. 28—WILLIAM BOWEN, Salem. To wife, all personal estate, after debts are paid, during life; then to my sons Joseph and Withnal. To wife Priscilla, the house and lot on Second Street, in Salem; after her death, to my youngest sons, Josiah H. and William S. Exec. wife. Wit. Daniel Miller, Ann Wright and George. M. Ward. Proved May 2, 1854. E-320

1854, May 2—SAMUEL WIBLE, Woodstown. To wife Ruth, furniture, and $180 yearly during life; sons John B. and Samuel to pay her $50 each, and son Joshua $200. Exec. to sell farm in Pilesgrove, and all real and personal estate not devised; receipts to be invested during wife's life; then to my children, son David's share to his son Thomas; also the further sum of $100. Exec.

sons-in-law Joseph Hackett and Elmer Reeve and son Joshua. Wit. W. M. Cawley, Proved May 18, 1854. E-322

1853, Nov. 9—GEORGE P. COX, Allowaystown. To stepfather Jesse Early and mother Mary Early, all estate during life; then to my three sosters and their children. Letters of administration granted to Jesse Early. Wit. Augustus Reeve, Joseph A. McKasson and William W. Foster. Proved June 5, 1854. E-325

1841, Sept. 15—HANNAH HUDDY (maiden), formerly of Philadelphia, but now of Mannington. To sister Martha, wife of John Mowers, apparel. Neice Maria Fry, apparel and furniture, and $30 to her and her mother, annually. Nephews John Robinson, Adam and Ephraim Mowers, each $50. Cousin Elizabeth Fisher, $20. Mary Tuft, $10. Neice Hannah Cline, $50. Sister Martha Mowers, remainder of estate. Exec. Caspar Wistar. Wit. Theophilus E. Beesley, Hannah W. Beesley and C. W. Beesley.

1852, Mar. 19—Codicil. Hannah Huddy and Mary Tuft being deceased, I bequeath $50 to Daniel Huddy Mowers, son of Ephraim Mowers, or Wilmington, Del., and $10 to Kesiah Bellville, of Philadelphia. Wit. Theophilus Beesley and Caspar Wistar. Proved July 27, 1854. E-326

1854, July 22—URIAH ACKLEY, Pittsgrove. To wife Sarah, $800. Real estate to be sold. Children Samuel, William, Joseph, Rachel wife of James Hanners, Hannah wife of Elam Mayhew, Ann wife of Josiah Ewing, Mary wife of Garret Langley, John, Jesse, Sarah wife of John Prime (?Pimm), Ruth wife of Jacob Creamer, Coombs, Jane wife of Nathaniel Ogden, and George. Exec. wife and sons Samuel and Joseph. Wit. Stephen A. Garrison, Richard Hanthorn and Isaac Hanthorn. Proved Aug. 18, 1854. E-329

1853, Apr. 13—CHARLES GRIER, Elsinborough. Farm to be sold. To George and Lydia Ann, children of Jonathan B. Grier, and Georgianna, dau. of Robert Grier, each $1000. Richard, son of John H. Patrick, $1500; remainder to George and Charles L., sons of John H. Patrick. To Ruth, dau. of Robert Grier, house and lot in Lower Alloways Creek, conveyed to me by my father, George Grier subject to my mother's life estate therein. Residue of estate to George, Lydia, Anna and Georgianna Grier and Richard, George and Charles L. Patrick. Exec. Jonathan B. Grier and Robert Grier. Wit. F. L. Macculloch, Isaac Hackett and John Kirby. Proved Sept. 9, 1854. E-331

1850, Feb. 23—JONATHAN SMITH, Woodstown. To wife Hannah, furniture, and house and lot in Woodstown for life and $1000 yearly to be paid by my dau. Jerusha White and my son Jonathan D. Smith. $1000 to be invested for benefit of my wife; at her death, to daus. Jerusha White and Elizabeth Fithian and my son Jonathan. Dau. Jerusha, land bot. of William White, the farm called Witherill Farm, meadow adjoining it, land bot. of David M. Davis, a house and lot in Woodstown, lands bot. of various others, $1000, and $150 to be paid her by my son Jonathan. Son Jonathan, land on road from Woodstown to Sculltown; he to pay dau. Elizabeth Fithian $150. Land in Pilesgrove to dau. Jerusha and son Jonathan. Land to grandchildren Hannah, Mary E. and Adelaide Fithian. Exec. daus. Jerusha White and Elizabeth Fithian, and son Jonathan. Wit. Richard F. Turner, Ephraim Walters, Jr , and Joseph L. Risley.

1853, July 11-.-Codicil. Whereas Adaline Fithian has died, her legacy is given to granddaus. Hannah, now wife of B. Lippincott, and Mary E. Fithian. Wit. Josiah W. Richman, Richard Turner and Joseph L. Risley. Proved Sept. 8, 1854. E-334

1852, Oct. 1—JOHN TORTON, Lower Penns Neck. To wife Sarah, all estate. Exec. William Dunn. Wit. Elijah Hancock, Sarah Garrison and William Dunn. Proved Sept. 18, 1854.
E-339

1854, June 6—JULIANA E. JOHNSON, widow of Robert G. Johnson. To Robert Carney Johnson, after the death of his sister Ann G. Hubbell, the house in which I live. Family portraits to nephew William C. Zantzinger, of Washington, D. C. To Madeline Henttenback, two cows. Sister Harriet, apparel; at her death, to Madeline Henttenback and her dau. Lependine. Residue of estate to sister Harriet Zantzinger. Exec. Robert Carney Johnson. Wit. John P. Bruna and Edward VanMeter. Proved Aug. 17, 1854. E-340

1854, July 19—WILLIAM WADDINGTON, Lower Alloways Creek. To wife Eliza M., during life, the house and lot at Hancocks Bridge; after her death, to Frances N. Waddington. To wife, furniture, store goods and fixtures and book accounts. Son William R., land and meadow in Alloways Creek Neck, he to pay $250 annually to my wife. Dau. Hannah Waddington, $500. Dau. Frances N. Waddington, $3500. Son William R., $2500, my library, bookcase. desk, watch, and a heifer calf. To the daus. of John M. Nelson, Eliza, $500, Catharine $250, and Mary Jane, $200. Exec. wife and bro.-in-law William H. Nelson. Wit. F. L. Macculloch, William Morrison and William C. Lanning. Proved Sept. 18, 1854. E-342

1852, Oct. 2—JOHN CURRY, Upper Pittsgrove. To wife Sarah, furniture, and house where I live, during life. and I order my sons John. William and Abraham to furnish firewood and the sum of $100 quarterly. Son John, land and buildings where I live. Son William, land on west side of turnpike, adjoining Ann J. Curry. Son Abraham land on road to Wig Lane and road leading to Pittstown. Grandchildren Elmer, Eliza and Margaret, land on Wig Lane road, and $173 to be paid them by sons John and William. Daus. Rachel Delks and Sarah Conly, $250 each. Exec. sons William and John. Wit. William Loper, Joseph C. Nelson and James H. Trenchard. Proved Sept. 19, 1854. E-345

1853, Apr. 14—JOHN SUMMERILL, SR. Upper Penns Neck. To wife Christiana. $300 and movables; each of my children to pay her $50 per year, except John, who shall pay $25. Son John, land at the Cove, and woodland. Residue of real estate, except the house on road from Biddle's Tavern to the Cove, to my widow during life; then to my children, Naomi, Garrett, William, Ann, Rebecca and Joseph. Exec. sons Garrett and William. Wit. Hudson A. Springer, Richard Somers and John Dickinson. Proved Sept. 25, 1854. E-349

1854, Oct. 3—JOB TYLER, Salem. To Hannah Dunham, during life, interest on $1000. At her death, the principal to my grandneice Rachel Tyler, and grandnephew James Tyler. Real estate to be sold. Exec. Joseph D. Test. Wit. John M. Cooper, Samuel Shimp and Benjamin Lloyd. Proved Oct. 13, 1854.
E-355

1853, May 20—MARY D. STRETCH, Lower Alloways Creek. Two houses to be sold, and proceeds to daus. Beulah Kiger and Sarah Mitten and sons William, John W., Mark D., and Charles Bradway. Exec. son Charles Bradway. Wit. William S. Carll, Sarah Stewart and Washington Bradway. Proved Nov. 11, 1854. E-356

1852, June 10—CHRISTIANA VANNEMAN, Pilesgrove. To dau. Mary, wife of Richman Dickerson, furniture, and $3300 which Richman Dickerson owes me; at her death, to her children Isaac V., John W. and Charles G. Dickerson. To above named grandsons, my farm in Upper Penns Neck, provided they pay my grandchildren James D. and Christiana Wallace each $1000, they being children of my dau. Clarissa, wife of Wesley W. Wallace. To grandsons Isaac V., John W. and Charles Dickerson, residue of estate. Exec. grandson Isaac V. Dickerson. Wit. William S. Vanneman, Caroline M. Vanneman and Hannah Vanneman. Proved Dec. 1, 1854. E-358

1854, Sept. 9—ELIZABETH FITHIAN, Woodstown. To son Daniel Smith Bowen, the house where I live, which my father, Jonathan Smith, dec'd, and my first husband, Dr. Daniel Bowen, bot. of David Davis, and 1/3 of woodland in Pilesgrove and Mandington, the house and lot adjoining the first mentioned lot, and

$800. To granddau. Mariah Elizabeth, dau. of Daniel S. Bowen, landscape and china. Grandson Randolph P., son of Benjamin B. and my dau. Hannah S. Lippincott, the secretary that belonged to his grandfather. Daus. Hannah S. Lippincott and Mary Fithian, remainder of estate. Exec. bro. Jonathan D. Smith. Wit. William Cra-amer, M. Oliphant and Benjamin H. Lippincott. Proved Dec. 1, 1854. E-360

1854, Sept. 18—JAMES S. SPRINGER, Upper Penns Neck. Exec to sell personal estate. To mother Christiana Springer, $150 per year during life. To wife Lydia L., bedding, furniture, and $120 per year during life. Residue of estate to my children, Anna L., Maria L., Mary Jane, Cornelia, and Wilber. After the death of Mother Springer, I give to son Wilber $1100; remainder to my daus. Cousin Thomas Flanigan grdn. of daus. Cousin John M. Springer exec., and grdn. of son Wilber and dau. Cornelia. Wit. James Stiles, John Justice and Jacob Stiles. Proved Dec. 2, 1854. E-362

1849, July 16—ISRAEL LONGACRE, Upper Penns Neck. To wife Martha, personal property, the homestead farm and woodland. Remainder of real estate to be sold; proceeds to my children, Elizabeth, wife of James McCollister, Andrew, Joseph, Israel, Anna Maria, Samuel, Peter and William. At death of my widow, real estate left to her to be sold; receipts to my children. Thomas Flanagin and William S. Vanneman grdn. of minor children and exec. Wit. Benjamin Smith, William S. Vanneman and John M. Springer. Proved Dec. 2, 1854. E-364

1854, Nov. 20—WILLIAM BROWN, Upper Pittsgrove. Stock and personal property to be sold and debts paid. To wife Sarah, the house and land on which I live, in Upper Pittsgrove, and land called Garrison Tract, with house thereon in Upper Alloways Creek. To bro. Mathew Brown, after the death of my wife, the estate where I live and the house in Upper Pittsgrove; at her death, the farm in Upper Alloways Creek to be sold; proceeds to my sisters, Sarah Ann Suttenger, Hannah Ann Burns and neice Mary Jane Peacock. Exec. Aaron D. Harris. Wit. Bacon Hutchinson, Providence Sheppard and Ebenezer Sheppard. Proved Dec. 4, 1854. E-366

1854, Dec. 4—CHARLES DALBOW, Upper Penns Neck. Estate to be sold. To wife Abigail, $500. Dau. Mary Elizabeth, $50. Residue after debts are paid, to sons Charles, Edward, Frederick and William. Reason for not leaving anything to the children by my first wife, Sarah, which are Ann, Sarah, John and Catharine: they are adults and capable of taking care of themselves. Thomas Flanagin, Sr., exec. and grdn. of Mary Elizabeth, Charles, Frederick and William. Wit. William H. Zane, Josiah Bowen and John K. Louderback. Proved Dec. 12, 1854. E-368

1854, Dec. 8—WILLIAM PATTERSON, Mannington. To wife Catharine, furniture and poultry. Son Benjamin, my gun. Dau. Ella Virginia, my watch. If they die, gun to John P. Lynn, and watch to Janetta Lynn. Mother Rebecca Patterson, wheat. John P., son of David Lynn, my sorrel mare. Residue to be sold and debts paid. Remainder to son and dau. Exec. William A. Casper. Wit. Edward VanMeter, Thomas J. Casper and Ezekiel P. Flanagin. Proved Dec. 27, 1854. E-370

1854, Dec. 19—WILLIAM REEVES, Upper Alloways Creek. To bro. Josiah H. Reeves, $800. Bro. Jacob P. Reeves, interest on $800; at his death, the principal to his children. Sisters Hannah, wife of James Baker, and Mary, wife of David P. Smith, each $200. Heirs of sister Sarah Ann, dec'd, wife of John Ballinger, Jr., $200. Residue of estate to bros. Charles A. and Stephen Reeves. Exec. John H. Lambert. Wit. David Bowen and Joseph C. Lambert. Proved Jan. 6, 1855. E-372

1841, Aug. 20—HOPE HAINES, Woodstown. To Hannah Kirby, the amount of her note held by me. Anna, wife of Samuel Holmes, silverware. Mary Elizabeth Pedrick, bedding. Residue of estate to Mary Elizabeth, Margaret and Anna Pedrick. Exec. Josiah Davis. Wit. Josiah Davis, Martha Kirby and William M. Cawley. Proved Jan. 23, 1355. E-374

1852, Jan. 28—WILLIAM ROBINSON, Salem. To wife Ann, during widowhood, the part of double dwelling where we live, $25, furniture, and an annuity of $100. Sons William, Noah and James S. to supply her with provisions. Son John P., meadow in Quaker Neck and land at Quintons Bridge. Dau. Mary Curliss, Silverware. Dau. Rebecca Ann bedding. Sons Benjamin O. and James, each $100. Jonathan H. Curliss and John P. Robinson, grdn. of my children. Rebecca Ann, Charles, Henry and Sarah B. Exec son John and son-in-law Jonathan H. Curliss. Wit. Benjamin Pine, Joseph Thompson and Joseph R. Lippincott. Proved Feb 12, 1855.   E-356

1854, Oct. 23—CHARLES HOGBIN, Allowaystown. Estate to be sold. To dau.-in-law Lidiann, widow of son John, 3/8 of estate. Remainder to sisters Elizabeth, wife of David Trullenger, and Ann, wife of Benoni Mills. David Sloan of Decater, Ind., married a dau. of my sister Elizabeth Trullender. Exec. John H. Lambert. Wit. John Lambert and Isaac T. Lambert. Proved Feb. 21, 1855.   E-380

1845, June 27—JAMES HARRIS, Lower Alloways Creek. To my children, Mary Simpkins, Isaac Harris, Rachel R. Jarman and Charlotte Harris, $3 each. Wife Mary, remainder of estate. Exec. wife Mary. Wit. John W. Maskell, Daniel Ashton and John Roork. Proved Apr. 13, 1855.   E-382

1844, Apr. 10—ELIZABETH W. MILLER, Salem. To exec. nephew Caspar Wistar and grandson Richard M. Acton, $21,000, in trust for dau. Sarah W. Acton during life; then to grandsons Richard M. Acton, Benjamin Acton and Caspar W. Acton, and granddau. Hannah H. Carpenter, each $2500; granddau. Charlotte, wife of Richard Wistar, $2000; granddaus. Letitia M., Sarah W. and Catharine Acton, each $3000. To exec. in trust for grandsons Richard, Samuel L. J. sons of my late son Josiah Miller, land in Mannington: $5000 in trust for dau-in-law Hettie H. Miller, during life; then to her sons Richard, Samuel and Wyatt: $20,000 in trust for education of said grandsons. To grandson Richard

M. Acton, 1/4 of undivided land and 1/2 of woodland in the glass-house tract; remainder to grandson Caspar W. Acton; granddaus. Hannah H. Carpenter and Sarah W. Acton, each 1/4 of undivided land. Grandson Richard M. Acton, land on west side of Broad Street, Philadelphia, and a horse and wagon. Grand dau. Sarah W. Acton, land on west side of Broad Street, above Coates Street, Philadelphia. Granddau. Charlotte Wistar, land on Ridge Road, Philadelphia. To exec. 8 shares of Salem Banking Co., in trust for granddau. Letitia Acton. Grandson Casper W. Acton, $3000. Granddau. Sarah, wife of Thomas Sheppard, land in Mannington, land on west side of Broad Street, Philadelphia, the house in Salem where I live, and land and store house in Salem. Land and meadow in Penns Neck to grandson Wyatt W. Miller, Part of glasshouse tract to grandson Samuel L. J. Miller. Exec. to sell Quaker Neck farm. Ann Lippincott, $200 and furniture. Samuel Smith, his bond and mortgage, held by me. Female Benefit Ass'n of Salem, $100. Rebecca Harding, $50. Wit. F. L. Macculloch, George C. Rumsey and Moses Crane. Proved Aug. 25, 1855. E-384

1855, Jan. 20--WILLIAM REASON, Bayleytown, Pilesgrove. After debts and expenses for repairs to a certain house are paid, remainder to be invested until my dau. Alice is 18 years of age; then to my children. To wife Maria, land adjoining where I live, during life; then to dau. Alice. Residue of estate to my children, Richard, Elizabeth wife of William Deal, Lavinia, Moses, and Mary Matthews. Exec. Jonathan Cawley. Wit. Howell B. Hoffman, Joseph McAltioner and W. M. Cawley. Proved Sept. 6, 1855. E-401

1851, Jan. 18—NATHAN WRIGHT, Mannington. Farm to be sold. To neice Hannah Lippincott, $1000, and to each of her children, $500. Remainder to children of my nephew Thomas Wright, dec'd. Land in Monmouth Co., and in Quaker Neck. To nephews George William and Charles Wright, each $600. Ruth Buzby, $1800. Nathan Buzby, $1200. Beulah Gaskill, $100 of an annual income from land that will go to Job and Harrison Wright.

SALEM COUNTY WILLS 125

Lewis Appleton $1300. George and Sarah Appleton, each $1200. Nephew Benjamin Wright, $1500, and to each of his daus. $800; to his son Stephen, $1000. To exec. in trust for Benjamin Wright and his wife, the house where they live; at their death, to their children. Almira H. Hoffman, dau. of Rebecca Guestner, $1800. Nathan, Joseph, Theophilus, Thomas and Benjamin Hews, nephew Ebenezer Wright and his sons Stephen and Richard and dau. Priscilla, his sons Edward, Ebenezer and Joseph H., each $1200. Neice Letitia Wright, $500. Anna Lippincott and Lydia Rogers, each $700. Neice Hannah Lippincott, $200, and $100 to each of her children. Thomas Lounsbury, Joshua Davis, George Dunn and James Ellis, each $75. James Seasor, William McDermott, Asher Mitchell, James Magill and Shedrick George, each $30. The sum that will come to Rebecca Jaquett, dau. of my nephew Thomas Wright, dec'd, shall be held in trust by Harrison Wright, and interest paid annually. Residue of estate to Harrison and Job Wright, who are appointed exec. Wit. William S. Boultinghouse, C. B. Hood and Anthony Elton. Proved Mar. 30, 1852.
E-405

1854, Jan. 17—JONAS KEEN, Lower Penns Neck. To dau. Margaret Pippin, all estate, and she is appointed exec. Wit. William A. Dick, Elijah Hancock and Edward Emery. Proved Sept. 2, 1855. E-412

1855, Sept. 18—JOHN R. POWELL, Upper Alloways Creek. Personal estate to be sold. Remainder to wife Lydia. Exec. wife and Richard H. Sparks. Wit. Oliver Smith, James Robinson and Edward S Carll. Proved Oct. 6, 1855. E-414

1853—MARGARETTA J. PRESCOTT. Exec. Andrew Sinnickson. To sister Mary S. Stoughten, land where I dwell, at Broadway and 3rd Street. Salem. Nephew Thomas S. Smith, Jr., woodland in Upper Alloways Creek. Bro. Thomas S. Smith, $4000. Mary C. Sprogell, Jr., and Richard B. Ware, each $500. Andrew Sinnickson, $1000 in trust for Clarissa Sinnickson; at her death, to her daus. Ruth and Maria. Dr. William P. Dexter, gold

watch. William H. Prescott, the Prescott family Bible. William H. Newbold my bookcase and library. Neices Margaretta Prescott Stoughton, and Maria Smith, silverware. Mrs. Cablebine, wife of William H Newbold, silverware. Nephew Thomas S. Smith, Jr., diamond pin. Remainder of estate to Mary S. Stoughten. Andrew Sinnickson, exec. Wit. William M. Roberts, William Patterson and Thomas Sinnickson. Proved Nov. 1, 1855.
E-416

1855, Nov. 12—JAMES GRIFFITH, Pilesgrove. Real estate in Baileytown to be sold and debts paid; remainder to bros. and sisters. Exec. Jonathan Cawley. Wit. John M. Clintock, John Ramsey and W. M. Cawley. Proved Nov. 28, 1855. E-418

1853, June 18—JOSIAH FLITCRAFT, Pilesgrove. Real estate to be sold. To wife Grace A., $1600, furniture, and the front room over the parlor. Children of dau. Ruth Ann Borden, dec'd, $1600, their father, Thomas J. Borden, grdn. of said children. Son Isaac, and dau. Lydia Borden, each $1600. To exec. $1600 in trust for son Charles. To granddau. Eliza, and grandson Pembroke, children of my son Isaiah R., each $700; Champion Atkinson to be grdn. of said children. Son Allen, the house where he lives, at Eldridges Hill. Remainder to my children, Ruth Anna Borden, Lydia Borden, Isaiah, Allen and Charles. Exec. sons Isaac and Allen. Wit. Isaac Shute, John Warrington and Richard Matlack.
1855, July 19—Codicil gives land in Rutherford Neck, to son Allen, he to pay estate $700. Same witnesses. E-420

1855, June 8—JANE APPLETON, Salem. House and lot to to be sold and debts paid. Residue to my children, Sarah A. Wright, Ruth, George and Lewis. Exec. sons George W. and Lewis R. Wit. Amelia R. Patterson and George Ward. Proved Dec. 6, 1855. E-424

1855, June 3—CHARLES BENNETT, Pilesgrove. To wife Margaret, furniture, grain, a cow, the house I now occupy, and the house in Sharptown on the road leading to the mill. Exec Hiram Shoemaker and Benjamin Lippincott to invest $1700 for benefit of my wife. Sarah wife of Hiram Shoemaker, $200. Amanda wife of Benjamin Lippincott, Joanna and Margaretta Humphreys, each $100. Charles and John Robinson, Jane Hewitt and George Robinson, each $50. Dau. Rachel Waters 1/2 of residue of personal estate; remainder to be invested for benefit of dau. Mary Humphreys Real estate, subject to wife's life interest, to Hiram Shoemaker and Benjamin Lippincott in trust for daus. Rachel and Mary. Wit. Moses Ale, Albert Bassett and W. S. Clawson. Proved Dec. 13, 1855. E-426

1855, Sept. 19—DAVID WALKER, Elsinborough. To be interred in the Friends' burying ground in Salem. Estate, after debts are paid, to friend Richard Grier, who is appointed exec. Wit. Charles H. Bradway and Isaac S. Sheets. Proved Jan. 26, 1856. E-430

1856, Jan. 11—JONATHAN WHITE, Upper Penns Neck. To wife Sarah, $30 yearly, to be paid by son Jonathan and dau. Rebecca, who inherit all estate. Exec. John M. Springer. Wit. John S. Sparks, Samuel Justice and Samuel Hortman.

1856, Jan. 26---John M. Springer renounces executorship. Proved Jan. 29, 1856. E-432

1855, Nov. 15—CHARLES A. REEVES. To bro. Jacob P. Reeves, $800. Bro. Stephen Reeves, watch, chest, horse, harness, carriage and sley. Sisters Hannah, wife of James B. Barker, Mary, wife of David Smith. Stephen R., Samuel E. and Thomas, sons of sister Sarah Ann and John G. Ballenger, Jr., $600. Wilhelmina, wife of bro. Josiah H. Reeves, $600. Exec. Josiah H. Reeves and David Smith. Wit. Jno. H. Lambert and Henry Saske. Proved Feb. 4, 1856. E-434

1851, Mar. 28—EDWARD LAWRENCE, Penns Neck. Land and house to children, Louisa, Edward, Elizabeth and Joseph.

Exec. Edward Emery. Wit. William A. Dick, John R. Dick and Samuel Wallen. Proved Feb. 20, 1856.　　　　　　　　E-436

1855, Aug. 8—MARY ALLEN, widow, Salem. To grandson Samuel H. Bacon, silver watch; if he should not survive me, to grandson Samuel son of son Edward Allen. Grandchildren, the children of son David Allen, dec'd, Mary, Hannah and Rebecca, silverware and $100. Son Jeremiah, furniture, and house and lot on 4th Street, Salem, where I now live. Sons Samuel and Edward silverware. Bro. Jacob R. Elfreth, during life, a house in Haddonfield; then to Samuel and Hannah, children of my dau. Hannah Bacon. Residue of estate to my sons. Exec. sons Samuel and Jeremiah. Wit. John Tyler, William B. Stretch and Josiah Wistar. Proved Feb. 28, 1856.　　　　　　　　E-438

1856, Jan. 31—SOLOMON COLEMAN. To exec., in trust for benefit of wife Anna during widowhood and after her remarriage, 1/3 of income of estate; at her death to sons Isaac and Moses. Exec. son Harris. Wit. Moses Bear and John McIntire. Proved Mar. 12, 1856.　　　　　　　　E-440

1856, May 13—WILLIAM NELSON, Pilesgrove. To wife Ann, during life, furniture, 2 shoats, a cow, rye, potatoes, and a house in Sharptown where I live; to be sold at her death. Exec. son William and nephew William Nelson. Wit. Samuel Hillman, John W. Wright, Jr., and W. M. Cawley. Proved May 30, 1856.
　　　　　　　　E-442

1856, Apr. 1—HUDSON A. SPRINGER, House and lot to be sold and $505.50 to be paid John R. Munion. To the public in general, a strip of land to be used as a highway. Exec. bro. John M. Springer. Wit. Shadrick Pedrick, Thomas Risner and Samuel M. Hunt. Proved May 21, 1856.　　　　　　　　E-444

1854, Mar. 16—JACOB SHOUGH, Upper Alloways Creek. To my children, David, Jacob, Elizabeth Swing, Margaret Lloyd,

and Christiana Shimp, all real estate. Exec. to sell rails off of the new ground that my son William leases. Remainder of estate to said children. Exec. son David and William House. Wit. John Shimp and Matthew Morrison. Proved June 28, 1856.
E-446

1856, Mar. 25—ISABELLA PARRETT. To nephews Richard P. and Joseph H. Thompson, $14,000 in trust to pay to Mary M. Starr the interest of $4000; Hedge, son of my nephew Thomas Thompson, dec'd, interest of $5000; and to Isabella P., dau. of said Thomas Thompson, interest on $5000. Nephew Joseph H. Thompson, M. D., $4000. Isabella P., dau. of Captain and Ann Lyman of Philadelphia, $200. Joseph H. Thompson, M. D., $500 in trust for Mary Ann Handy. Residue of estate to Richard P. Thompson. Exec. Joseph H. Thompson. Wit. William Otis, S. C. Harbert. Proved July 3, 1856. E-448

1850, Mar. 13—SARAH HILLIARD, Salem. To Susan Thompson, a straw trunk. Ann Bacon Ware, large soup tureen. Neice Elizabeth Hilliard, apparel. House where I live to be sold. Residue of estate to neice Elizabeth Hilliard. Exec. George M. Ward. Wit. Job Ware and Henry D. Hall. Proved July 12, 1856. E-450

1855, Feb. 28—BENJAMIN SPRINGER, Upper Penns Neck. To my neice and housekeeper Jane Erwin, all household goods (except the arm chair, clock and spy glass) and $1000. Granddau. Maria Walker, residue of estate. Exec. nephew Hudson A. Springer. Wit. Richard Somers and William H. Pedrick.

1856, Aug. 1---Letters of administration granted to John M. Springer. E-452

1856, Apr. 27—HENRY FREAS, Salem. To son James, $1700. Dau. Ann, wife of Sylvanus B. Sheppard, $2000. Sons Henry, Johnson and Reuben J., each $2000. Son Daniel J., $1700. Daus. Elizabeth wife of Smith Bacon and Lusianna, widow of Jeremiah

Fox, each $2000. Son William, land in Lower Penns Neck. Grandchildren, children of son Samuel R., dec'd, Mrs. Sarah Tuft, Mary Sickler, Ellen, Hannah, Charles, Elizabeth and George Freas, each $300. Exec. to sell real estate. Remainder of estate to Ann Sheppard, James, Henry, Johnson William R., Daniel and Reuben J. Freas, Elzabeth Bacon and Louisiana (the marriage records call her Lucy Anna) Fox. Exec. sons Johnson, William and Reuben. Wit F. L. Macculloch, Thomas Cattell and Joseph Robinson. Proved Aug. 12, 1856. R-453

1854, Jan. 10—JOHN RIDGWAY, Mannington. To my son Joseph, apparel. Dau. Hannah, wife of Mayhew Sparkes, $1. Personal estate to be sold and debts paid. Joseph Ridgway, remainder of proceeds from sale of the Keech tract. Residue of estate to my children, Daniel, Samuel, John, Caroline Githens and Joseph Ridgway. Exec. Edward VanMeter. Wit. Charles Benner, C. Wood VanMeter and Thomas I. Yarrow. Proved Aug. 30, 1856. E-456

1856, June 8—JOHN OGDEN, Pittsgrove. Exec. Enos Veal and son Richard G. Ogden to sell real estate; proceeds to my children, Elizabeth R. Bowen, Sarah Jane Baker, Richard G., Oliver, Deborah, James S. and Henry C. Son John T., $100. Wit. James G. Ford and Adam Kandle, Jr. Proved Aug. 15, 1856.
E-458

1856, Jan. 22—MARY SMITH (widow), Upper Alloways Creek. Apparel to daus. Mary Ann, wife of Ephraim Carll, Sr., Elizabeth, wife of Oliver Smith, Luetta, wife of Richard Mulford, Lydia, wife of John Mills, and granddau. Ann Eliza, wife of George Hires, Jr. To grandson Phineas, son of Phineas Smith, a double coverlid; if he dies, to his sister Margaret. To Elizabeth, wife of Oliver Smith, and my granddau. Ann Eliza Hires, bedding. Residue of estate to be sold; Proceeds to granddau. Ann Eliza Hires, and sons and daus. Exec. son Abner Smith. Wit. William S. Carll and Mordica Cuff. Proved Aug. 11, 1856. E-460

1854, Apr. 15—ADAM URBAN, Pittsgrove. To wife Eunice furniture. Estate to be sold and debts paid. Residue to wife, dau. Eunice and son John. Exec. William S. Clawson. Wit. Smith Hewitt, Ephraim Coles and Joseph Urion. Proved Sept. 10, 1856.   E-462

1856, Sept. 21—THOMAS MARSHALL, Mannington. Personal estate to be sold. To exec., all real estate, in trust for son Thomas. Wife Mary, 1/4 acre of land during life. Exec. wife Mary, son Jacob, and Thomas Hinchman. Wit. David Bassett, Samuel J. Moore and John R. Cooper. Proved Oct. 1, 1856.   E-464

1855. Sept. 29—WILLIAM DAVIS, Upper Alloways Creek. To dau. Hannah. $10. Dau. Mary Banks, bedding and cow. Residue of personal estate to be sold; proceeds to daus. Ruth Edwards, Harriet Redrow, sons Henry V., James, Mary Banks, Sarah Clark, and granddau. Rachel Pedrick (nee Nichols). Exec. nephew Arthur Davis of Deerfield. Wit. John Shimp and William House. Proved Oct. 4, 1856.   E-466

1856, Oct. 7—WILLIAM BARNETT, Sculltown. To wife Rachel, house, lot and furniture. A clock and furniture to be sold; proceeds to my children, Samuel, Mary Ann, Amanda and Henrietta. Exec. Benjamin Darlington. Wit. James Hoffman and A. T. Jester. Proved Dec. 6, 1856.   E-469

1849, Mar. 31—REBECCA HARRIS. To granddau. Hannah, dau. of deceased dau. Anne Fogg, a bureau and apparel. Grandson John H , son of dau. Anne Fogg, $500. Granddau. Rebecca, dau. of son Amos, $200. If either of grandchildren dies under age, their legacies go to my sons Hiram and Amos, who are appointed exec. Wit. Dalymore Harris, Elizabeth H. Clarke and George R. Morrison. Proved Dec. 22, 1856.   E-470

SALEM COUNTY WILLS

1842, Aug. 2—DAVID BOWEN, JR. To neice Hannah, dau. of deceased sister, Rachel Horner, land in Lower Alloways Creek. If she dies a minor, to Matilda Chester. Exec. James Butcher. Wit. George Githens, Silas Harris and Robert Butcher. Proved Jan. 8, 1857. E-472

1852, May 11—SOLOMON HARKER, Upper Alloways Creek. Estate to be sold. Children Jonathan, Elias, Albert, Hester wife of Jonathan Crandall, Hannah wife of George Vanlier, Philemon, and grandson Jacob G. Johnson, money advanced to them. Dorcas S. wife of Hiram Carll, $40. Dau. Barbara Ann, $28. If Jacob G. Johnson dies under age, his share goes to the rest of my children. Sons Jonathan and Albert grdn. of Jacob G. Johnson and exec. Wit. Benjamin L Horner, Isaac Hall and Belford M. Bonham. Proved Jan. 13, 1857. E-474

1857, Feb. 4—ABIGAIL SNELL, Salem. Bro.-in-law Samuel Smith exec. and grdn. of dau. Phebe Snell. Wit. John M. Treen, John Ramsey and John Noble. Proved Feb. 21, 1857. E-475

1857, Jan. 23—BENJAMIN N. SMITH. Exec. John M. Cooper to sell real estate and pay debts; remainder to wife Rebecca. Wit. Charles C. Clark, William Robertson and M. C. Clark. Proved Feb. 12, 1857. E-476

1857, Mar. 27—JOHN HOMAN, Lower Alloways Creek. To wife Heta R., remainder of estate, after debts are paid, during life; then to my children, Abel and Mary Elizabeth. Exec. Amos Harris. Wit. Joseph Pancoast, Horner Nicholson and Hannah Homan. Proved Apr. 15, 1857. E-477

1854, Nov. 13—WILLIAM STRETCH, Woolwich. To bro. John Stretch of Michigan, $1000. Children of my bro. Thomas, dec'd, Sarah, Joseph, Anna Maria, Elizabeth, Margaret, James, Hannah, Beulah and Thomas Stretch, $300 each. Neice Mary Jane Stretch, cousin Samuel Stretch and cousin Caroline Y.

Sprogell, each $50 per year. Elizabeth, widow of my bro. Thomas Stretch, land bot. of exec. of estate of said Thomas, during widowhood; at her death, to children of said Thomas. Residue of estate to exec. bro. Robert Stretch. Wit. Joshua S. Thompson, Charles Garrison and Asher Bower. Proved Apr. 23, 1857.

E-478

1856, Jan. 26—CATHARINA PETERSON, Wilmington, Del., Exec. to sell house and ground in Philadelphia. Proceeds to my children and grandchildren, Amy Conrow, Rebecca Perry, Catharine Cole. Samuel Biddle, son Abel Biddle, children Louisa Halter; Charles Holton, Rebecca Till, Mary Butler, John, William and Ephraim, children of my dau. Sarah Holton, dec'd. Son Abel Biddle to pay my funeral expenses. $28 to be deducted from share of Rebecca, wife of David Perry. Dau. Mary Lippincott and granddau. Catharine Weiss, to have no share in my estate. Exec. John L. Louderback. Wit. Thomas Titus, William Stilley, and John C. Thomas. Proved Apr 23, 1857. E-479

1857, June 15—JOHN HAMBLY, Salem. Personal estate to be sold and debts paid. To daus. Mary, wf. William Ough, and Grace Ann, wife of Benjamin Link, all real estate. Son William, $10. Exec. son-in-law William Ough. Wit. Elisha Bassett, Robert M. Boon and James M. Hannah. Proved July 13, 1857. E-481

1856—JACOB DAVIS, Bordentown. To my children, Martha, wife of Henry D. Moon, Hannah P. and William N. Davis, all real estate. Exec. son William. Wit. J. Beck, M. Hutchinson and William W Allen. Proved Aug. 12, 1857. E-482

1856, Aug. 28—SMITH HEWITT, Pilesgrove. To wife Rebecca furniture, interest on $1000 and $10 yearly, to be paid by each my sons John and William, daus. Elizabeth wife of Charles Robinson, and Rebecca Jane, and son Josiah. Son Josiah, $75 and my watch. Remainder of estate to children. Exec. son Smith Hewitt,.

Wit. Isaac Ridgway, John Woolman and William Cawley. Proved Aug. 13, 1857. E-483

Not Dated—JOHN G. ELWELL, To wife Mary, all estate. At her death, to my children, Elizabeth, Ellen, Caroline and Samuel. Exec. John Casperson Wit. Thomas D. Bradway, John W. Lumley and Joseph Yonker. Proved Sept. 5, 1857. E-485

1857, June 7—BURTIS BARBER, Mannington. Land on Hutchen Street to be sold. Personal estate (except library to be sold) to my children. Exec. sons Henry A. and John W. Wit. Richard Somers and George M. Ward. Proved Sept. 29, 1857. E-487

1857, Apr. 29—ANDREW BELL, Mannington. To wife Hannah, $500, furniture, a cow and grain. Bushland in Hopewell to be sold. Son Joseph, $200. Son Andrew, $100 and gun. Daus. Hannah Ann, Lydia and Harriet, $75 each. Son Samuel to invest $100 for benefit of Sarah, wife of James Darlington. Residue, after debts are paid, to my children, Samuel, Benjamin, Mary, Joseph, Robert, Hannah Ann, Andrew and Harriet. Exec. wife and son Samuel. Wit. David D. Armstrong, Josiah H. Reeves and Edward VanMeter. Proved Sept. 17, 1857. E-488

1856, July 3—EDWARD H. ROBBINS. Marble stock and everything pertaining thereto to be sold and debts paid; remainder to be invested until dau. Caroline is 21 years of age; then divided among my children. Son Edward owes me $250 in consideration of my taking him in copartnership. Property in Bridgeton to be sold; when children are of age, to be divided among them. Son Edward, my gold watch and gun. Bro.-in-law W. F. Rackliff, a gold watch. Dau. Caroline and housekeeper Elizabeth Adams, furniture. Exec. to sell the monument erected to my deceased wife Catharine at Laurel Hill, the proceeds with $200 not otherwise appropriated to purchase a monument to our united memories. Exec. bro.-in-law William F. Rackliff. Wit. Francis Hand and Edward VanMeter. Proved Oct. 17, 1857. E-490

SALEM COUNTY WILLS 135

1857, July 6—SAMUEL CORLISS, To wife Ann, furniture and yearly profit from my house and lot in Hancocks Bridge and my farm near Jno. S. Wood's upper mill. To Henry Kline, Samuel B. Corliss and Rebecca, wife of Joseph Fox, after death of my wife, all real estate. Powell Baker and Ann his wife, farm in Lower Alloways Creek; said farm to pay my wife $150 in half-yearly payments. Tombstones to be placed at my grave. Exec. Thomas A Maskell. Wit. Theophilus Patterson and Edward VanMeter. Proved Oct. 24, 1857. E-492

1854, Apr. 28—EDITH THOMPSON, (wid. of James, Sr.) To Sarah Jane, dau. of Andrew T. Thompson, $50 at 18 years of age. Eliza Sparks, Edith Ann Ware and dau. Mary Baker, silver ware. Mary, wife of Samuel Thompson, lookingglass. Son John W. Thompson, clock. Grandson Joseph Baker; $20 at 21 years of age. Ann E. Thompson, Edith A. Thompson dau. of James, Martha Baker, Mary Emma Baker and Sarah Hall Thompson, each $6. Jane Draper, $26. Mary Thompson and Mary Baker, each a rocking chair. Mary W. Baker, Sarah Laurence, Sarah Jane, dau. of Andrew Thompson, Mary wife of Samuel Thompson and Jane Draper, apparel. Mary Ett Osgood, a bureau. Remaining furniture to be sold. House in Pennsville to be rented for five years; then to be sold; proceeds to my children, Mary Baker, Samuel S., James, Daniel, John W. and Andrew. Exec. John W. and Andrew Thompson. Wit. John K. Louderback, Andrew J. Lawrence and George Denny. Proved Oct. 29, 1857. E-494

1851, Apr. 29—TERASE RIDGWAY. To grandson Isaac R., son of dau. Charlotte Morgan, $1. Remainder of estate to my children, Joseph P., Isaac, and Levi Ridgway and Elizabeth R. Petit. Exec. son Levi. Wit. Jonathan B. Grier and David Petit. Proved Sept. 12, 1857. E-497

1844, July 30—CLARISSA BURROUGHS (widow of Edward Burroughs, dec'd, and late widow of William Parrett), Salem. To relative Harriet Howell Ingham, dau. of my late neice Mary C.

Sinnickson, dec'd, bedding and furniture. Residue of estate to Thomas Sinnickson of Philadelphia, son of Mary C. Sinnickson, and John Sinnickson. Exec. Thomas Sinnickson. Wit. Robert C. Johnson, Mason VanMeter and Josiah Harrison. Proved Nov. 24, 1857. E-499

1857, June 6—REBECCA LAWRENCE, Salem. Exec. to invest $1500 for benefit of my sister Mary, wife of Abraham Johnson; after her death, the sum to her daus. Mary and Margaretta; if they die before their mother, then to children of my bro. George W. Connarroe, sister Margaret Rumsey and of my deceased sister Sarah Little. Sister Mary Johnson, book case and books and bust of my bro. George. Sister Margaret Rumsey, stove and chairs. Nephew Henry M. Rumsey, portrait of my mother and aunt Ellen Mecum. Nephew George M. Connarroe, bedding. Neice Maria Connarroe, rocking chair. Neice Ellen M. Connarroe, work stand. Sister Charlotte, wife of George W. Connarroe, shawl, Neice Margaret Sheppard, pier table. Cousin John W. Mecum, Henrietta Harrison and bro. George, pictures. Cousins Anna Connarroe, Margaretta Curliss and Ann Lawrence, and friend Rev. John Burt, $25 each. Residue to bro. George Connarroe, children of my deceased sister, Sarah Little, sister Margaret Rumsey, and nephews George M. Connarroe and Henry M. Rumsey. I desire to be buried in the same grave with my mother. Exec. bro. George M. Connarroe. Wit. William Bassett and Joseph B. Heishon. Proved Nov. 25, 1857. E-501

1857, Nov. 11—JOHN T. BROWN, Upper Pittsgrove. To wife Mary, farm on which I live and timber land on Blackwater Branch, an money remaining of my personal estate. To sons John Henry and Moses R., each $1. Residue of estate to wife, who is appointed adm. Wit. Henry Harding, Elmer Newkirk and Israel Conover. Proved Nov. 26, 1857. E-505

1857, May 6—DAVID WILEY, Upper Penns Neck. Estate to be sold. Wife Mary, $250 and $240 yearly. Remainder of estate to son John, children of son Joseph B., dec'd, and children of dau. Rebecca, late wife of Burden Danser. Notes held against sons John and George to be deducted from their shares. Exec. sons John and George. Wit. John K. Louderback, Sedgwick R. Leap and Matthew N. DuBois. Proved Dec. 10, 1857. E-507

1852, Sept. 29—HENRY JOHNSON, Upper Alloways Creek. To grandchildren Henry J., Mary E. and Cutisoaf Pilgrim, children of dau. Rebecca, dec'd, each $200. In case said grandchildren should die before reaching the age of 21 years, same shall be divided between my children, Joseph, Elias, Harriet Mickle, Anna Gibson and Margaret Johnson. Residue of estate to said children. Exec. son Elias and son-in-law Henry Mickle. Wit. William H. Brown, Caroline VanMeter and Edward VanMeter. Proved Dec. 16, 1857. E-50

1851, Dec. 17—BENJAMIN MUNION, Upper Penns Neck. To wife Maria, furniture. Son Thomas, bedding and $10. Son Samuel, bedding and 1/2 of threshing machine. Dau. Mary Ann, bedding. Son William Henry, bedding and 1/2 of threshing machine. Exec. son Samuel. Wit. Jacob Justice. Samuel Hortman and William S. Vannaman. Proved Jan. 15, 1858. E-511

1856, Mar. 20—JOHN PEDRICK, Lower Penns Neck. To wife Elizabeth, dwelling on Main Street, Pennsville and $250 during life. Son Jacob, during life, real estate on road to Penns Grove; after his death, to his children. Real estate devised to wife, after her death, to be sold; receipts to daus. Mary Straughn and Margaret Borden, sons Jacob and Francis, and daus. Rebecca Armstrong Hannah Ann Newcomb and Elizabeth Whitesell. Residue of estate to above named daus. and Joseph Henry Pedrick and Elmer Fox. Tombstones to be placed at my grave and that of my wife. Exec. Dr. William Vanneman and my son Francis. Wit. William M. Roberts and William Patterson. Proved Jan. 18, 1858. E-513

1855, Oct. 26—HANNAH BRICK, Pilesgrove, To nephews Samuel S., Mark and Warner Miller, and neice Ann Elizabeth Paul, my house in Woodstown, which after the death of my sister, Mary S Miller, is to be sold. Exec son-in-law William Pancoast. Wit. James Lawrie and Sidney Averill. Proved Jan. 18, 1858. E-517

1858, Jan. 1—CATHARINE FREAS, Upper Alloways Creek. To granddau. Margaret Bell, $10. George T. Freas, my clock, desk and $50. Grandson Charles W. Freas, looking glass bedding, and $50. Dau. Elizabeth Freas, apparel. Exec. son-in-law William Freas. Wit. Sarah Gosling, Ephraim B. Freas and Jonth. L. Brown. Proved Jan. 19, 1858. E-518

1858, Jan. 7—AARON VALENTINE, To sister Ann Valentine, my right to the homestead. Bros. John and Asa, each $1. Bro. Silas and sister Ann Valentine, residue of estate. Exec. bro. Silas, Wit. Robert Butcher and Waddington Bradway. Proved Feb. 8, 1858. E-520

1857, Mar. 7—ELIZABETH SIGER, Upper Alloways Creek. To son Lewis, $100, family Bible, clock and furniture. Son Peter, $100, clock and furniture. Dau. Elizabeth Sweatman, $100, furniture and silverware. Market wagon, cows and bees and residue of personal estate to sons Lewis and Peter, who are appointed exec. Wit. John Burroughs and Samuel Mickel. Proved Mar. 2, 1858. E-522

1857, Dec. 28—WILLIAM PALMER, Sculltown. To wife Mary, all moneys and interest arising therefrom, furniture and all personal estate. House and lot in Lower Penns Neck to be sold; proceeds to wife; at her death or marriage, remainder to my children, Sarah, David and William. Exec. Joseph Humphreys. Wit. John S. Locke, Joseph F. Hoffman and Alfred T. Jester. Proved Mar. 16, 1858. E-524

SALEM COUNTY WILLS 139

Not Dated—JEDEDIAH G. DUNN, Lower Penns Neck. To wife Sarah, furniture and silverware. Remaining personal estate to be sold. Residue of estate to bros. Ebenezer P. and John. Exec. bro. Ebenezer. Wit. Benjamin Hewitt and William A. Dick. Proved Mar. 27, 1858. E-526

1854, Oct. 27—JAMES FRAZER. Farm on which I live to be sold and debts paid; residue to my children, John, Daniel, heirs of son Caleb, dec'd, heirs of son David, dec'd, Richard S., Robert M., Joseph H., Fuller H., and Rachel. Son Fuller to have $50 more than the others. Granddau's. neices Amanda M. and Ruth Ann Frazer. Dau.-in-law Matilda Frazer, silver spectacles. Exec. son Joseph and John S. Lewallen. Wit. Joshua Mickle and William R. Parvin. Proved Mar. 30, 1858. E-528

1853, Dec. 21—MARY WARE. $2000 in trust for Jane, dau. of son Job Ware dec'd. Residue of estate to dau. Mary, wife of William Carpenter, Benjamin Beesley and Elijah Ware. Exec. William Carpenter and Elijah Ware. Wit. Benjamin Lloyd, Benjamin Lippincott and John M. Brown. Proved Apr. 3, 1858.
E-530

1856, Apr. 29—WOODNUTT PETIT, Salem. Son James, gold watch and library. Bonds against sons David and James to be collected. House and land which I occupy, on Market Street, and meadow on Hancock Street to be sold. Principal and interest on said bonds and proceeds of sale of property to my children, Rachel Beesley, David, Joseph, Anna wife of Elihu Roberts, James and in trust for dau. Sarah B., wife of Edward P. Cooper. Exec. dau. Rachel Eeesley. Wit. F. L. Macculloch, Maskell Ware and John N. Cooper. Proved Apr. 8, 1858. E-533

1858, Mar. 8—ISAAC HOLETON, Lower Alloways Creek. To son John E., $150. Wife Elizabeth, residue of estate. Daniel Danser, grdn. of son. Nephew James E. Keever to inherit money left to son if he dies a minor without issue. Exec. wife.

Wit. Enoch Ayars, Joseph A. Mills and Job Sullivan. Proved Apr. 18, 1858. E-536

1858, Apr. 16—ARCHER STACKHOUSE, Lower Alloways Creek. To wife Charlotte, all estate. She is appointed exec. Wit. Belford E. Wood, Samuel Dowlin and William S. Carll. Proved May 5, 1858. E-538

1855, Oct. 26—HANNAH W. BRICK and MARY S. MILLER, Pilesgrove, sisters. (Joint will). To nephews William, Samuel, Mark and Warner T. Miller, and neice Ann English Paul, all personal estate. Eliza, wife of John Clifton, who was brought up in the family of our father, Abraham Miller, dec'd, $100. Exec. William Pancoast, son-in-law of Hannah Brick. Wit. James Lawrie and Sidney Averill. Proved Apr. 28, 1858 E-540

1857, July 30—JOHN S. BARBER, Upper Penns Neck. To wife Sarah, house and lot in which I live. in Penns Grove, during life, and $150 in furniture. Personal estate and farm to be sold, debts paid and tombstones erected; remainder of proceeds of sale to be invested. Dau. Hannah Guest, the house and ground bequeathed to my widow, at her death. At death of wife, all personal estate to be sold; proceeds to daus. Hannah Guest and Sarah Jane Denny. Dau. Sarah Jane, $750. Sons Elijah S., David D., John S. and Job, all money secured in my farm. Exec. William Summerill, Jr. Wit. John L Louderback, Samuel M. Rain and Gerard Sparks. Proved June 3, 1858. E-543

1858, May 1—WILLIAM DUNN, Salem. To wife Eliza, furniture. Bro. Samuel Dunn, bookcase. $3000 to be investe for benefit of wife; she to select tombstones. Movables to be sold; Proceeds to be invested for maintenance and education of dau. Saaah until she is 18 years of age; then the principal to her. If she dies without issue, $1000 to my wife and remainder to my sisters Sarah and Phebe, bros. Thackray and Samuel, and nephews

Ebenezer and John, sons of Thomas Dunn. Exec. bro. Samuel Dunn. Wit. Jonathan Ale and Edward VanMeter. Proved July 3, 1858. E-547

1858, May 6—HENRY HUTCHINSON, Salem. To wife Mary Ann, all personal estate, and real estate consisting of three houses, during life; then to sons John Henry and Antrim. Exec. James Newell. Wit. John H. Hutchinson and Samuel Brown. Proved July 7, 1858. E-552

1858, May 27—JONATHAN BELTON. To wife Rebecca, $100 worth of furniture, a silver watch, a cow, $3000 and meadow at foot of South Street, during life, and a house on Union Street, jointly with dau. Harriet N. Low, the house I now live in, in Salem, during their lives. Said dau., $100 worth of furniture, a gold watch, $2000, a lot bot. of William B. Otis, and a dwelling and store occupied by Benjamin Lippincott. To wife and dau. Harriet, land in Alloways Creek. Grandson Clement B. Low, the house and lot, after the death of my wife and dau. Harriet; also the house adjoining, meadow in Tilbury Meadow Co., and land bot. of Aaron Treadway and Jacob Brown. Granddau. Ellen M. Low, the house on Union Street, at the death of my wife, and the above mentioned house and store. To Aute Pedo Baptist Society in Salem, $2000. Woodstown and Woodbury Baptist Churches, each $500. Sarah Collins, $6, and $6 every six months. Exec. wife. Wit. Jno H. Lambert, Robert Guestner and William Nicholson. Proved July 22, 1858. E-554

Not Dated—CATO GRANT. To wife Beulah, furniture and house and lot, during life; then to the African Beneficial Society. Exec. wife. Wit. Job. S. Dixon and William Finlaw. Proved July 24, 1858. E-558

1858, July 23—GRACE ANN McDOUGALL, Lower Alloways Creek. To children Anna Rogers McDougall, James and Mary Emma, timber land in Fairfield; if they die without issue, then to my cousins William P., Charles W., Robert F. and

Joseph E. Sheppard, sons of Dr. Edmund Sheppard. Exec. husband John W. McDougall. Wit William B. Willis and J. Reeves Daniels. Proved Aug. 21, 1858.   E-559

1858, Apr. 10—KETURAH GOODEN, Upper Penns Neck. To nephew Joseph P. Tomlin, $100   Neice Mary Dawson (nee Shute), $150. Residue of estate to nephew Jacob G. Tomlin. Exec. nephew Jacob G. Tomlin. Wit. Samuel M. Hunt   Francis Davis and Sarah H. Davis. Proved Aug. 30, 1858.   E-561

1853, May 27—JOHN CLARK, Lower Pittsgrove. To wife Lydia, dwelling and $50. Personal estate to be sold. Real estate to be sold after death of wife; proceeds to my children. Exec. sons Isaac and Benjamin. Wit. John E. Hann and Robert G. Hann. Proved Aug. 31, 1858.   E-564

1858, Aug. 5—ELISHA WHEATON, Pennsville. To wife, all estate; she to take charge of William Henry and Rosanna and give them schooling until the son is 21, and the dau. 18 years old. Exec. Samuel Urion. Wit. J. B. Yoken, Michael Powers and John W. Lumley. Proved Sept. 2, 1858.   E-566

Not Dated—JAMES VANMETER, SR., Upper Pittsgrove. To wife Sarah, furniture, during life; then to daus. Son James, the farm south of the run coming from the Baptist parsonage swamp, between the run and the road from Pole Tavern to Daretown. Residue of estate to be sold; proceeds to my children, John, Joseph, Rebecca Garrison, Eliza Conover, Catharine Heritage and Sarah Ann VanMeter. Exec. Thomas R. Clement. Wit. Charles Elwell, Charles F. H. Gray and James A. Reed. Proved Oct. 18, 1858.   E-568

1858, Sept. 21—EZEKIEL DUBOIS, Penns Neck. To son Joshua M., $400. Grandchildren Lorena Madara, Clement and Joshua Hinchman, remaining estate. Exec. son-in-law Rheuben Hinchman. Wit. Theophilus Patterson, Jonathan Scattergood and Charles Robinson. Proved Oct. 23, 1858.   E-573

1858, Jan. 13—THOMAS BILDERBACK, Salem. To dau. Phebe A., $100. Wife Eunice, residue of estate. Exec. wife and son Smith. Wit. Isaiah Conklyn and John N. Cooper. Proved Dec. 6, 1858.   E-575

Not Dated—AMY RICHMAN, Upper Pittsgrove. To son William, a desk, clock and corner cupboard. Dau. Priscilla Dean, a mirror, carpet and dishes. Dau. Sarah Sparks, $100. Dau. Experience Burt, dining table. Grandsons Jonathan R. Dean, Charles R. Burt and George W. Richman, each $100. Monument to be erected. Residue of estate to son and daus. Exec. son William. Wit. Moses Richman, Jr., and Stephen Sarish. Proved Dec. 14, 1858.   E-577

1859, Feb. 9—ROBERT GUESTNER, Salem. All estate to daus. Rebecca and Anna E. Dau. Mary G. Adams (a widow), shall receive $100 from my daus. Exec. daus. Rebecca and Anna. Wit. John M. Carpenter and George Ward. Proved Feb. 23, 1859.   E-579.

1859, Feb. 26—JONATHAN CAWLEY, Pilesgrove. To dau. Amy B. Mattson, $100. She has children, Alfred and Christiana Lippincott Dau. Anna Maria Lippincott, a farm in Pilesgrove, subject to payment of $2000 to my dau. Esther H. Lippincott. Dau. Sarah Hillman, $250 yearly during life. Children of dau. Sarah: Charles, Jonathan C. and Joseph Peterson the farm on which she lives and woodland. Son Jonathan P., the homestead farm, livestock and farming implements. Dau. Esther H. Lippincott, $10,000. Grandson Alfred Lippincott, $750, woodland and farm in Harrison Township, Gloucester Co. Granddau. Christian B. Lippincott, $2600. Nephew William M. Cawley, $100. Residue of estate to be sold; receipts 1/4 to children of dau. Sarah, 1/4 to son Jonathan P., 1/4 to dau. Esther H. Lippincott. Exec. son Jonathan P. Wit. David C. Pancoast, John H. Lippincott and W. M. Cawley. Proved Mar. 29, 1859.   E-581

1854, Mar. 28—WILLIAM STRATTON, Clayville. Personal estate to be sold; after debts are paid, 1/3 to dau. Sarah, 1/3 to son Eleazar, and remainder to grand son John, and granddau. Rachel Stratton. Real estate to be sold when Rachel is 18 years of age; 1/3 of proceeds to William Woodnutt, in trust for dau. Sarah; if she dies without issue, 1/2 to son Eleazar, and remainder to said grandchildren. Exec. William G. Woodnutt. Wit. Joseph R. Chew, Edwin Nicholson and Henry F. Chew. Proved Apr. 11, 1859. E-588

1859, Jan. 29—THOMAS CLEAVER, Salem. Estate to be sold and debts paid. Dau. Rachel L. Hall, $90. Residue to my children, Sarah M. wife of James Smith, Hannah wife of Joseph Paullin, Elizabeth wife of Charles Lolley, William L. Cleaver, Caroline N. wife of Charles Ware, Ann wife of Francis Hand, and Rachel L. Hall. Exec. son-in-law Francis Hand. Wit. Samuel Dilmore and John N. Cooper. Proved Apr. 18, 1859. E-590

1859, Mar. 26—JOSIAH HARRIS, Upper Penns Neck. To wife Sarah Ann, $200, residue of personal estate and proceeds of sale of real estate, while she remains my widow; then to my children, Mary wife of Edward Smith, James, William H., Edward S., Catharine and Anna M. Harris. Exec. wife and John M. Springer. Wit. John K. Louderback and Alfred Springer. Proved Apr. 28, 1859. E-592

1858, June 11 — JONATHAN BARNES, Lower Alloways Creek. Wife Lydia Jane, estate, after debts are paid. Exec. Thomas A. Maskell. Wit. Charles B. Ayres and Loransy Hogate. Proved May 14, 1859. E-594

Not Dated—RICHARD SPARKS. Wife Margaret, in addition to $200 allowed her by law, a cow and pig. Son David, my 8-day clock and my horse shed at the M. E. Church, in Lower Penns Neck. Dau. Jane Anna, bedding. Samuel Callahan, son of my wife by a former marriage, my brown horse called Boby. Exec. to sell residue of personal estate and pay debts; remainder to son Samuel and dau. Jane Anna. Exec. and grdn. of children, wife and bro.-in-law Martin Patterson. Wit. John F. Elwell and William A. Dick. Proved May 16, 1859. E-596

1859, June 30—SAMUEL TOMLIN, Upper Penns Neck. To wife Henrietta, all personal estate; at her death to my children, Clement F., Baker D., Hiram S., Mary Ann Curry, and Robert H. D. Exec. John K. Louderback. Wit. William D. Burden and John S. Dolbow. Proved July 18, 1859. E-599

1859, July 8—FRANCIS L. MACCULLOCH, Salem. To dau. Mary, all estate. Stephen H. Brooks, grdn. of dau Mary. Exec. Stephen H. Brooks amd William H. Roberts. Wit. Mary L. Miller, Charlotte P. Roberts and Elizabeth B. Heberton. Proved July 28, 1859. E-601

1857, June 7—BURTIS BARBER, Mannington. Lot on east side of Hutchen Street and houses on Hutchen and Taylor Streets, and personal estate to be sold. Exec. sons Henry A. and John. Wit. Richard Somers and George M. Ward. Proved Aug. 13, 1859. E-603

1859, July 19—REBECCA BELTON, Salem. To dau. Harriet N. Low, apparel, furniture, horse, carriage, wagon, hay, grain and feed. Benjamin Lippincott. $1000 in trust for dau. Harriet N. Low; at her death, to neice Amanda, wife of said Benjamin. To said Amanda, $1000. Cousin Maria, wife of David Williams, $300, Dau. Harriet and Benjamin Lippincott, grdn. of Clement and Ellen, children of said Harriet. Exec. to erect stones and enclose burrial lot with an iron fence. Residue of estate to Benjamin Lippincott. Exec. dau. Harriet and Benjamin Lippincott. Wit. Rosanna G. Prior and George A. Morrison. Proved Aug. 25, 1859. E-606

1859, Aug. 7—SAMUEL HACKETT, Pilesgrove. Wife Elizabeth, movables, except goods given to me by my mother, Mary Hackett and aunt Ann Walmsley, which I give to her during her life; then to my nephews and neices, William E. and Edward H. Hackett's children, Aaron and Ellen Hackett, Mary Ann Thompson and Sarah G. Hackett. To said nephew and neices, $825, being a note held against Jonathan D. Smith, after debts are paid, and money due on a mortgage from William F. Lippincott. Exec. Jonathan E. Smith. Wit. James Woolman, W. M. Cawley and Isaac S. Fogg. Proved Aug. 26, 1859. E-608

1859, Sept. 6—DANIEL PLATT, Upper Alloways Creek. To nephew Noah Sheppard, the house and land where I now live, during life; then to his oldest son. Personal estate to said Noah, after debts are paid. Dau. Anna Maria Platt, $1. Exec. Noah Sheppard. Wit. Ephraim C. Harris, Gabriel P. Kirk and Josiah T. Harris. Proved Sept. 22, 1859. E-611

1859, May 16—JAMES RICHMAN, Whig Lane. To children of son William, $800. Dau. Rachel wife of Providence Sheppard, $1200. Granddaus. Rebecca Dean, and Achsa Ann, wife of John Krom, each $300. Residue of estate to be invested; Achsa, widow of my deceased son John C., to be comfortably maintained from the interest. $1000 each to grandsons Alfred and Francis, and $300 each to granddaus. Alynda and Emma Richman. Exec. Harmon Richman. Wit. J. C. Weatherby and Joseph L. Risley. Proved Sept. 29, 1859. E-612

1859, July 25—JOHN H. PATRICK, Elsinborough. Estate to be sold and debts paid. Residue to son Morris G. Exec. Amos Harris. Wit. Thomas Y. Hancock and R. P. Thompson. Proved Oct. 27, 1859. E-614

1859, Oct. 26—THOMAS COOPER, Pilesgrove. Wife Ann, all estate; at her death to daus. Frances and Rebecca. Exec. John Hunt. Wit. William H. Reed and Jacob Urion. Proved Nov. 12, 1859. E-616

1855, Jan. 30—NATHAN SHEPPARD, Elsinborough. Exec. to sell meadow in Stow Creek and invest $1200 for benefit of Emeline, widow of my son Isaac Sheppard, until her son Gilbert D. is 21 years of age; then to Gilbert, $400; remainder to be invested benefit of said Emeline until her son Henry H. is 21; then to him, $400; income of remainder to her youngest son, John E., at 21. Residue of estate to my children, Joseph C., Albert H., Leander W., Theodore W. Sheppard, and Maria E. Stelle. Exec. son Joseph E. Wit. F. L. Macculloch, Smith Darmon and Maskell Ware. Proved Nov. 12, 1859. E-618

1857, Dec. 21—BENJAMIN R. MORGAN, Sharptown. To nephew Richard Stanton, house and land in Sharptown, bushland in Upper Alloways Creek, and cedar swamp on Blackwater. To nephew James Wardsworth, a house and ground in Sharptown, known as the Dickinson Lot, and a house on the back street in Sharptown. Richard Stanton is to pay my sister, Sarah Hackney, $100; Jacob Wardsworth is to pay my friend, Margaret, wife of Oakford Nixon, $100. Administration cum testo annexo granted to Richard Stanton. Wit. David C. Pancoast, David M. Davis and James Lawrie. Proved Nov. 22, 1859. E-622

1859, Apr. 23—MARGARET ROBINSON, Pilesgrove. To son Robert P., my 8-day clock. Son Reuben, residue of estate; at his death, to my children. Exec. son Robert. Wit. Samuel Hillman and W. M. Cawley. Proved Nov. 22, 1859. E-623

1859, Nov. 3—LYDIA L. SPRINGBR, Salem. To my children, Anna L., Maria L., Mary Jane, Cornelia C., and Wilber F., $2000. To said daus., furniture. To son Wilber, my watch. House and lot on Union Street to be sold and debts paid. Exec. John M. Springer. Wit. Moses Richman, Jr., and Maria Lodge. Proved Nov. 11, 1859. E-625

Not Dated — JOHN MICHAEL KUMMERLE, Salem. To wife Katrina, all estate. Exec. wife and Christian F. Brown.

SALEM COUNTY WILLS

Wit: Christian F. Brown and Robert Gwynne. Proved Dec. 13, 1859. E-628

1859, Nov 5—ELWOOD JEFFERIS, Salem. To wife Sarah, furniture during widowhood; then to my children. Son William, carpenter's tools. Son Elwood, silver watch. To exec. in trust for my wife and children, all real estate. Exec. bro. Joshua Jefferis and John C. Dunn. Wit. Isaac Smith and Benjamin F. Wood. Proved Jan. 7, 1860. E-630

1859, Dec. 29—CHARLES PLUMMER, Elsinborough. Exec. to sell estate and pay debts; residue to my wife Ann Eliza, and children Elizabeth M., Ann Eliza, Henry and John C. Exec. George R. Morrison and Joseph Waddington. Wit. William H. Nelson and Jacob Mulford. Proved Jan. 13, 1860. E-632

1859, Apr. 28—CHARLES SWING, Sharptown. To wife Hannah B., all real estate in Mannington, the house and land where I live, and all personal estate; at her death, to Charles P., Margareta A. and Abigail S. Swing. Exec. wife. Wit. Richard Gordon, Samuel Hillman and George A. Robbins. Proved Jan 21. 1860. E-634

1858, Nov. 28—DANIEL R. SHOCKLEY, Mannington. To wife Margaret all estate after debts are paid; after her death or marriage, to sons Edward James and Robert Henry Shockley. Exec. wife. Wit. James F. White, Mayhew Sparks and W. M. Cawley. Proved Feb. 2, 1860. E-636

1859, Jan. 6—CHRISTOPHER McALEER. To wife Mary, all estate after debts are paid. She is appointed exec. Wit. Cornelius Connor, William O'Brien and Patrick McCabe. Proved Feb. 17, 1860. E-638

1859, Apr. 18—BENJAMIN WRIGHT, Salem. To wife Martha Ann, all estate, after debts are paid; after her death, to my children Stephen M. Wright and Sarah M. Tusse. Exec. son Stephen. Wit. Caroline VanMeter and Edward VanMeter. Proved Mar. 14, 1860.   E-639

1859, Nov. 12—SAMUEL WHITE, Pilesgrove. To wife Jerusha, interest on $3000, to be paid annually by my children, Elizabeth B. Hinchman, David White and Walter Wilson White. Dau.-in-law Lydia, widow of son Jonathan White, $400. Grandchildren Clarence Hinchman, Ada and Franklin Waddington, each $100. Granddau. Gertrude White, $1300, to be invested until she is 18 years of age. Son Walter Wilson White, the farm bot. of Jacob Davis, part of a tract of chestnut timber land, 1/2 of live stock, farm implements to the amount of $40, and one share of B. and L. Assn. at Woodstown. Dau. Elizabeth B. Hinchman and son David White a farm and the house and lot in Newtown, and remainder of personal estate. Exec. dau. Elizabeth and son David. Wit. Omar Borton, Joseph K. Riley and L. A. D. Allen. Proved Mar. 12, 1860.   E-640

1860, Feb. 28—ROBERT CHAMLESS, Upper Pittsgrove To son Charles R., my desk, clock, and a note for $100 held against Andrew and Enoch Newkirk. Daus. Harriet and Sarah, furniture, Dau. Sarah and son Charles, $50. Personal estate to be sold; after debts are paid, residue to daus. Charlotte Newkirk, Emeline Heacock, Harriet and Sarah Chamless, and son Charles R. Chamless. Exec. and grdn. of son Charles, Benjamin F. Burt. Wit. William Richman and George Wamsley, Preved Mar. 17, 1860.
E-644

1853, June 22—DAVID CLAWSON, Upper Alloways Creek. To wife Jane H., all estate. She is appointed exec. Wit. Belford E. Davis and Am ni Davis. Proved Apr. 6, 1860.   E-646

150   SALEM COUNTY WILLS

1858, Oct. 17—MARY FINLAW, Lower Alloways Creek. To nephew Enos P. English, all estate, after debts are paid, during minority of his dau. Anna; when 18 years of age, she shall have household goods. To Enos P. English, all notes and money. If Anna dies under 18, estate to Enos P. English, who is appointed exec. Wit. Edward Hancock, Elizabeth Emerson and William S. Carll.   Proved Mar. 26, 1860.   E-648

1857, Aug. 4—ELIZABETH GOODWIN, Salem. To sisters Sarah, wife of Jonathan Woodnutt, and Abigail Goodwin, a house on the west side of Market Street; after their death, to Richard and William G. Woodnutt, in trust that Mary E., wife of Edward A. Acton may have use and rents thereof during life; if she dies without issue, or before reaching 21 years of age, then to the children of Richard and William Woodnutt. Sister Abigail Goodwin, two bonds of $1000 each against the Susquehanna Canal Co. during her life; then to Mary and Sarah Ann Conrow; at their death, one bond to Margaret, dau. of James Woodnutt, and Anna, dau. of William G. Woodnutt; the other to Mary Emily and Sarah, daus. of Richard Woodnutt. Exec. nephews Richard and William G. Woodnutt. Wit. Richard M. Acton, F. H. Archer and Joseph B. Lawrence   Proved Apr. 16, 1860.   E-650

1858, Mar. 20—MAHALAH HORNER, Sculltown. To wife Sarah, during life, furniture, stock, farming implements, house and lot in Sculltown, where I now live, land on road from Sculltown to Sharptown, adjoining the M. E. Church lot, land on the Woodstown-Pedricktown road, and $180 yearly. $3000 to be placed on mortgage on the farm occupied by my son Benjamin. Daus. Abigail, Susan and Sarah D., and sons George W. and Charles, each $125 and bedding. All real estate to be sold, except the house and lots devised to my wife, and divided between my children, Elijah B., Asa R., Benjamin L., Malachi, Joseph L., Mary R. Kirby, Meshack, Sybilla D., Abigail Ann, Susan, George W., Charles P. and Sarah D. Exec. sons Elijah B. and Joseph L., and son-in-law Josiah B. Beckett. Wit. Robert R. Robinson, Smith Hewitt and W. M. Cawley.   Proved May 11, 1860.   E-652

1858, June 24—MICHAEL NULL, Woodstown. To wife Ann $500 an annuity of $300, and the homestead during widowhood. Sister Hannah Rocap, during life, an annuity of $60. Dau. Sarah, wife of Joshua Barnes, $3000. Grandson-in-law Edward B. Humphries of Sharptown, trustee to manage all legacies and hold in trust all money bequeathed to children of son William Null, dec'd, the four children by his first wife, $3000, to the four children by his second wife, $3400. Son George, 2 houses on Beach Street, Kensington. and a house and lot in Camden. Dau. Caroline, wife of Joseph L. Harris, woodland in Pilesgrove, stock in the Salem Banking Co., and my gold watch for her son, Michael N. Harris. Elmer and Clinton H., sons of my dau. Margaret Hancock, dec'd, $3000. The farm occupied by Morris R. Elwell, and all other real and personal estate to be sold. Exec. wife Anna, son George and grandson-in-law Edward B. Humphries. Wit. James Best, Howel. B. Huffman and W. M. Cawley. Proved June 7, 1860   E-657

1858, Aug. 3—SARAH S. FOGG, Lower Alloways Creek. To husband Edward Fogg, $200. Sisters Elizabeth and Mary Stewart, $300 each. Residue of estate to bros. John D., Samuel, Joseph and William Stewart. Exec. Joseph Test. Wit. William Powell and Josiah L. Smith. Proved June 9, 1860.   F-1

1860, Mar. 17—REBECCA DIXON. To bro. Samuel DuBois, all estate. He is appointed exec. Wit. Joseph Nelson, Andrew Hann and Francis B. Harris. Proved June 13, 1860.   F-2

1858, Aug. 2—RICHARD HANTHORN, Pittsgrove. To wife Rebecca, furniture, $500 and all real estate. Son Isaac, 3 lots of land in Pittsgrove. Dau. Ann, wife of Lewis Hays, house in Millville, after the death of my wife. Dau. Emily, wife of Joseph West, $10. After the death of my wife, all real estate devised to her is to be sold; receipts to daus. Ann Hays, Rachel, wife of Daniel Brown, Rebecca, wife of Isaac Bowen, and Elizabeth wife of Thomas Brown. Exec. son Isaac and son-in-law Isaac Bowen. Wit. Jacob R. Shimp, Jonathan Hogate and James H. Trenchard. Proved June 30, 1860.   F-5

1859, June 6—FIRMAN FOGG, Salem. Real estate to Samuel W. Miller and John N. Cooper, in trust during the life of my father, David Fogg; then to my bro. James P., and to the use of the heirs of my bros. James P. and Isaac Fogg. After the death of David Fogg, $100 to James P. Fogg annually during life. Residue to James P. and Isaac Fogg. Exec. Samuel W. Miller and John N. Cooper. Wit. John W. Maskell, Elijah Ware and John P. Robinson. Proved June 5, 1860. F-9

1853, May 19, JOSEPH HARKER, Pilesgrove. To wife Margaret S., all estate. She is appointed exec. Wit. Elizabeth Ann Kirby, Mary A. Hilliard and W. S. Clawson. Proved July 12, 1860. F-12

1860, June 23—JOHN RICHMAN, Pilesgrove. Farm to be sold; receipts to be invested for benefit of wife Sarah Ann during widowhood. At her marriage or death, principal to my children. To wife, a cow, and furniture. Son John R., $800 at 21 years of age. Dau. Margaret $50, and daus. Sarah Elizabeth and Emily Jane, each $150 to finish their education. Exec. to sell residue of estate; proceeds to my cnildren. Exec. Joseph K. Riley. Wit. Enoch Boon and Hannah Boon. Proved July 12, 1860. F-13

1856, Oct. 4—JOHN ARMSTRONG, Mannington. To son Mark, my farm where I now live and part of woodlot in Bushtown, subject to payment of $400 to my dau. Pheby Riley, and $100 each to my grandchildren, John S., Eliza and Joseph Armstrong. Son David D., land adjoining John Woodside, land south of Guineatown, and remainder of woodland in Bushtown, subject to payment to grandson Thomas B. Armstrong, $100 at 21 years of age. Dau.-in-law Phebe Ann Armstrong, my house and lot in Guineatown, during life; then to grandson Thomas B. Armstrong. To sons Mark and David, my claim to an undivided right in meadow in Greenwich, Cumberland Co., woodland in Lower Alloways Creek, and remainder of personal estate, after debts are paid. Exec. sons Mark and David. Wit. John Miller, Jacob Lippincott and James Patterson. Proved July 18, 1861. F-16

1855, Aug. 9—MOSES CRANE, Salem. To wife Priscilla, all estate. She is appointed exec. Wit. H. B. Ware, Moses Richman, Jr., and Samuel H. Clement. Proved July 23, 1860.   F-18

1848, Jan. 19—MARY ANN THOMPSON, Salem. To Anna Maria Thompson, Rebecca Caldwell and Rebecca I. Thompson, silverware. Isabella P., dau. of R. P. Thompson, a gold watch, to be bot. by my exec. Real estate to be sold; proceds to Joseph Thompson, $2000 in trust for benefit of Hedge and Isabella, children of my deceased son, Thomas Thompson. Sons Richard P. and Joseph H. each 1/4 of proceeds of sale of real estate, after deducting $2000 in trust for daus. Mary M. Starr and Rebecca H. Thompson. To my children, Richard, Joseph, Mary and Rebecca, all personal estate. Exec. sons Richard and Joseph. Wit. Andrew Sinnickson, Jno. Johnson and Jno. Ingham. Proved Aug. 31, 1857.   F-20

1858, Feb. 25—JOHN S. MULFORD, Hopewell, Cumberland Co. To wife Maria Louisa, all personal estate to which she is entitled, and 1/2 the remaining real estate and 1/2 of rents of real estate. To Lydia dau. of Rachel Waithman, and wife of Jeremiah Welden, $200. Remainder of personal estate to wife and dau. Margaret Kogle. Real estate to be rented; 1/2 of rent to wife; remainder to dau. Margaret. At death of wife, estate to Margaret, wife of John Kogle; at her death, to her children. Exec. wife and sister's son, Thomas, son of John W. Maskell. Wit. James S. Thomas and H. R. Merseilles. Proved Sept. 14, 1860.   F-24

1859, May 13—ANDREW SMITH, Elsinborough. To grandchildren, Prudence, Richard and Sarah Dare, $1800. Granddau. Sarah M. Smith, meadow in Elsinborough and bushland in Upper Alloways Creek. Andrew Smith Reeves, Mary Elizabeth Reeves and Thomas B. Reeves, children of my dau. Mary Reeves, dec'd, land in Elsinborough. Grandson Andrew Smith Reeves, $200. Dau. Hannah, wife of Hiram Harris, land in Elsinborough, where they now live, she to pay my granddau. Sarah M. Smith, $1000 at

21 years of age, Grandchildren Rebecca N., Hannah Jael and Stretch Harris, children of my dau. Catharine Harris, dec'd, land occupied by me, in Elsinboro, and an undivided share in Money Island, in said township. Exec. to invest $2500 for benefit of granddau. Sarah M. Smith at 21 years of age. Remainder of estate, after debts are paid, to grandchildren, excepting children of Hannah Harris. Exec. Amos Harris, who was the husband of my deceased dau. Catherine. Wit. Caroline VanMeter and Edward VanMeter. Proved Dec. 8, 1860. F-26

1855, Mar. 12—BENJAMIN GRISCOM, Salem. To children of my deceased son John, Ephraim, Job, John, William, Henry, Clarkson, Joseph and Ann Elizabeth, $400 each. Elizabeth, widow of son John, the stock, farming utensils and personal estate which I bot. at assignee's sale of said son, on condition that she maintains the 3 youngest children. Grandson Joseph Jeffries, $100. Dau. Beulah, wife of John Tyler, $300. Remainder, after debts are paid, to my children, Sarah Pancoast, Andrew, Benjamin, Beulah Tyler, and George Griscom. Exec. son Andrew and sons-in-law John Pancoast and John Tyler. Wit. Joshua Jefferis, Elwood Jefferis and Edward VanMeter. Proved Dec. 11, 1860.
F-30

INDEX TO TESTATORS

Abbit, John, 18, 19.
Abbott, Lydia, 67.
  Martha, 81.
  Mary Ann, 59.
  Samuel, 21.
Ackley, Uriah, 117.
Adcock, Isaac, 106.
Allen, Jedediah, 24, 93.
  Mary, 128.
  Samuel, 70.
Andrews, Clarissa, 109.
  Mary, 50.
Antrim, William N., 106.
Aplen, Jesse, 23.
Appleton, Jane, 126.
Applin, Joseph, 52.
Archer, Benjamin, 68.
Armstrong, John, 152.
Ashton, Daniel, 77.
Austin, Samuel, 19.
Ayres, Susan D., 111.
Bacon, David 39.
  John, 102.
  Thomas, 110.
Baker, Thomas, 33.
  William D., 110.
Balanger, Valentine, 26.
Barber, Burtis, 134, 145.
  John S., 140.

Barnes, Jonathan, 144.
  Joseph, 114.
Barnett, William, 131.
Bassett, David, 64.
  Joseph, 76.
Bee, Elizabeth, 10.
Beesley, William G., 49.
Bell, Andrew, 134.
Belton, Jonathan, 141.
  Rebecca, 145.
Bennett, Charles, 126.
Benson, William, 116.
Bevis, Job, 65.
Biddle, Isaac, 9.
  Thomas, 92.
Bilderback, Jonathan, 36.
  Peter, 41.
  Thomas, 143.
Black, Elizabeth, 81.
  Job, 80.
Blackwood, John, 99.
  Rebecca, 13.
Bolton, Joseph, 16.
Bond, Samuel, 110.
Boqua, John, 59.
Borton, Elizabeth E., 75.
  William, 29.
Bowen, Anna M., 76.
  David, Jr., 132.

George, 105.
Joseph, 108.
Thomas S., 74.
William, 116.
Bradway, Edward, 113.
  Sarah, 90.
  Susannah, 11.
Brick, Hannah, 138.
  Hannah W., 140.
  Samuel, Jr., 13.
Brown, John T., 136.
  William, 121.
Buck, Henry, 81.
Burch, John, 93.
Burroughs, Clarissa, 135.
  Clarissa Parrett, 56.
  Cornelius, 26.
Butcher, James, 97.
Calehopher, Susannah, 29.
Camp, Mary, 109.
Carney, Catharine, 20.
Carpenter, John, 16.
  Mary, 88.
  Powell, 96.
  William, 28.
Caspar, John, 103.
Casperson, John, 40.
Cawley, Jonathan, 143.
Chamless, Robert, 149.
Chase, Mary, 94.
Christopher, Elizabeth, 14.
Clark, Jacob, 30.
  John, 142.
  William, 9.
Clawson, David, 149.
Cleaver, Thomas, 144.
Clement, Ruth, 20.
Cole, George, 76.
Coleman, Solomon, 128.

Connarroe, Margaret, 69.
Cook, Mary, 43.
  William, 35.
Cooper, Thomas, 146.
Corliss, Samuel, 135.
Corcoran, Thomas, 65.
Counsellor, John, 91.
Cox, George, 117.
  Peter, 38.
Craig, James D., 114.
Crane, Moses, 153.
Creemer, Jacob, 32.
Currey, Dorcas, 107.
Currie, Sarah, 68.
Curry, John, 119.
Cuff, Meriam, 12.
Dalbow, Charles, 122.
Dallas, Jonathan, 81,
Dare, James, 96.
Davis, David, 17.
  Elizabeth, 91.
  Francis, 12.
  Jacob, 133.
  Joseph, 29.
  Mary, 92.
  Rebecca, 31.
  Thomas, 63.
  Thomas, Sr., 15.
  William, 131.
Dehart, Harvey S., 74.
Denn, John, 19.
  Rhoda, 68.
Dickeson, Samuel, 90.
Dickinson, John, 99.
Dixon, Rebecca, 151.
Dolbow, Gabriel, 99.
Drew, Rebecca, 47.
DuBois, Ezekiel, 142.
  Jonathan, 31.

INDEX TO TESTATORS

Dukemineer, Thomas, 34.
Dunlap, John, 77.
Dunn, Jedediah G., 139.
  Mary, 49.
  Samuel, 27.
  Thomas, 43.
  William, 140.
Earley, Sarah, 66.
Elwell, John G., 134.
  Joseph, 97.
Emley, John, 112.
Emmel, John, 84.
Engle, Levi, 97.
English, Anthony, 111.
  David, 94.
  Isaac, 113.
  Joseph L. F., 110.
Field, Benjamin, 104.
Fields, Christiana, 88.
Finlaw, Mary, 150.
Finley, Job, 8.
Fish, James, 74.
Fisher, William, 88.
Firth, Ann, 49.
Fithian, Elizabeth, 120.
Flitcraft, Josiah, 126.
Fogg, David, 22.
  Ebenezer, 20.
  Firman, 152.
  Hannah, 72.
  Lydia, 34.
  Miller, M., 17.
  Sarah T., 151.
Fox, George, Sr., 73.
  Jacob, 5.
Franklin, Benjamin, 98.
Freas, Catharine, 138.
  Henry, 129.
Frazer, David, 112.
  James, 139.
Fries, George, 58.
Gardiner, Patience, 67.
Garrison, Daniel, 98.
  Jedediah, 73.
  Josiah, 50.
Gibbon, Rachel, 102.
Gibson, Elizabeth, 93.
Gill, James, 46.
  John, 57.
Gilmore, Samuel, 58.
Gooden, Keturah, 142.
  Jacob, 25.
Goodwin, Elizabeth, 150.
  Huldah, 71.
Gosling, John, 56.
  Samuel, 32,
Gould, George, 19.
  Wilcher, 32.
Grant, Cato, 141.
Grier, Charles, 117.
  George, 84.
Griffith, James, 126.
Griffiths, Elijah, 77.
Griscom, Benjamin, 154.
Groff, Asa, 113.
  Edith, 23.
  Elizabeth, 86.
Guestner, Robert, 143.
Hackett, Samuel, 101, 146.
Haines, Drusillia, 63.
  Hope, 122.
  Thomas P., 75.
Hall, Ann, 41.
  Amy G., 77.
  George, 103.
  John, 55.
  Morris, 39.
  Sarah, 37.

William, 32, 72.
Hamby, John, 133.
Hance, John, 51.
Hancock, Rabecca, 52.
   Sarah, 52.
Hanthorn, Richard, 151.
Harbeson, Adam, 115.
Harding, Thomas, Sr., 100.
Harker, Joseph, 152.
   Solomon, 132.
Harmer, Ebenezer, 89.
   Leven, 83.
Harris, Abraham, 42.
   James, 123.
   Josiah, 144.
   Lydia, 54.
   Rebecca, 131.
   Stretch, 82.
Heritage, Hannah, 95.
Heward, Benjamin, 10.
Hewitt, Smith, 133.
High, Andrew, 86.
Hiles, Richard, 70.
Hilliard, Sarah, 129.
Hillman, David, 110.
   Patience, 17.
Hinchman, Lot, 15.
Hitchner, George, 67.
Hoffman, Jacob, 57.
   Martha, 82.
Hogbin, Charles, 123.
Holeton, Isaac, 139
   William, 99.
Holton, John, 87.
Homan, John, 132.
Horner, Mahalah, 150.
Hortman, Jonas, 100.
Hubbs, Rebecca, 107.
Huddy, Hannah, 117.

Hudson, Abraham, 9.
Hughs, Benjamin, Jr., 22.
   Richard I., 39.
Humphreys, Isaac, 115.
Hunt, Mary W., 26.
Hutchinson, Henry, 141.
James, Samuel S., 66.
Jaquett, Hance, 32.
   Paul, 27.
   Peter, 61.
   Samuel, 84.
Jarman, Martha, 82.
Jeffris, Elwood, 148.
Johnson, Henry, 137.
   James, 27.
   Juliana E, 118.
   Robert G., 94.
   Samuel M., 7.
Jones, Thomas, 77.
Kandle, Henry, 32.
   John, 71.
Keasbey, Prudence, 105.
Keen, James, 72.
   Jonas, 125.
Kiger, Henry, 11.
Kinsey, James, 15.
   Rebecca, 62.
Kirby, Asa, 36.
   Jedidah, 14.
   John, 12.
   Maria, 77.
Knowles, George, 54, 55.
Kummerle, John Michael, 147.
Lambson, Moses, 79.
Ladow, Ann, 105.
Langley, John, 31.
Laurence, Rebecca, 136.
Lawrence, Andrew, 40.
   Edward, 127.

INDEX TO TESTATORS

Leeds, Noah, 107.
Lindsey, Sarah, 42.
Lindzey, James, 17.
Lippincott, Christiana, 100.
   James, 5.
Little, Sarah, 111.
Lock, Israel, 41.
   Samuel, 46.
Locuson, Clayton, 63.
Longacre, Israel, 121.
Low, Samuel, 83.
Macculloch, Francis, 145.
Manning, Thomas, 18.
Marshall, Thomas, 131.
Martin, Elizabeth, 112.
   Henry, 86.
Mason, Ann, 27.
   John G., 37.
May, John, 8.
Mayhew, Elisha, 111.
   Lydia, 64.
McAleer, Christopher, 148.
McBride, Mathew, 113.
M'Calla, Jane H., 45.
McCallister, Rachel, 50.
   Thomas, 108
McCollister, Isaac, 33.
McDonnol, Thomas, 46.
McDougall, Grace Ann, 141.
Mecum, Elenor, 82.
Miles, Rebecca, 105.
Miller, Elizabeth, 123.
   Franklin, 46.
   Lydia, 9.
   Mary, 140.
   William, 28.
   William F., 80.
Minch, Mary, 10.
Minters, Abigail, 92.

   Andrew, 89.
Mires, Christopher, 14.
Moncreef, Catharine, 88.
Moore, Joseph, 30.
Morgan, Benjamin R., 147.
   Samuel, 7.
Morris, Eliza, 79.
Morrison, Matthew, 101.
   Sarah, 107.
Mulford, James W., 23.
   John S., 153.
   Rachel, 26.
   Stephen, 72.
Munion, Benjamin, 137.
Murphey, John, 94.
Nealey, James, 76.
Nelson, Davis, 103.
   Samuel, 35.
   Sarah, 53.
   William, 44, 128.
Newcomb, Josiah, 89.
Newkirk, Andrew, 91.
   Jacob, 83.
   Joast, 116.
   Joseph, 107.
Nichols, Norton, 105.
Nicholson, Elizabeth, 67.
   Joseph, 47.
   Samuel, 62.
   Sarah, 43.
Null, Michael, 151.
Ogden, John, 130.
Palmer, Samuel W., 68.
   William, 138.
Pancoast, Samuel, 13.
Parrett, Isabella, 129.
Patrick, Abner, 14.
   George K., 21.
   John H., 146,

Patterson, Joseph, 10, 50.
  William, 122.
Paulling, Lydia, 45.
Pedrick, John, 137.
  Sarah D, 93.
  Silas, 15.
Penton, Daniel, 115.
Perry, Lydia, 61.
  Wells, 69.
Peterson, Amos, 7.
  Catharina, 133.
Petit, Sarah, 59.
  Woodnutt, 139.
Pimm, Mary, 52.
Platt, Daniel, 146.
Plummer, Charles, 148.
  William, 71.
Polson Jeremiah, 5.
Powell, Elkanah, 94.
  Jeremiah, 51.
  John, 57.
  John R., 125.
  Sarah, 74
Powner, Apacarius, 36.
Prescott, Margaretta J., 125.
Press, Sarah, 91.
Prickitt, Joel S., 96.
Ray, Rebecca, 34.
Read, Catharine, 57.
Reason, William, 124.
Reed, James, 47.
Reeve Martha, 64.
  Thomas, 11.
Reeves, Charles A., 127.
  Edward A., 73.
  Enos P., 104.
  Hannah, 112.
  Isaac, 104.
  Stephen, 58.

  William, 46, 122.
Richman, Amy, 143.
  Daniel, 30.
  James, 146.
  John, 152.
  Matthias, 38.
  Rachel 101.
Ridgway, John, 130.
  Terase, 135.
Robbins, Edward H., 134.
  John, 109.
  Obadiah, 8, 34.
  Sarah, 35.
Roberts, Rebecca, 87.
Robins, Mary, 48.
Robinson, Margaret, 147.
  William, 123.
Royal, William, 45.
Scull, Paul, 60.
  Sarah, 24.
Seagrave, Artis, 24.
  William, 40.
  William K., 87.
Seeds, Mark, 109,
Seers, Samuel, 44.
Selby, Samuel, 23.
Sheppard, Elizabeth W., 47.
  Enoch, 41.
  Nathan, 147.
Sherron, James, 102.
Shimp, George, 108.
  William, 54.
Shockley, Daniel, 148.
Shough, Jacob, 128.
Shute, Isaac, 64.
  Ruhama, 104.
Siger, Elizabeth, 138.
Simkins, Ellis, 17.
  Joel, 86.

INDEX TO TESTATORS 161

Simpkins, Ezekiel, 56.
Sims, James, 84.
Smart, Hannah, 93.
    Mary, 24.
Smith, Andrew, 153.
    Asa, 75.
    Benjamin N., 132.
    Jail, 71.
    James, 68.
    Jane, 31.
    John, 25.
    Jonathan. 118.
    Joshua, 44,
    Mary, 33, 130.
    Oliver, 14.
    Prudence, 11.
    Sarah, 43.
    William B., 83.
Snell, Abigail, 132.
Somers, John, 63.
    Samuel, 91.
Sparks Gerrard, 57.
    Richard, 144.
Springer, Benjamin, 129.
    Hudson, 48.
    Hudson A , 128.
    James S., 121.
Stackhouse, Archer, 140.
Stanton, David, 112.
    George, 44.
Steelman, Isaac, 40.
Stevenson, John, 100.
Stewart, James, 24.
    Joseph, 53.
Stratton, William, 144.
Stretch, Elisha, 12.
    Mark, 79.
    Mary D., 120.
    William, 132.

String, David, 100.
Summerill, John, Sr., 119.
Swing, Abraham, 13.
    Charles, 148.
Taylor, Samuel, 45.
Teel, Samuel, 20.
Test, Joseph, 97.
Thompson, Ann, 96.
    Edith, 135.
    James, 53, 98.
    Joshua, 5.
    Mary, 55.
    Mary Ann, 153.
    Mary N., 108.
    Rebecca, 6.
    Samuel, 22.
    William, 94.
Tomlinson, Samuel, 145.
Torton, John, 117.
Townsend, Jonathan, 88.
    Peter, 72.
Tredway, Joseph, 75.
Truss, Thomas, 22.
Tuft, Elizabeth, 37.
    Mary, 52.
Tussey, Joseph, 115.
Tyler, Benjamin, 18.
    Job, 120.
Valentine, Aaron, 138.
    James, 23.
VanMeter, Bathsheba, 7.
    David, 18.
    James, Sr., 142.
    Joel, 61.
    Rachel, 35.
    Robert H., 34.
    Sarah, 15.
Vanneman Christiana, 120.
    Daniel, 85.

Waddington, Aaron, 48.
  Edward, 60.
  Hannah, 62.
  Jesse, 85.
  William, 119.
Walker, David, 127.
  James, 20.
  Rebecca, 8.
  William, 90.
Wallace, Ann, 103.
Walmsley, Ann, 12.
Ware, Bacon, 109.
  Mary, 139.
Waters, Anthony, 65.
Watson, Robert, 16.
Wattson, Isaac, 22.
Westcott, Sarah, 87.
Westerbeck, Remmers, 114.
Wheaton, Elisha, 142.
White, Hannah, 54.
  Isaac, 79.
  Jonathan, 127.
  Samuel, 149.
  William, 26.
Whitsel, Conrad, 36.

Wibie, Samuel, 116.
Wick, Margaret, 43.
Wiley, David, 136.
Williams, Job, 33.
  Mark, 65.
  William, 48.
Willit, Edmond, 69.
Wintzell, Charles, 49.
Wiser, George, 16.
Wistar, Clayton, 42.
Wood, Auley B., 96.
  Bathsheba, 113.
  Henry, 66.
  Joseph H., 36.
  Josiah, 12.
  Maria R., 61.
Wright, Benjamin, 149.
  Hezekiah, 30.
  Nathan, 124.
  Peter, 60.
  Steven, 73.
Urban, Adam, 131.
Yarrow, Thomas, 46.
Young, William, 36.

GENERAL INDEX

A

Abbit—Hannah, 19; Isaac C., 18; John, 18, 19; Mary, 18.

Abbot—Samuel, 80, 81.

Abbott—Amy A., 67; Ann, 83; Catharine, 100; George, 21, 59, 60, 67, 68, 81; John, 81; Lydia, 21, 60; Martha, 21, 60, 67; Mary A., 67; Mary Ann, 21; Ruth S., 81; Samuel, 21, 46, 59, 60, 67, 68; Sarah W., 81, Susan, 25; William G., 21, 81.

Accoo—Julian, 32.

Ackley, Coombs, 117; Daniel R., 30; George, 117; Jesse, 117; Joseph, 117; Nancy, 31; Samnel, 117; Sarah, 117; Thomas T., 25; William, 100, 117.

Acton, Ann, 36; Benjamin, 68, 123; Caspar W., 123, 124; Catharine, 123; Clement, 80; Edward A., 150; Hannah, 38; Isaac, 19, 67; Jane, 36; Letitia, 123, 124; Mary, 150; Richard, 52; Richard M., 31, 41, 69, 93, 108, 123, 124, 150; Samuel, 28; Sarah W., 9, 123, 124; Sarah W., Jr., 93; William, 55.

Adams—Eli, 96; Elizabeth, 134; John, 19; Mary G., 143.

Adcock—Elizabeth, 106; Isaac H., 22; Isaac P., 106.

Ale—Jonathan, 141; Moses, 127.

Allen—Chambles, 93; David, 70, 71, 128; Edward, 70, 128; Eliazbeth, 62; Hannah, 21, 44, 59, 67, 81, 93, 128; Hannah G., 67; Isaac, 72; Jedediah T., 19, 81; Jeremiah, 70, 81, 128; John W., 44; L. A. D., 149; Lettice, 24; Lydia, 19; M. R., 83; Margaret, 43, 44; Mary, 128; Mathew, 26; Michael, 79; Rebecca, 19, 128; Richard, 19, 90; S. A., 116; Samuel, 37, 70, 128; Samuel Austin, 19; William W., 133.

Allwas—Benjamin, 9.

Altemus—P., 89.

Anderson—Elizabeth T., 92; Rebecca A., 52; Rebecca Ann, 6, 55.
Andrews—Clarissa, 50, 51; Martha C. 109.
Antrim—Tabitha, 106.
Aplen—Joseph, 23.
Aplin—Charles, 23; Peter, 23.
Applegate—Amelia, 75; Israel, 101, 115; Lavinia, 75, 90; Margaret, 10, 11; Richard, 75.
Appleton—George, 125, 126; Lewis, 125, 126; Ruth, 126; Ruth W., 60; Sarah, 125.
Applin—Emma, 52.
Archer—Benjamin, 6, 20, 31, 52, 84; Benjamin, Dr., 49; F. H., 150; Fenwick, 20; Fenwick H., 68; Rachel, 6, 68; Rachel T, 52.
Armstrong—David D., 134, 152; Eliza, 152; Hannah, 137; John, 26, 34, 40, 43, 152; John, Jr., 19; Joseph P., 46, 152; Mark, 40, 152; Mary, 43; Phebe Ann, 152; Thomas B., 152; Thomas Brown, 8; William, 8.
Ashton—Daniel, 123; Hannah Steel, 78.
Atkinson—Abbit, 19; Benjamin H., 95; Champion, 97, 126; Elizabeth H., 95; Hannah, 38, 95; Samuel, 38; Samuel C., 11, 81; Sarah, 81.
Atwood—Anthony, Rev., 85; Rebecca C., 85.
Austin—David N., 22; Lewis W., 87; Lydia, 19; William, 19, 115.
Averill—Sidney 138, 140.
Avis—George, Jr., 105; Rebecca, 74; Ruth, 74; Sarah, 74; William, 74.
Avise, John L., 26.
Ayars—Charles B., 89; Daniel Ashton, 78; Enoch, 140; Joseph Ashton, 78; Mary, 78; Susannah, 87.
Ayres—Charles B., 144; Ellis, 38, 49, 58, 59, 67, Hannah, 87; Isaac S., 67. John B., 111; Lucretta M, 111; Rachel, 100; Rebecca Jane, 111; Robbins, 109; Susanna, 86; Winfield S., 111.

B

Bacon—Charles, 39, 113; David, 11; Elizabeth, 7, 73, 110, 129 130; Francis, 70; Hannah, 70, 102, 128; Jacob, 7; John, 89, 40, 92, 102; John S., 110; Lot, 7; Mary, 73; Samuel H., 128; Sarah, 102; Smith, 129; Thomas, 39, 46; Thomas S., 72, 80; William C., 102; William, Dr., 61.

GENERAL INDEX

Baker—Ann, 66, 135; Hannah, 122; Jacob, 110; James, 122; John, 110; John S., 48; Joseph, 12, 110, 135; Judah, 33; Maria, 89; Martha, 135; Mary, 135; Mary Emma, 135; Mary Jane, 99; Mary W., 135; Powell, 135; Sarah Jane, 130: Susannah, 110; William A., 66; William M., 64.

Ballenger—Elizabeth, 26; Isaac, 13; Isaac, Jr., 13; John G., 97, 127; Joshua, 26; Josiah, 13; Mary, 75; Samuel E., 127; Sarah, 100; Sarah Ann, 58; Stephen R., 127; Thomas, 127; Valentine, 26, 57.

Ballinger—Emma, 95; John, Jr., 122; Joseph, 95; Priscilla, 95; Sarah Ann, 122, 127.

Banks—Jacob, 27, 44, 84, 107; Mary, 131.

Barber—David D., 140; Elisha S., 79, 140; Henry A., 134, 145; Isaiah, 77; Job, 140; John, 145; John S., 140; John W., 134; Joseph, 11; Sarah, 140; William, 59.

Barker—Hannah, 127; Hannah Ann, 58; James C., 58, 127.

Barnes—Arrabella, 115; Elizabeth, 18; Ephraim 18, 41; Hannah, 41; Joseph, 7, 29; Joshua, 151; Lydia Jane, 144; Mary Jane, 115; Phebe Ann, 114, 115; Sarah, 151.

Barnet—George, 34.

Barnett—Amanda, 131; Henrietta, 131; Mary Ann, 131; Rachel, 131; Sarah, 131.

Barratt—Asa, 97; Prudence, 60.

Bassett—Albert, 127; Amanda, 76; Anna C., 64; Benjamin, 6, 64, 76; David, 38, 76, 131; Davis, 64; Elisha, 76, 80, 133; Hannah D., 64; Hannah Ann, 60; John, 62; Joseph, 6, 33, 37, 43, 65, 67, 71; Margaret Johnson, 62; Martha, 41; Mary, 76; Rebecca, 76; Samuel, 64, 76; Sarah, 39; William, 62, 64, 72, 76, 83, 95, 136.

Bates—M. W., 43.

Batten—Anna Jane, 61; Thomas I, 61; Thomas J., 70.

Beck—J., 133.

Beckett—Josiah B., 150.

Bee—George, 10, 11; George C., 112.

Beesley—Benjamin, 38, 49, 50, 139; C. W., 117; Hannah, 50; Hannah, W., 117; Mary, 52; Rachel, 49, 59, 139; Theophilus E., 117; William G., 38, 41.

Belair—Lewis D., 93.

Belden—Calvin, 49; Rebecca, 65.

Bell—Andrew, 134; Benjamin, 108, 134; Elizabeth, 101; Hannah, 108, 134; Hannah Ann, 134; Harriet, 134; Henry, 49; Joseph, 68, 134;

Joseph Henry, 108; Lydia, 124; Margaret, 138; Mary, 134; Rachel, 108; Rachel J., 113; Robert, 134; Samuel, 101, 108, 134; Sarah H., 49.

Belton—Jonathan, 47, 83, 86; Rebecca, 141.

Bellville—Kesiah, 117.

Benner—Charles, 130.

Bennett—Margaret, 126.

Benson—Elmer, 116; Josiah, 116; Lewis, 116; Morris, 116; Samuel, 116.

Best—James, 151.

Bevis—George Washington, 25, 65; Job, 15, 25, 30, 44, 48, 50, 52, 58; Sarah, 58, 65.

Biddle—Aaron, 92; Abel, 133; Beulah, 92; Elizabeth, 23, 57; Elmer, 96; Evelina, 9; John, 23; Miller, 9; Maria, 92; Samuel, 133; Sarah, 9; Susannah, 92; Thomas, 92.

Bilderback—Alpheus, 36, 37; Edward, 36, 70; Eunice, 143; Jane, 41; Joseph, 36, 37; Lucy, 36; Phebe, 8; Phebe A., 143; Sarah, 27, 41; Sarah S 91; Smith, 143.

Bishop—John, 15.

Bivins—Elizabeth, 109.

Black—Edward, 80; Elizabeth, 11; Job, 48, 67, 80; Joseph, 20, 39, 48, 101; Mary, 67; Thomas, 89.

Blackwood—Beulah, 13; Clarissa, 99; Fannie, 99; John, 13, 99; Joseph, 13; Miranda, 99; Rosanna, 99; Roxanna, 99; Saloma, 99; Sheppard, 70; William, 13.

Blondeau—Maria, 65.

Bolton—Beulah S., 16; Charlotte H., 16; Elizabeth I, 16; Ellen 16; Joseph L., 16; Richard B., 16; Samuel, 14, 24, 44, 60, 63, 115.

Bond—Elizabeth, 110; Harriet, 110; Jesse, 6, 7; Mary Jane, 110; Rebecca Ann, 110.

Bonham—Belford M., 132.

Boon—Enoch, 152; George T., 88; Hannah, 152; Lauren, 99; Mary Ann C., 114; Robert M., 133; Sarah, 13.

Boots—Martha, 68.

Boqua—Ann, 59; Catharine, 59; Hannah, 59; Hannah Ann, 59; John, 40; Margaret, 59; Martha, 59.

Borden—Clement A., 115; Lydia, 126; Margaret, 137; Ruth Ann, 126; Susannah, 16; Thomas J., 126; William, 86.

Borton—Aaron, 29, 75, 97; Elizabeth, 29, 30; Hannah, 57, 92;

GENERAL INDEX 167

Joel, 29, 30; Omar, 149; Rachel, 92; Thomas, 30.

Boultinghouse—William S., 125.

Bowen—Clinton, 105; Daniel, Dr., 120; Daniel S., **121**; Daniel Smith, 120; David, 16, 26, 59, 74, 76, 104, 122; David M., **74, 76**; David Madison, 47; Elizabeth R., 130; George, 105; Isaac, **151**; Jane, 28; Joseph, 116; Joseph, Jr., 90; Josiah, 122; Josiah H., **116**; Keziah, 74; Maria Elizabeth, 121; Priscilla, 116; Rebecca, **151**; Thomas, 105; Thomas S., 76; William, 32; William S., **116**; Withnal, 116.

Bower—Asher, 133; Theodotia, 48.

Bradway, Adna, 11; Beulah, 24; Charles, 120; Charles H., **127**; Elizabeth, 113; Mark, 24, 42, 72; Mary, 113; Rebecca, **45**; Samuel B., 106; Thomas D., 36, 134; Waddington, 11, 113, 138; **Washington**, 90, 110, 120; William W., 113.

Branson—Rebecca, 93.

Brick—Deborah, 13, 25; Hannah, 140; Samuel S., **138**; Thomas, 115.

Bright—Deborah, 34; James, 51, 67; Nicholas, 14.

Brinton—Ann C., 98; Daniel Garrison, 98; Lewis, 98.

Britton—Hannah, 97.

Brogan—Samuel D., 88.

Brookfield—Hannah, 34.

Brooks—Eliza, 99; Isaac S., 47; Mary, 47; Pheby, 57; Sarah, 47 Stephen H., 145.

Brown—Ann C., 38, 67, 87; Christian, 55, 67; Christian F., **147**; Daniel, 152; Ebenezer, 21; Elgar, 87; Eliza, 22; Eliza F,, 21, Elizabeth, 87, 151; Hannah, 33; Henry, 38; Israel, 87; Israel E., 38; Jacob, 141; John Henry, 136; John M., 36, 50, 52, 53, 62, 67, 68, 81, 87, 92, 93, 110, 139; John W., 38; Jonth. L., **138**; Joseph, 32; Joseph E., 19, 37, 39, 42; Mary, 102, 136; Mathew, 121; Moses R., 136; Nancy, 87; Rachel, 151; Samuel, 141; Sarah, 114, 121; Thomas, 151; William, 14; William H., 137; Zacheus, 21, 22.

Bruna—John P., 119.

Buck—Caroline, 66; Dayton, 81; Deborah, 93; Henry, 81; **James**, 81, 87; Mary, 81; Mary Jane, 81; Robert, 81, 87; Robert S., 66.

Buckman—Dilworth, 27.

Bullock—Charles, 89; Edward R., 49.

Bunting—Jesse D., 26.

Burch—Ann, 93.

Burden—William D., 65, 145.
Burdsall—Abel, 14
Burns—Hannah Ann, 121.
Burroughs—Benjamin, 26; Clarissa, 56; Cornelius, 26; Cornelius, Jr., 26; Edward, 135; Elizabeth, 100; John, 87, 138; Jonathan, 91; Joseph, 26.
Burt—Benjamin F., 149; Charles R., 143; Experience. 143; John, 61; Richard, 109.
Burtt—John, Rev., 106, 136.
Butcher—Hannah. 97; Isabella I., 97; James, 7, 72, 132; James, Jr., 88; Jervis, 11; Lydia Ann, 97; Mary 97; Rachel, 76; Robert, 78, 97, 132, 138; Sarah B., 101.
Butler—Mary, 133; William, 25.
Buzby, Asher, 21; Nathan, 124; Ruth, 124.

C

Caldwell—Rebecca, 153.
Calehopper—Charles, 29; F. T., 110.
Callahan—Samuel 144.
Cammack—Joseph, 44.
Camm—Agustus, Jr., 87; Hannah, 102; John C., 102.
Camp—Joseph, 50.
Campbell—Christopher M., 74; James, 14.
Camplett—Hannah R., 93.
Carll—Dorcas, 132; Edward S., 125; Ephraim, Jr., 76; Ephraim, Sr., 130; Hiram, 132; Jesse, 14, 76, 90; Mary Ann, 130; William, 76; William S., 120, 130, 140, 150.
Carman—John A., 65.
Carney—Amy, 20; Peter, 20; Phebe, 20; Rachel, 10.
Carpenter—George W., 39; Hannah A., 88; Hannah H., 123, 124; John, 28; John M., 143; Mary, 28, 49, 50, 96, 139; Mary B., 16; Samuel P., 17, 89; Samuel Pseston, 28, 29; William, 16, 17, 28, 29, 50, 57, 72, 80, 88, 89, 93, 96, 105, 139.
Carrel—Amy, 77.
Carrol—Amy, 77.
Carter—John, 91; Mary, 57; Sarah Ann, 10.
Caspar—Anna, 104; Charles, 104; Clement, 104; John, 103;

GENERAL INDEX

Joseph, 104; Mary, 104; Sarah, 103; Thomas, 104; Thomas J., 103, 122; William A., 122.

Casperson—Catharine, 40; John, 134; John E., 40; Margaret, 40; Samuel, 40; William, 40.

Cassaday—Ruth, 31.

Casseday—Elisha, 83.

Cattell—Alexander G., 54, 55; Elizabeth, 53, 61; Thomas, 7, 130; Thomas W., 24, 77, 85.

Cauley—Esther, 95; Esther H., 95; William, 101, 102, 104, 106; William M., 108.

Cawley—Amy, 76; Emily S., 86; Jonathan, 11, 83, 124, 126; Jonathan P., 143; William, 92, 134; William M., 86, 122, 143; W. M., 117, 124, 126, 128, 143, 146, 147, 148, 150, 151.

Challis—Ann, 47; James M, 47; John W., 47; Lydia, 28.

Chamless—Charles R., 149; Harriet, 149; Sarah, 149.

Champneys—Benjamin, 35.

Charlesworth—Elizabeth, 19.

Chase—Daniel, 49; Samuel, 94; Stephen, 94.

Cheesman—William, 48.

Chester—Matilda, 132.

Chew—Henry F., 144; Joseph R., 144.

Clark—Anne, 73; Benjamin, 142; Charles C., 132; Edward, 78; Eli, 30; Elizabeth, 30; Ellenor, 30; George, 73; Gideon, 30; Isaac, 142; Jacob, 30; Jacob, Jr., 36; James G., 89; John, 32; John L., 30; Lydia, 142; Martha, 20; Mary, 9, 92; M. C., 132; Rachel, 88; Rosanna, 84; Samuel, 20, 30; Sarah, 131; Thomas, 28, 30.

Clarke—Elizabeth H., 131.

Clarkson—W. S., 78.

Clauson—W. T., 104.

Clawson—F. S., 99; Jane H., 149; J. R., 16; William S., 131; W. S., 115, 127, 152.

Clay—Joseph C., 66.

Clayton—Beulah, 43.

Cleaver—William L., 144; William S., 111.

Clement—Dewitt Clinton, 90; Elizabeth, 20; Mary, 20, 75; Samuel, 20; Samuel H., 71, 153; Thomas R. 100, 113, 142.

Clifton—Christian, 63; Eliza, 140; Hannah, 63; John, 140; Joseph B., 63.

Cline—Hannah, 117; Josiah, 94; Lucy, 94.

Clintock—John M., 101, 126.

Cobb—Hannah, 75, 90; Paul, 102; Samuel, 75.

Cock—Mary, 88; Samuel, 88.

Cole—Catharine, 133; Elizabeth, 77, 109; George M., 64; Samuel, 109.

Coleman—Anna, 128; Harris, 128; Isaac, 128; Moses, 128.

Coles—Elizabeth, 52, 103; Elmer, 53; Elmer K., 103; Ephraim, 131; Ephraim S., 30, 89; George M., 29; Joseph, 15; Margaret, 7; **Martha**, 7; Martha Ann, 7; Morgan, 7; Rebecca, 7; Samuel, 52, 53, 64; William, 7.

Collier—Elmira, 104.

Collins—Elisha, 6; Freeman, 65; Sarah, 141.

Comminskey—John, 113.

Conaroe—Ellen, 82; George, 82; Margaret, 82; Maria, 82; Sarah, 82.

Conarroe—George, 69; Margaret, 62; William M., 69.

Conklyn—Isaiah, 103, 143.

Conly—Sarah, 119.

Connarroe—Charlotte, 136; Ellen M., 136; George W., 136; Maria, 136.

Connor—Cornelius, 148.

Conover—Eliza, 142; Israel, 41, 136; John M., 98.

Conrow—Amy, 133; Ann, 38; Emily, 38; Mary, 38, 150; Prudence, 38; Sarah Ann, 38, 150.

Cook—Eliza, 35; John, 18, 46, 90; Joseph, 35, 43, 61, 107; Mary, 35, 43; Mary Louisa, 43.

Coombs—Elizabeth, 11; Henrietta, 81; James, 15, 81; Williame 39.

Cooper—Ann, 146; Edward P., 139; Frances, 146; John A., 81; John M., 13, 72, 93, 120, 132, 139, 143, 144, 152; John R., 131; Joseph H., 88; Margaretta, 52; Mary, 47; Rebecca, 146; Rebecca Ann, 13; Samuel L., 109; Sarah B., 139; Thomas B., 107.

Copner—Samuel, 102.

Corcoran—Susan, 82; Susannah, 65.

Corliss—Ann, 135; John, 91; Maria, 91; Samuel B., 135.

Cosens—Ann, 107; Sarah, 107.

Costill—Charles, 14.

Couch—Adam, 10.

Councillor—John, 111.

Counsellor—James, 20; Rhoda. 20; Samuel, 20; Stephen, 19.
Cox—Ann, 38; David, 38; Edmund, 38; Rachel, 38; Rebecca, 38.
Craft—Mary, 76.
Craig—Gilbert, 45; Gilbert H., 105; Harriet, 105; Mary, 7; Pamela. 114; Samuel. 114.
Crandall—Hester, 132; Jonathan 132.
Crane—Moses, 124; Priscilla, 153.
Crammer—William, 121.
Cranmer—Burdin, 8.
Craven—John, 57.
Creamer—Jacob, 117; Ruth, 117.
Creemer—Enos, 32; Mary, 32; Rodah, 32.
Crow—Edith, 75, 90; Jonathan, 75; Sarah, 90.
Crowe—Johnson, 90.
Cuff—Emma Ann, 12; John, 66; Jonathan, 67; Mary 66; Mordica, 130.
Curliss—Jonathan H., 123; Margaretta, 136; Mary, 123.
Currey—Abraham, 107; John, 107.
Curriden—John P. H., 40.
Currie—James, 68.
Curry—Abraham. 119; Ann J., 119; Dorcas, 32; Eliza, 119; Elmer, 119; Jacob, 23, 72; John, 119; Margaret, 119; Mary, 72; Mary Ann, 72; Mary Jane, 145; Neal, 20, 36, 110; Sarah, 119; William, 119.

D

Dalbow—Abigail, 122; Ann, 122; Catharine, 122; Charles, 122; Edward, 122; Frederick, 122; John, 122; Mary Elizabeth, 122; Sarah, 122; William, 122.
Dallas—Holmes, 81.
Dalrymple—James, 8.
Daniels—John B., 65; J. Reeves, 142.
Danser—Burden, 137; Daniel, 139; Rebecca, 137.
Danzenbaker—Elizabeth, 109.
Dare—Benjamin, 94; Beulah, 69; David D., 105; Hannah A., 96; James A., 96; Josiah A., 96; Prudence, 153; Richard, 153; Samuel A., 96; Sarah, 153.
Darlington—Benjamin, 131; James, 134; Sarah, 134.
Darman—Smith, 88, 147; William, 8, 21.

Darragh—Ann, 41; Margaret S., 41; Susan, 41.

Davis—Ammi, 149; Amy, 99; Ann, 92; Arthur, 131; Belford E., 109, 111, 149; Benjamin, 49; Caleb, 109; Clarissa, 74; Clarra, 9; David, 11, 28, 29, 64, 120; David M., 17, 64 147; Eli, 67; Elisha, 15, 31; Elizabeth, 12, 31, 91, 97; Esther, 31, 63, 64; Francis, 91, 142; George, 61; George A., 84, 109; Hannah, 131; Hannah P., 133; Henry V., 131; Horace B., 109; Horatio G., 61; Isaac, 109; Jacob, 64, 149; Jacob C., 48; James, 131; Jeremy, 111; Joseph, 5, 7, 11, 29, 92; Joseph P., 99; Joshua, 125; Josiah, 17, 64, 122; Keziah, 109; Martha, 92; Mary, 29; Mary Ann, 64, 81; Mary, 111; Mordecai, 111; Rebecca, 15; Richard, 64; Sarah, 31, 62, 64, 109; Sarah, 142; Silva, 84; Thomas, 17; Thomas W., 17, 64; William N., 133.

Dawson, Mary, 142.

Dayton—Mary B, 52; Mary T., 52.

Deacon—Sarah, 68; Stacy F., 68.

Deal—Catharine, 86; Elizabeth, 124.

Dean—Jonathan R., 143; Priscilla, 143; Rebecca, 146.

Dehart—William, 74.

Delahay—William, 49.

Delks—John, 116; Rachel, 119.

Denn—Ann, 19; Clayton, 73; Elizabeth, 19; James, 57; John, 19; Margaret, 19; Mary, 19, 24, 38; Rachel, 13, 19, 38; Rebecca, 19; Rhoda, 38; Sarah, 38; Susan, 60, 69; William, 24.

Dennals—John B., 52.

Dennis—Albert, 11; Elizabeth, 11; John, 36, 70; Lucy Ann, 11; Mary, 28; Rachel, 11.

Denny—George, 135; Sarah Jane, 140.

Dexter—William, 125.

Dick—John R., 123; Maria, 62; Sarah, 62; William A., 8, 41, 47, 61, 68, 69, 125, 128, 139, 145.

Dickerson—Charles G., 120; Isaac V., 120; John W., 120; Mary, 120; Richman, 120.

Dickeson—Anna F., 90; David, 90; Grace, 90; Mary H., 90; Samuel, 90; Sarah, 90; Thomas, 90.

Dickinson—Ann, 44; George, 43, 61; John, 16, 36, 58, 114, 120; John J., 99; Mahlon D., 99, 114; Martha D., 114; Mary, 32, 55, 114; Richman, 99; Samuel, 14; Sarah, 99; Thomas, 80, 109, 116; Thomas, Jr., 80; William, 14, 32.

Dilmore—Samuel, 144.

Diver—Jacob, 30; Joseph, 93, 104.

Dixon—Job S., 141.

Dodgson—Joseph, 26.

Dolbo—Margaret, 100.

Dolbow—Eli, 99; Gabriel, 40; Gabriel VanBuren, 99; George, 99; John Bennet, 100; John S., 125.

Doran—Francis, 64; William H., 64.

Dorton—Richard, 29; William, 29.

Doughton—Sarah, 75; Thomas, 75.

Dowdney—Henry, 45.

Dowlin—Samuel, 140.

Downs—Catharine, 71; Jesse, 71.

Draper, Jane, 135.

DuBois—Amy, 106; A. N., 75; David, 13, 31; Edmund, 31; Elanor, 21; Hope M, 10; Jacob, 26; Jedediah, 35; Jeremiah, 10, 106; Jonathan, 31, 106; Joshua M, 142; Josiah, 110; Lydia, 31; Martha O., 106; Mary, 71; Matthew N., 137; Nathan, 10; Rachel, 10; Richard, 26, 74; Samuel, 151; Sarah, 107; Thomas, 13; Uriah, 71.

Dumont—Caroline, 88; Samuel B., 88.

Dunham—Hannah, 140; John, 25.

Dunlap—Amy, 77; Elizabeth Harriet, 77.

Dunn—Abigail, 94; Ann, 27, 46; Ebenezer, 27, 43, 53, 54, 109, 141. Ebenezer P., 139; Elijah, 27; Eliza, 140; Elizabeth, 43; Ellenor, 43; George, 18, 125; Hope, 69; Jedediah, 43; John, 27, 43, 139, 141; John C, 54, 148; Mary, 27, 43; Mary Ann, 45, 109; Nehemiah, 27; Phebe 140; Rachel, 49; Rhoda, 49; Samuel, 21, 45, 46, 140, 141; Samuel, Jr., 74; Sarah, 27, 45, 139, 140; Susan, 49; Susannah, 43; Thackray, 140; Thomas, 27, 141; Wllliam, 118.

Dyer—John G., 78; Mary Groff, 78; Reeves S., 78.

E

Eakin—Elisa, 102; Mary, 87.

Eakins—Alphonso L., 8, 12, 85

Earley—Caleb, 66; James, 66; Jesse, 66, 117; John, 66; Mary, 117; Robert, 66; William, 66.

Edwards—Aaron, 57, 89; Barclay, 89; Charles, 75: Joseph, 75; Rachel, 75; Ruth, 131; Samuel, 75; Sarah, 92; Thomas, 13, 22, 30, 40, 53, 55, 57, 75, 82, 89, 92, 97, 100; William, 29, 75.

Eggman—Abraham, 5.
Eldridge—Esther, 29, 75.
Elfreth—Jacob R., 17, 128.
Elkinton—John, 78.
Ellet—Maria Chamblis, 33.
Elliot—Mary Anne, 94.
Ellis—James, 125.
Elton—Anthony. 125.
Elwell—Abraham, 19, 97; Caroline, 134; Charles, 43, 74, 142; Elizabeth, 134; Ellen, 134; Enoch, 97; Henry H., 34; Isaac, 97; Jacob, 97; John, 97; John F., 145; Joseph, 41; Margaret, 9. Martha, 44; Mary, 97, 134; Morris R., 151; Samuel, 35, 134; Thomas, 97, 103, 104; William C., 113; William H., 79.
Emerson—Elizabeth, 150.
Emery—Edward, 125, 128.
Emlen— Maria, 55.
Emley—Job C., 23.
Emmel—Albert S., 114; Elizabeth, 114; Emanuel, 84; John, 84; Lydia Ann, 84; Philip, 84; William, 84.
Engle—Joseph, 33, 97; Josiah, 97; Sarah, 36.
English—Ann, 53; Anna, 150; Anthony, 94, 110; Anthony N., 53; Aulay, 113; Charles H., 114; David, 10, 53; David S., 111; Enos P., 94, 111, 150; Hannah, 114; Hannah S., 111; Isaac, 45, 87, 88, 115; Jael, 94, 111; James, 114; Mary Jane, 114; Mary S., 111; Samuel Southard, 111; Sarah, 94, 111; Sarah D., 113; Theodore, 110; Timothy Craft, 94; William McCalla, 114; William S., 111.
Erwin—Jane, 129.
Evans—James D., 34.
Ewan—Maria, 82.
Ewing—David, 57; Josiah, 117.

F

Feller—Lois, 33.
Felty—Margaret, 29.
Fennemore—Ann, 113; Edward B., 113.
Ferguson—William, 50.
Ferris—Benjamin; 27; Eliza M., 27; Hannah, 43; John, 27, 43; Ziba, 27.

GENERAL INDEX 175

Fields—Benjamin, 88; James, 88; Joseph, 88; Patrick, 88; Samuel, 88.

Finlaw—Isaac, 76; John, 76; William, 141.

Finley—Ann, 9; David L., 42; Elizabeth, 47, 53; Horatio, 8; John, 8, 54.

Firth—Ann, 6, 55; Elizabeth, 49; Elizabeth C., 55; Hannah, 49; John, 49, 55; Samuel, 49, 55; Thomas, 16, 17, 49, 55.

Fish—Benjamin, 106; James, 9, 74; Richman, 74; William, 74.

Fisher—Elizabeth, 88, 117; William, 82.

Fisler—Ann, 100.

Fithian—Adelaide, 117; Elizabeth, 118; Hannah, 118; Mary, 45, 121; Mary E., 118.

Flanagan—James, 75; Robert, 90; Sheppard H., 90.

Flanagin—Ezekiel P., 122; Patience, 17; Sarah Ann, 8; Thomas, 52, 64, 121; Thomas, Sr., 122.

Flemings—Adaline, 36; Eliza Jane, 36; Mary, 36.

Flitcraft—Allen, 126; Bevan, 15, 30, 31, 40, 57, 75. Charles, 126; Eliza, 126; George, 91; Grace A., 126; Isaac, 126; Isaiah, 15; Isaiah R., 126; Pembroke, 126; Sarah, 75.

Fogg—Ann, 37, 38, 82; Anne, 131; Catharine, 49; David, 17, 21, 40, 152; Edward, 22, 72, 151; Elizabeth, 17; Hannah, 21, 82, 131; Henrietta, 22; Holme, 34; Isaac, 152; Isaac S., 146; James, 94; James P., 152; John H., 131; Mary, 39; Mary Ann, 57; Samuel, 16, 17, 72; Thomas, 57; William, 17, 39; William B., 75.

Folwell—Joseph D., 29, 92; Martha, 29; William D., 29.

Ford—James G., 130; Martha Kandle, 38.

Foster—A. H., 104; Barbara, 86; Harriet, 86; Jane, 86; Jeremiah, 45; John, 81; Joseph, 98; Judah, 35, 91, 96; Margaret S., 77; Ruth, 22; Sarah, 98; William W., 112, 117.

Fowler—John, 101.

Fowser—Ann, 45; Mary, 45.

Fox—D. M., 112, Elmer, 137; Frederick, 5; George, 6, 66, 73; Henry, 5, 116; Isaac, 6; Jacob, 5; Jeremiah, 5, 65, 129; Joanna, 79; Job, 73; John, 112; Joseph, 111, 135; Lucy Ann, 130; Louisiana, 130; Lusianna, 129; Mary, 15; Rebecca, 135; Rebecca Cline, 111.

Franklin—Hannah, 52.

Frazer—Adam N., 112; Amanda M., 139; Caleb, 139; Caleb N., 112; Charles G., 109; Charles P., 112; Daniel, 139; David, 139; David S., 112; Elizabeth, 112; Fuller H., 139; Hester, 112;

Isaac N., 112; Jacob M., 112; John, 112, 139; Joseph H., 139; Joseph K., 112; Lydia, 112; Matilda, 139; Rachel, 139; Richard S., 139; Robert M., 139; Ruth Ann, 139; Samuel M., 112.

Freas—Charles, 130; Charles W., 138; Daniel J., 112, 129; David, 101; Elizabeth, 130, 138; Ellen, 130; Ephraim B., 138; George, 130; George T., 138; Hannah, 130; Henry, 72, 99, 129, 130; Jacob, 26, 101; James, 47, 129, 130; Johnson, 83, 129; Mary, 101; Reuben J., 129; Samuel R., 130; William, 130, 138.

Freed—Mary, 50.

Freedland—Jonathan, 46, 49, 71, 73, 93 107.

French—Charles, 68; Elizabeth, 86; Hewlings, 86; Mary Elizabeth, 86; Samuel E., 57, 86.

Friant—James, 57.

Fries—Daniel, 59; Elizabeth, 68, 59; Henry, 34; Henry J., 59; Jacob, 58; John, 59; Margaret, 58, 59; Thomas, 59.

Frost—Lydia, 93.

Fry—Maria, 117.

Fursman—Mary, 109.

G

Gagers—David, 86.
Gamble—John, 33, 100.
Gardiner—Ann, 17.
Gardner—Ruth, 28.
Garnel—Catharine, 15.
Garrett—Mary, 36.

Garrison—Ann, 51, 73; Ann T., 31; Catharine, 9, 32; Charity, 50; Charles, 133; Daniel, 6, 37, 44, 65, 69, 91, 94; Daniel I., 37, 69; Daniel J., 98; Eliza, 50; Elizabeth, 8, 50; Ephraim, 37; Gamaliel, 73; George W., 31; Jedediah, 73; John, 73; Louisa Jane, 31; Mary, 69, 98; Milliscent, 72; Neh., 21; Nehemiah, 37; Rebecca, 6, 142; Rebecca F., 6; Samuel, 73; Sarah, 118; Stepeen A., 117; Thomas, 50.

Garton—Mark, 113; Mary H., 47.
Garwood—Elizabeth, 103; Samuel, 103.
Gaskill—Job, 124.
Gaw—Ann, 53.
George—John, 116; Mary Jane, 116; Shedrick, 124.

GENERAL INDEX 177

Gibbon—Ann, 73; Edward Keasbey, 102; George, 73; Leonard 102; Mason Seeley, 102; Quinton, 44, 102; Sarah Ann, 102; Thomas, 73.

Gibbons—Anne, 49, 69; Edmond, 98; Grant, 27, 98; Lurina, 98; Sarah A., 106.

Gibbs—Clarissa, 14; Edward, 14; John, 12; Rebecca, 12; Richard, 14.

Gibson—Anna, 137, Hezekiah, 93, 109; Thomas, 54.

Gill—Ann, 57; David, 57; Elizabeth, 46; Hannah, 46; John M., 67; Joseph, 57; Sarah Ann, 57.

Gillingham—Thomas, 7.

Gilman—Samuel, 46.

Gilmore—Alexander, 53, 54; Esther, 54; Esther C., 54; Samuel, 54; Samuel C., 53; Sarah, 53.

Githens—Caroline, 130; George, 91, 132; Sarah Elizabeth, 66.

Goforth—Hannah B., 83; Rachel, 10; Robert, 83.

Gooden—Kitturah, 25.

Goodwin—Abby, 38; Abigail, 150; Hannah T., 71; Jacob, 15; Mary M., 71; William T., 71.

Gosling—Ann, 32; Boston, 56; Hannah 56; Hiram, 32, 56; John Fenwick, 56; Richard, 115; Sarah, 56, 138; William, 32, 56.

Gould—Joseph, 32; Mary, 12; Sarah, 19; Susannah, 32.

Graham—Jacob, 46.

Grant—Beulah, 141.

Gray—Charles F. H., 142.

Green—Arthur H., 15; Elizabeth, 67, 80, 100; Emily Ann, 74; Lewis, 51, 67, 80; Silas, 74.

Grice—Amy, 92.

Grier—Anna, 118; Charles, 85; George, 17, 53, 117, 118; Georgianna, 117, 118; Jonathan, 85; Jonathan B., 117, 118, 135; Jonathan Butcher, 84; Lydia Ann, 117, 118; Richard, 117, 118, 127; Robert, 84, 85, 111, 117, 118; Ruth, 84, 118; Sarah, 94.

Griffing—Edmund, 42; Hannah, 42.

Griffith—Amos W., 93; Ellen M., 111; Joseph, 111; Sarah Jane, 111; Thomas, 111·

Griffiths—Elijah S., 77; Eugenia Holly, 77; Henry H., 77; Joseph M., 77; Mary Ann, 77; Rebecca Ann, 77; Thomas S., 77.

Grimshaw—Hugh, 103.

Griscom—Andrew, 154; Ann, 74; Ann Eliza, 154; Benjamin, 154;

Benjamin, Sr., 83; Clarkson, 154; Ephraim, 154; George, 154; Henry, 154; Job, 154; John, 154; Joseph, 154; Samuel, 74; Rachel J., 69; William, 154.

Groff—Amasa, 86; Anna J., 78; Arrabella, 86; Benjamin, 86; Benjamin A., 113; Charles, 99; Charles F., 78; Charles H., 78; Garret, 24; George, 24; George T., 114; Hannah, 86; John, 113; Joseph, 86; Richard, 24; Maria, 99; Sarah Ann, 24, 86; Stephen, 86; William, 24; William M., 113.

Guest—Elizabeth, 107; Hannah, 140; Henry, 32; John, 32.

Guestner—Anna E., 143; Mary, 82; Owen, 32, 44, 63; Rebecca, 125, 143; Robert, 66, 141.

Gwynne—Robert, 148.

H

Hackett—Aaron, 146; Edward, 12; Edward H., 146; Elizabeth, 101, 146; Ellen, 146; Emily Ellen, 12; Hope, 12; Isaac 77, 87, 92, 118; Jonathan, 12; Joseph, 117; Joseph R., 101; Mary, 146; Mary 12; Samuel, 12, 101; Sarah Ann, 12; Sarah G., 146; William E., 146; W., 12.

Hackney—Sarah, 147.

Haines—Aaron, 19; Adelia, 75; Charles, 40, 49, 63; Eleanor, 40; Elizabeth, 31 43; Empson, 22, 36; Ephraim, 59; Hope, 31; John, 40; Margaret, 19; Marian, 63; Rachel, 63, 95; Thomas P., 50; William, 95.

Hains—Lydia, 77.

Hall—Ann, 12, 55; Ann G., 32; Clement, 39; David, 39; Emley, 89; George, 18; George W., 103; Hannah A., 37; Henry D., 80, 129; Horatio, 55; Isaac, 132; James W., 37; John, 20, 37, 39, 62, 71, 75; Joseph, 78; Josiah, 32, 55; Margaretta, 39; Margaret W., 37; Mark, 28; Mary, 39, 55; Matilda Stiles, 103; Lewis M., 39; Lydia, 39; Morris, 20, 37, 39; Prudence, 37; Rachel, 28; Rachel L., 144; Rebecca, 115; Rebecca K., 37; Samuel, 55; Thomas, 39; Thompson, William, 55, 76.

Hamby—William, 133.

Hammitt—Rebecca, 17; Thomas, 17.

Hampton—Benjamin, 44; Mary Ann, 44.

Hance—Isaac, 51; James, 51; John, 11; Milton, 11; Rebecca Ann, 51.

GENERAL INDEX 179

Hancock—Aaron, 76; Anna K., 106; Cornelia Artemesia, 106; Caroline, 52; Chambles, 52; Charles Gilbert, 106; Clinton H., 151; Edward, 150; Elijah, 118, 125; Elmer, 151; Hannah M., 52; Joseph A., 85; Margaret, 151; Martha, 62; Mary Ann, 76; Morris, 11; Percival Araby, 106; Sarah, 52, 76; Susan G., 94; Thomas Y., 67, 147; William, 74.

Hand—Ann 144; Ann W., 87; Francis, 134, 144.

Handy—Eliza 54; Mary Ann, 129.

Hanes—Edward, 57, 91.

Hann—John E., 142; Robert G., 142; Samuel, 73.

Hanna—Rebecca, 75; Reuben, 75.

Hannah—Annah K., 106; James M., 106, 133; Rebecca A., 106.

Hannas—David, 45; Lydia, 45.

Hanners—Rachel, 117.

Hanthorn—Bathsheba, 113; Henry W., 113; Isaac, 117, 151; John, 39; Mary D., 113; Rebecca, 151; Richard, 73, 117; Simon, 113.

Harback—Ann Eliza, 65.

Harbert—S. C., 129.

Harbeson—Ann Elizabeth, 70; David, 115; Elijah, 115; George 115; Isaac, 115; Margaret, 117; Robert, 115.

Harding—Benjamin, 100; Eli, 100; Henry, 100, 107, 136; John, 74, 100; Rebecca, 124; Thomas, 100.

Harker—Albert, 132; Barbara Ann, 132; Benjamin, 53; Daniel, 53; Deborah, 113; Elias, 132; Elizabeth, 53; Jonathan, 132; Joseph, 65; Philemon, 132; Rebecca, 108; Samuel, 53; Samuel Coles, 53; William, 87.

Harmer—Elwood, 89; Hannah B., 89; Joseph, 40, 89; Letitia, 40; Lydia, 89; Mark, 40, 90; Mary Ann, 89; Mary B., 89; Rebecca, 90; Sarah, 40; William, 89, 90.

Harris—Aaron D., 122; Amos, 82, 131, 132, 146, 154; Anna M., 144; Benjamin, 12; Caroline, 151; Catharine, 144, 154; Charlotte, 123; Dalymore, 16, 21, 23, 42, 53, 54, 64, 82, 131; Ebenezer, 13, 86; Edward S., 144; Elizabeth, 16, 54; Ephraim, 84; Ephraim C., 94, 146; Francis B., 151; Hannah, 153, 154; Hiram, 82, 131, 153; Isaac, 123; Jacob, 78; Jael, 154; James, 7, 76, 144; John P., 46; Johnson, 41; Joseph, 12; Joseph L., 141; Josiah T., 146; Lettis, 23; Margaret S., 152; Mary, 97, 123; Michael N., 151; Oliver, 94; Parmenas, 23; Rachel, 96; Rebecca, 82, 131; Rebecca N., 154;

Samuel, 42; Sarah, 13; Sarah Ann, 144; Silas, 132; Stretch, 154; William, 32; William H., 144.

Harrison—Henrietta, 136; Josiah, 136.

Hartnock—Catharine, 58.

Haun—Andrew, 104, 105, 114, 151.

Hays—Ann, 151; Lewis, 151.

Headly—Samuel, 29.

Heberton—Elizabeth B., 145.

Heacock—Emeline, 149.

Heishon—Joseph B, 136.

Henley—Abigail 34; David, 34.

Henry—Amelia, 105; Elizabeth, 105; Maria, 105; William, 38.

Henttenback—Madeline, 119.

Heritage—Benjamin F., 95; Catharine, 66, 142; Jonathan, 95; Joseph, 16, 95; Priscilla M., 95; Sarah, 66; William, 95.

Herson—Elizabeth, 39.

Heward—Joseph, 10; Mary, 10; Richard, 10.

Hewart—Sarah, 87.

Hewes—Benjamin, 125; Thomas, 125.

Hewitt—Benjamin, 139; Benjamin, Jr., 8; Jane, 127; John, 139; Joshua, 26; Josiah, 133; Rebecca, 79, 133; Rebecca Jane, 133; Robert, 46; Smith, 10, 79, 131, 133, 150; William, 133; Wiliam F., 36; William S., 8.

Hews—Ann, 66; Joseph, 125; Nathan, 125; Theophilus, 125.

High—Cilas, 87; Elizabeth, 86; Joseph, 87; Lot, 86.

Hildreth—Anna, 62.

Hiles—Abigail, 70; Ann Eliza, 70; Catharine, 70; Elizabeth, 70; John, 70; Joseph, 70; Mary Ann, 70; Priscilla, 70; Richard, 70; Samuel K., 70; Sarah, 70; Sarah Elizabeth, 70; William, 70.

Hill—Sarah Ann, 48; Thomas, 31.

Hilliard—Elizabeth, 129; Hannah, 13; Mary A., 152.

Hillman—Catharine, 20, 110; Hannah N., 110; Martha C., 110; Samuel, 128, 147, 148; Sarah, 143; Theophilus H., 114.

Hinchman—Catharine, 15; Clarence, 149; Clement, 15, 142; Elizabeth B., 149; Joshua, 142; Lot, 6, 11; Margaret, 15; Mary, 53; Reuben, 14; Rheuben, 142; Ruth, 15; Thomas, 15, 53, 131.

Hires—Ann Eliza, 130; George, Jr., 130; John, 86.

Hitch—Spencer; 49.

Hitchner—Hannah, 67, 115; Henry, 49; Jacob, 35; John H., 101

Hitchner—Matthias, 35, 39; Philip, 79; Rebecca, 79; Sarah, 49.

Hoffman—Abigail, 82; Almira H., 125; Howell, 102; Howell B., 124; Isaac, 97; James, 131; Job, 73; Joseph F., 138; Sarah, 24.

Hogate—Jonathan, 113; 151; Loransy, 144; Sarah, 34.

Hogbin—Charles, 101; John, 123; Lidiann, 123; Mary, 59.

Holdcraft—Letitia, 113.

Holdshorn—Mary, 94.

Holdskins—Joseph, 9; Sarah, 9; William, 9.

Holeton—Elizabeth, 139; John, 139; Matilda, 99; William, 99, 115.

Holliday—Joseph, 46; William, 85.

Hollinshead—David E., 17; George, 17; Hagar, 45; Hannah, 17; Mary, 17.

Holme—Benjamin S., 37; Margaret W., 37.

Holmes—Anna, 122; Samuel, 122.

Holton—Andrew, 87; Charles, 133; David, 85; Ephraim, 133; Jesse, 87; John, 87, 133; Louisa, 87; Mary Ann, 23; Philip, 87; Samuel, 87; Sarah, 133; Thomas, 87; Thomas C., 23; William, 87, 133.

Homan—Abel, 132; Mary Elizabeth, 132; Hannah, 132; Heta R., 132.

Hopkins—Charles, 11.

Hood—C. B., 125.

Horn—Jain, 49.

Horner—Abigail, 150; Abigail Ann, 150; Ann, 7; Asa R., 150; Benjamin, 150; Benjamin L., 132; Charles, 150; Charles P., 150; Elijah B., 150; George W., 150; Hannah, 132; Joseph L., 107, 150; Malachi, 150; Meshack, 150; Rachel, 132; Sarah, 84, 150; Sarah D., 150; Susan, 150; Sybilla D., 150.

Hortman—Peter Andrew, 100; Samuel, 100, 127, 137; Sarah, 100; Sarah Ann, 100.

House—William, 101, 108, 112, 116, 129, 131.

Howard—Asbury, 73; Charles, 73.

Howell—Samuel, 33.

Howey—Elizabeth, 106: Henrietta, 92; Isabella, 92; Jacob, 16, 48, 86, 106.

Hubbell—Anna G., 95, 118; Anne, 95; Anne Ladow, 95; Helen, 95; Johnson, 95.

Hubbs—Beulah, 107; John, 107; Paul K., 15; Rebecca, 25.

Hudson—Abraham, 9; Samuel, 9.
Huddy—Hannah, 117.
Huffman—Howel B., 151.
Hughes—John, 71, 88, 101; Rebecca, 96.
Hughs—Almira, 39; Ann, 39; Christiana, 22; Elam, 39; Eliza, 39; Harriet, 39; Henry, 22; Ira, 39; John, 22; Margaret, 22; Mary, 22; Oliver, 39; Permelia, 39; Rachel, 22; Rebecca, 35.
Hulick—Cornelius, 9.
Humphreys—Joanna, 127; Joseph, 138; Lydia, 115; Margaretta, 127; Mary, 127; Rachel, 79; Samuel, 34.
Humphries—Charles, 79; Edward B., 150; Hannah, 79; Isaac, 79; John, 79; Josiah 79; Mark, 79; Samuel, 79.
Hunt—Hannah, 26; Jacob, 34; James B., 42; John; 26, 146; Mary, 26; Naomi, 26; Samuel W., 110, 128, 142; Willlam, 26.
Hunter—Julian, 69; Sarah, 15, 35.
Hurley—Abigail, 35; David, 35; Rachel, 63; Samuel, 63.
Hurse—James, 74; Michael, 74.
Husted—James, 103.
Hutchens—Ellen, 88.
Hutchinson—Antrim, 141; Bacon, 122; Daniel, 12; Henry, 141; John H., 141; M., 133; Mary Ann, 141; Rebecca, 35.

I

Ingham—D. K., 96; Harriet H., 55. 62, 135; I., 95; Jno., 163; Jonathan, 65, 62; R. T., 96; S. D., 96.
Ireland—David, 47; Elizabeth, 47; Emma, 88; Samuel C., 99; William, 15, 88.
Ivins—H. B., 71; Sarah, 113; Thomas, 53.

J

Jackson—Holiday, 80.
James—Elizabeth, 78; 101; James, 66; Lewis, 105; Mary, 66; Samuel, 66; Sarah, 24.
Janvier—E. J., 78; Eliza, 41; George W., 13.
Jaquett—Abraham, 84; Ann, 27; David, 84; Dorcas Amy, 27; Drusilla, 27; Eliza, 61; Elizabeth, 26, 32; Hance, 27, 61; Hannah, 84; Jacob, 84; Jane Ann, 27; John, 27, 84; Julian, 32; Kitts, 26, 32;

GENERAL INDEX 183

Lott, 24, 37, 70; Paul, 61; Peter, 27, 61; Robert, 61.

Jarman—Catherine, 82; Daniel, 113; Elizabeth, 34; George, 34, Henry Freas, 34; Rachel, 123; Sarah Jane, 34.

Jarnell—Catharine, 35.

Jefferis—Elwood, 148, 154; Joseph, 154; Joshua, 148, 154; Sarah, 148; William, 148.

Jeffers—W. N., 27, 34.

Jenkins—Charlotte, 108.

Jester—Alfred T., 131, 138.

Johnson—Abraham, 28, 69, 136; Alexander, 28; Andrew, 49; Ann, 8, 101, 115; Elias, 137; Elizabeth, 44; Isaac, 112; Isaac, 2nd, 15, 35, 83; Jacob, 132; James, 44; John, 28, 100; John, 3rd, 96; Jno., 153; Joseph, 137; Juliana E, 95; Margaret, 44, 111, 137; Margaretta, 136; Mary, 69, 111, 136; Robert, 118, 135; Samuel, 115; William, 28, 44.

Jones—Aquilla, 17; Christeen, 71; Elizabeth, 55; Hannah, 96; Jacob, 26; Jeremiah, 47; Joanna, 79; Joseph, 39; Rachel, 91; Rebecca, 47; Samuel, 71; Thomas, 78, 93; Zipporia, 31.

Jordan—Anthony A., 107; John, 84.

Justice—Emeline, 70; Hannah, 70; Jacob, 70, 137; John, 50, 70, 121; Mary Ann, 70; Rebecca, 125; Samuel, 100, 127; Wilson Lee, 70.

K

Kaats—William, 38.

Kandle—Adam, 31, 71, 88; Adam Jr., 130; Christeen, 71; Harriet, 38; Henry, 71; Jacob, 32; John, 22, 32, 33, 71; Joseph, 32, 33; Katharine, 32; Lydia, 71; Margaret, 33; Mary Ann, 33; Rebecca, 33; Samuel, 32; Sarah, 33, 71.

Katts—Henry, 25, 30, 65; Joseph, 20.

Kean—Samuel, 58.

Keasbey—A. D, 75, 96; Anne, 106; Anthony, 106; A. Q., 80; Caroline, 106; Charles, 106; Delzil, 102; Edward, 56, 62, 96, 106; Elizabeth, 106; Helen, 106; John, 106; Keziah, 102; Mathew, 56, 106; Prudence, 102

Keen—Elijah, 72; James, 27, 84; Levi, 109; Lorenzo Dow, 104; Mary, 14; Moses, 72; Rebecca, 14; William, 72.

Keever—James, 139.

Kelton—George, 112.

Keren—John, 109.
Kelty—Hannah, 5; Jonathan, 15.
Ketcham—Henry, 45; Ruth, 45.
Kidd—John, 27.
Kiger—Adam, 11; Barbara, 11; Beulah, 120; Daniel, 11; Henry, 11; John, 11; Margaret, 11; Nathan, 11, 104; Rebecca, 11.
Kille—Ann, 62.
Kinsey—James, 55; Rebecca, 15, 54, 55, 56.
Kirby—Asa, 12; Chalkley, 12; Deborah, 12; Ebenezer, 12, 115; Elizabeth, 36, 77; Elizabeth Ann, 152; Emily, 12; Hannah, 12, 36, 77, 122; Harriet, 107; Henry, 11; Hill Smith, 11; Jacob, 12; John, 118; Lucy, 11; Margaret, 17; Margaret, 17; Maria, 36; Martha, 122; Mary, 150; Nicholas, 11; Priscilla, 36, 77; Richard, 9; Robert, 12; Samuel, 11; Sarah, 14; William, 11, 82.
Kirk—Gabriel, 146; George, 13.
Kitchen—Christiana, 100; Sarah, 100.
Kline—Henry, 135; Mary, 69.
Knight—Mary Ann, 17
Knowles—Mahalah, 54.
Kogle—John, 153; Margaret, 153.
Krom—Achsa Ann, 146; John, 146.
Kummerle—Katrina, 147.

L

Lake—Mary, 31, 113; William, 25.
Lambert—Elizabeth, 97; Isaac 123; John H., 50, 56, 97, 101, 104, 108, 110, 114, 122, 123, 127, 141; Joseph, 122; William, 13.
Lambson—Caroline, 80; Clarissa, 80; John, 80; Merrick, 80; Michael, 80; Rebecca, 80; Sarah, 80; Thomas, 101; William, 80.
Langley—Garrett, 117; Hannah, 31; Isaac, 38, 109; John, 33; Mary, 117; Richard, 31; William, 109.
Lanning—Charles, 30; William, 119.
Laurence—John, 116; Rebecca, 69; Sarah, 135.
Lawrence—Alpheus, 67; Ann, 82, 136; Andrew, 40, 135; Edward, 127; Elizabeth, 127; Franklin, 40; Gideon, 40; Isaac, 48; Joseph, 127, 150; Kiturah, 48; Louisa, 40, 127; Mary Ann, 40; Mary Jane, 40; Nathan, 114; Prudence, 115; Rebecca, 40; Richard, 40; Samuel, 40; William, 34, 40, 112.

GENERAL INDEX

Lawrie—James, 40, 138, 140, 137.

Lawson—John, 34, 40.

Layton—Albert, 15, 42; Jonathan, 60; Lydia, 62; Stacy, 54.

Leap—Jacob, 72; John, 48; Sedgwick, 137.

Lecroy—Asher, 106.

Leeds—N., 105.

Lewallen—John, 139.

Lewis—Isaac, 10. 108.

Likins—Margaret, 44.

Linch—David, 14; Samuel, 16, 63.

Link—Benjamin, 133; Grace Ann, 133.

Lindsey—James, 42; John, 42; Mary, 42; Sarah, 28.

Lindzey—Hannah, 97; John, 97; Mary, 17; Sarah, 17.

Lippihcott—Alfred, 143; Amanda, 145; Amy, 100; Ann, 124; Anna, 69. 125; Anna Maria, 143; B., 118; Benjamin, 46, 53, 121, 127, 139; 141, 145; Caleb, 18; Caroline, 5; Christiana, 67, 80, 100, 143; Elizabeth, 53; Emily 5; English, 5; Esther, 143; Hannah, 118, 121, 124; 125; Isaac, 5, 79; Jacob, 152; John, 108, 143; Joseph, 54, 70, 123; Mary, 63, 133; Randolph, 121; Samuel, 54, 100; Sarah, 59; Thomas, 5, 80, 109; William, 145.

Little—Archibald, 62; Benjamin Franklin, 111; Ellen, 69, 82; Robert, 111; Sarah, 62, 69, 136.

Lloyd—Ann, 65; Benjamin, 8, 40, 120, 139; Furman, 8; James, 52; John, 8; Margaret, 47. 57, 128; Nathan, 65; Nathaniel, 65; Stacy, 10, 11, 36, 42, 47, 57, 99.

Lock—Abigail, 46; Alice, 41; Samuel, 41.

Locke—John, 138.

Locuson—Clayton, 63; George, 63; Joseph, 63; Nathaniel, 43; Rachel, 63.

Lodge—Maria, 147.

Lolley—Elizabeth, 144; Charles, 144.

Long—Mary, 91; Thomas, 91, 92.

Longacre—Andrew, 121; Anna Maria, 121; Sarah, 121; Joseph, 121; Martha, 121; Peter, 121; Samuel, 121; William, 121.

Loper—Ezekiel, 12; John, 109; Robert, 87; William, 119.

Lott—Ebenezer, 41.

Loudenslager—Charles, 114.

Louderback—John, 30, 65, 100, 115, 122, 133, 135, 137, 140, 144, 145; Susan, 44.

Lounsbury—Thomas, 125; Walker, 100,
Low—Clement, 141, 145; Ellen, 141, 145; Harriet, 83, 141, 145.
Ludiam—Jacob, 71, 101.
Lumley—Edmund, 68; John, 134, 142.
Lyman—Ann, 129; Captain, 129; Isabella, 129.
Lynn—David, 122; Janetta, 122; John, 122.

M

Macculloch—F. L., 19, 31, 42, 49, 52, 55, 68, 76, 79, 80, 93, 97, 102, 105, 108, 118, 119, 124, 130, 139, 147; Sarah, 145.
Madara—John, 79; Lorena, 142.
Madkiff—Daniel, 108; Elizabeth, 108.
Magill—James, 125.
Manes—Hannah, 102.
Mankin—Jacob, 69; Joseph, 102; Mary, 102.
Marshall—Jacob, 131; Mary, 131; Thomas, 131.
Mart—Henry, 66.
Martin—George, 86, 100, 112; Henry, 86, 112; Jacob, 86, 112; John, 86; Mary, 9, 112; Peter, 83, 86, 112; Ruth, 83; Samuel, 112.
Maskell—John, 7, 14, 41, 69, 76, 78, 97, 123, 152, 153; Thomas, 135, 144, 153.
Mason—Anna, 27; Charles, 27; John, 5, 17, 19, 20, 25, 27, 30, 32, 33, 36, 78; Lewis, 27; Mary, 27; William, 27.
Matlack—Richard, 75, 126.
Matson—Mary, 109.
Matthews—Elizabeth, 92; Mary, 124.
Mattson—Achsa Ann, 48; Amy, 143; Ann, 48; Elias, 48; Hannah, 48; Mary, 24; Sarah, 72.
May—George, 9; Jacob, 9; John, 9.
Mayhew—Ann, 107; Bathsheba, 7; Clarence, 64, 72; David, 111; Elam, 117; Edward, 23; Eleazar, 19; Elizabeth, 23; Isaiah 64; Isaac, 22; Jacob, 19; James, 64, 101; John, 64; Lydia, 46; Margaret, 107; Maria, 111; Mark, 64, 107, 111; Mary, 111; William, 8, 100.
McAleer—Mary, 148.
McAltioner—Abigail, 91; John, 91; Joseph, 124.
McBride, Ann, 113; John, 113; Mary, 113.
McCabe—Patrick, 148.
McCain—Keziah, 66.

GENERAL INDEX

M'Calla—Auley, 45; Elizabeth, 45; Joseph, 45; Margaret, 45; Robert, 45; William, 45.

McCall—James, 102.

McCalla—Aulay, 114.

M'Callister—Deborah, 108; Harriet, 108; James, 108; Jane, 108; Mary Isabella, 108; Thomas, 108; William, 108.

McCallister—Aaron, 33; Benjamin, 33; Charles, 50; Janeway, 50; Moses, 33; Rachel, 33.

McChalliff—John, 91.

McClintock—Charles Henry, 75.

M'Collister—Isaac, 108.

McCollister—Benjamin, 87; Charles, 104; Deborah, 10; Elizabeth, 121; James, 121; Thomas, 10, 33.

McConner—Clement, 10; Mary, 10; Matthias Kiger, 10; Rachel, 10; William, 10.

McCune—John, 23, 78, 112; Ruth, 94.

McDaniel—William, 72.

McDermott—William, 125.

McDonnol—Catharine, 46; Edward, 46; John, 46, 83; Samuel, 46; Thomas Harrison, 46.

McDougall—Anna, 141; James, 141; John, 142; Mary Emma, 141.

McFarson—Sarah, 45.

McIlvain—Keziah, 112.

McIntire—John, 128.

McKasson—Joseph, 117.

McNichols—William, 68.

Mead—Robert 35.

Macum—Ann, 102; Ellen, 62, 65, 82, 136; Ellener, 23; James, 32, 82; Jane, 111; John, 136; Mary, 86; William, 82.

Mench—Elizabeth, 86; Henry, 86; Mark, 86.

Merseilles—H. R., 153.

Mickle—Harriet, 137; Henry, 137; Joshua, 139; Samuel, 138.

Micksner—Susannah, 18.

Miles—Adaline, 105.

Miller—Abraham, 140; Ann, 49; Catharine, 49; Daniel, 116; Elizabeth, 9, 71, 75; Esther, 46, 66, 80; George, 28; Hannah, 80; Hettie, 41, 123; John, 28, 86, 152; Joseph, 71; Josiah, 28, 123; Kesiah, 89; Levi, 49; Lewis, 28; Lot, 108; Lydia, 9; Mark, 138, 140; Martha,

45; Mary 28, 49, 138, 145; Richard, 123; Samuel, 75, 123, 124, 140, 152; Sarah, 30, 31; S. L. J., 41; Susan, 28; Warner, 138, 140; William, 9, 21, 75; Wyatt, 123, 124.

Mills—Adaline, 45; Andrew, 39; David, 39; John, 91, 130; Joseph, 39, 140; Mary, 39; Michael, 101; Rebecca, 39; Richard, 39; Sarah, 39.

Minters—Abigail, 89; Andrew, 89; Barzillai, 89.

Mitchell—B. G., 8; George, 46.

Mitten—Sarah, 120.

Moncreef—Catharine, 88; Edward, 88; Henry, 88; Hugh, 88; Margaret, 88; Robert 88

Moon—Henry, 133; Martha, 133.

Moore—Charlotty, 105; Daniel, 109; David, 47; Dickason, 109; Enoch, 55, 62; Esther, 98; Hannah, 29; Isaac, 105; John, 79, 109; Joseph, 30; Mary, 30, 52, 55, 62; Mary Ann, 30; Mary Jane, 54; Mathias, 32; Rachel, 30; Samuel, 29, 30, 53, 131; Thomas, 53.

Morgan—Alice, 41; Ann, 7; Charlotte, 135; Isaac, 135; Joseph, 7; Kimsey, 75; Samuel, 7.

Morris—Charles, 49; Elizabeth, 79; Mary, 79; William, 8, 60, 79.

Morrison—George, 131, 145, 148; Matthew, 107, 129; William, 21, 52, 73, 85, 101, 119.

Mowers—Adam, 117; Catharine, 10; Daniel, 117; Elizabeth, 11; Epharim, 117; John, 10, 101, 117; Joseph, 10: Martha, 56, 117; Rebecca, 101.

Mugway—Owen, 20, 21; Ruth, 20.

Mulford—Abigail, 23; Ann, 28; Charles, 86, 87, 105, 114; Elizabeth, 23; Ephraim, 26; Jacob, 103, 148; John Edward, 51; John, 114; Joseph, 46; Luetta, 130; Margaret, 6; Margaret Millicent, 51; Mary, 23; Mary Ann, 51; Mary Louisa, 153; Millicent, 51; Rachel, 26; Rebecca, 28; Richard, 23, 130; Rody, 51; Samuel, 68; Sarah, 26; William, 25, 40, 47, 61.

Mullica—Maria, 93; Thomrs, 72.

Munion—John, 128; Maria, 137; Samuel, 137; Thomas, 65, 137; William Henry, 137; Tnomas, 60.

Murphey—John, 83, 94; Phebe, 94; Rachel, 94; Sarah, 24.

Murrey—John, 66: Sarah, 12.

Myles—Thomas, 104.

N

Nail—Elizabeth, 20; Horatio, 20.

Naylor—Joseph, 14.

Nealey—David, 76; James, 76; Sarah, 76; William, 76.

Nelson—Abraham, 27; Ann, 128; Anthony, 17; Catharine, 119; Eliza, 119; Elizabeth, 35; Jane, 27; John, 35, 119; Joseph, 18, 35, 61, 91, 105, 116, 119, 151; Mary, 35; Ruth Ann, 91; William, 53, 103, 111, 119, 128.

Nesmith—Solomon, 23.

Newbern—Elizabeth Ann, 101.

Newbold—Cablebine, 126; William, 126.

Newcomb—Hannah Ann 137; John, 89; Josiah, 61; Keziah, 89; Reuben, 89; Sarah, 89; William, 89.

Newell—Artemesia, 98; Charles, 98; James, 45, 87, 141.

Newkirk—Absalom, 31; Anorew, 149; Ann, 97; Charlotte, 149; Clement, 96, 107; Cornelius, 107, 116; Edmond, 91; Elmer, 136; Elizabeth, 96; Enoch, 91, 149; Isaac, 107; Jacob, 12, 83; Joast, 83 107; Joseph, 107; Lorenzo, 96; Mariah, 97; Mary, 116; Rebecca, 91; Ruth Ann, 96; Susannah, 107; William, 83, 91, 96, 107.

Nicel—David, 59.

Nichols—Abigail Ann, 105; Benjamin, 33, 50; Dan, 91; David, 94; Joseph, 33; Rachel, 131; Sarah, 108; William, 94.

Nicholson—Caspar, 71; Charles, 47; Daniel, 43; Edwin, 144; Elizabeth, 5, 38, 55, 71; Hannah, 55; Horner, 132; I. T., 83; James, 71; John, 55; Joseph, 55; Joseph, 94; Josiah, 55; Joshua, 67; Mary, 55; Rachel, 43, 51, 62, 67; Samuel, 43, 55, 62; Sarah Ann, 38, 67; Washington, 47; William, 43, 67, 141.

Nixon—Margaret, 147; Oakford, 147.

Noble—John, 132.

Noblet—Joseph, 11; Rebecca, 11.

North—Benjamin, 54.

Null—Ann, 151; George, 151; Michael, 10, 55; William, 151.

O

O'Brien—William, 148.

Offiey—Michael, 53.

Ogden—Deborah, 130; Hannah, 73; Henry; 130; James, 130;

Jane, 117; John, 130; Miranda, 38; Nathaniel, 73, 117; Oliver, 130; Richard, 130.

Ogee—Jonathan, 48.

Oliphant—M., 121.

Olmstead—Nicholas, 22; Sarah, 22.

Otis—William, 129, 141.

Ough—Mary, 133; William, 113, 133.

Owens—Elizabeth, 29, 75; Griffith, 110.

Ovenbaker — Lydia, 38; Matthias Pitman, 38; Michael, 38; Sophia, 38.

P

Palmer—David, 138; John, 68; Mary, 138; Sarah, 68, 138; William, 138.

Pancoast—Ann, 13, 29; Ann, 92; Ann Elizabeth, 92; Catharine, 25; Charles; 13, 92; David, 29, 92, 143, 147; Dorcas, 13; Edward, 25; Eliakim, 13; Elizabeth, 13; James, 13; John, 154; Joseph, 13, 29, 92, 132; Josiah, 13; Martha, 92; Mary, 92; Samuel, 13; Sarah, 154; Susan, 37, 38; William 13, 138, 140; William Henry, 92.

Parker—Mary, 42.

Parrett—William, 78, 135.

Parvin—Daniel, 19; Elizabeth, 19; Garret, 106; Mary, 22; Samuel, 32; William, 139.

Patrick—Anna, 21; Charles, 118; Elizabeth, 14; Ephraim C., 60; George, 117; Hannah, 14; Jesse, 14; John, 60, 84, 118; Mary Ann, 14; Morris, 146; Rachel, 84; Samuel, 111; William, 14.

Patterson—Amelia, 126; Benjamin, 60, 122; Catharine, 122; Elizabeth, 10; Ella Virginia, 122; Esther, 80; James, 46, 111, 152; Martin, 27, 145; Mary, 50; Rebecca, 50, 122; Robert, 107; Theophilus, 135, 142; William, 50, 93, 126, 137.

Paul—Ann Elizabeth, 138; Ann Engiish, 140.

Paullin—Hannah, 144; Joseph, 144; Mary, 38; Parvin, 50.

Paulling—Matilda, 75.

Paulson—Joseph, 115.

Peacock—Mary Jane, 122.

Pearson—Benjamin, 26.

Peaslee—Sarah, 43.

Pedrick—Anna, 122; Chalkley, 15; Charles, 52; Ebenezer, 58;

GENERAL INDEX 191

Edith, 58; Elizabeth, 137; Francis, 137; Hannah, 93, 115; Jacob, 63, 65, 77, 137; John, 93; Joseph, 93; Joseph Henry, 137; **Margaret,** 122; Martha, 15; Mary Elizabeth, 122; Miles, 15; Rachel, 131; R. C., 52; Robert, 86; Shadrick, 128; Thomas, 17; William, 26, 40, 70, 77, 129.

Penton—Abner, 72; Eliza, 21, 72; Elizabeth Ann, 101, 115; Jane, 101; Rachel, 21; Sarah, 116.

Perdue—John, 46.

Perry—Caroline, 20; David, 133; Elizabeth, 69; Rebecca, 133; Susan, 69.

Peterson—Achsah, 55; Amos, 7, 30, 41; Anna, 75; Benjamin, 21, 24, 63; Charles, 143; David, 59, 99; Deannis, 99; Elizabeth, 58; George, 9; Gerrard, 58; James, 44; John, 40, 115; Jonathan, 143; Joseph 7, 143; Margaret, 115; Samuel, 75; Sarah Ann, 90; Stacy, 7; Susannah, 41; Thomas, 58; William, 13, 43; Zaruh Maris, 56.

Petit—David, 59, 93, 135, 139; Elizabeth, 135; James, 59, 139; Jonathan, 59; Joseph, 59, 139; Martha, 97; Ruth, 59; Samuel, 59; Sarah, 59; Woodnutt, 59.

Phillips—Elias, 68.

Pidgeon—Ann, 91; Nicholas, 91.

Pierpoint—William, 72.

Pierson—Lydia, 92; Sarah, 66.

Pilgrim—Cutisoaf, 137; Henry, 137; **Mary,** 137; **Rebecca,** 137.

Pimm—Jonathan, 53; Samuel, 103.

Pine—Benjamin, 94, 123; Martha, 40; Samuel, 40.

Pippin—Margaret, 125.

Pirnell—Gemima, 26.

Platt—Anna Maria, 146; Lydia, 14.

Plumley—Ruth, 68.

Plummer—Amy, 72; Ann Eliza, 148; Charles, 72, 103; Edward, 72; Elizabeth, 148; Emley, 72; Henry, 148; Janetta, 72; **John,** 72, 148; Rachel, 71; Samuel, 42; Sarah, 72; William, 72.

Polson—Ann, 5.

Potter—Michael, 31.

Powell—Anna, 94; Daniel, 94; Elias, 57; Elizabeth, 57; Elkanah, 21; Henry, 101; Jeremiah, 21, 22, 51, 57; John, 5, 13, 38, 51, 52, 57, 82, 94; Joseph, 57; Lydia, 125; Samuel, 51, 57; Sarah, 51; **William,** 51, 52, 72, 74, 111, 151.

Powers—John, 74; Michael, 54, 142; **Rebecca,** 27, 52; **Samuel, 69.**

Prescott—Edward, 54, 62; William, 126.
Press—William, 91.
Preston—John, 109.
Price—Eli, 17; Rebecca, 23; Thomas, 23.
Prickitt—Garrett, 96; Hannah, 96; Job, 96, 97; Lydia, 100; Thomas, 97.
Prime—John, 117; Sarah, 117.
Prior—Rosanna, 145; Samuel, 42.

Q

Quicksall, John, 67; Sarah, 67.

R

Rackliff—W. F., 134.
Raft—Elizabeth Cray, 102.
Rain—Margaret, 18, 42; Samuel, 42, 140.
Rammel—Henry, 81.
Ramsey—John, 126, 132.
Ray—Johnson, 59; Zacheus, 10, 11, 14, 66.
Read—Josiah, 32; Stephen, 57.
Reason—Alice, 124; Lavinia, 124; Maria, 124; Moses, 124; Richard, 124.
Redman—Rachel, 28.
Redrow—Harriet, 131.
Reed—Catharine, 47; Enoch, 19, 36; James, 82, 99, 142; William 90, 146.
Reeve—Anthony, 11; Augustus, 117; Clarissa, 66; Elizabeth, 108 Elmer, 117; Elwood, 11; Isaac, 11; Mary, 81; Milicent, 64; Priscilla, 9; Samuel, 28, 29; Sophia, 11; Thomas, 11.
Reeves—Abraham, 11; Andrew Smith 153; Anna, 112; Anthony, 65; Biddle, 60; Caleb, 104; Charles, 58, 104, 105, 122; David, 66; Ebenezer, 107; Elizabeth, 46, 73; Enos, 58, 112; Hannah, 104, 112; Isaac, 104; Jacob, 58, 122, 127; James, 58, 112; Jefferson, 104, 112; Jeremiah, 73; Joshua, 11, 15, 103; Josiah, 58, 73, 122, 127, 134; Keziah, 109; Margaret, 58; Mary, 153; Micajah, 11; Samuel, 72, 104, 105; Sarah, 60; Sarah, 104, 112; Scull, 11; Stephen, 14, 58, 99, 122, 127; Thomas, 22, 153; Wilhelmina, 127; William, 58, 104, 109,

112; William Henry, 104.

Remster—Benjamin, 108; Mary, 108; Eliza, 10; Sarah, 108.

Remington—Sarah, 71.

Restine—Frederick, 102; Josephine, 102.

Reve—William, 43.

Reynolds—Hannah, 49, 55; Thompson, 55.

Rich—Joseph, 65.

Richman—Achsa, 146; Achsah Ann, 105; Alfred, 146; Alynda, 146; Amanda, 101; Andrew Jackson, 30, 31; Ann, 43; Anna, 29; Bathsheba, 31; Emily Jane, 152; Emma, 146; Francis, 146; George, 143: Harmon, 61, 146; Henry, 15, 86, 104; Isaac, 30, 31; James, 7, 29; John, 30, 146, 152; Jonathan, 9; Joseph, 7; Josiah, 118; Margaret, 152; Maria, 8; Martha, 15; Matthias, 31, 48; McKendric, 38; Moses, 43; Moses, Jr., 41, 46, 53, 83, 107, 110, 143, 147, 153; Nehemiah, 22; Phebe, 53; Sarah, 43; Sarah Ann, 152; Sarah Elizabeth, 152; William, 61, 143, 146, 149

Richmond—Elizabeth, 90; Hannah, 101; Samuel, 90.

Ridgway—Ann, 41; Daniel, 130; Isaac, 52, 134, 135; John, 48, 130; Joseph, 130, 135; Levi, 135; Samuel, 130; Tracy; 52.

Riley—Anna. 103; Catharine, 18; Jonathan, 16; Joseph, 56, 115, 149, 152; Pheby, 153; Thomas, 106.

Risley—J. F,, 14; Joseph, 14, 22, 33, 43, 61, 68, 88, 90, 115, 118, 146; John, 107; Oliver, 96.

Risner—Elizabeth, 70; Thomas, 70, 128.

Robbins—Alfred, 35; Caroline, 134; Catharine, 134; Edward, 134; Furman, 79; George, 8, 35, 148; Harriet, 63; Nancy, 34, 35; Nathan, 48; Nathaniel, 48; Obadiah, 8, 35; Sarah, 9; Sarah Ann, 35; Thomas, 34, 35.

Roberts—Ann, 59; Anna, 139; Charles, 49, 95; Charlotte, 145; Elihu, 139; Rebecca, 23, 82; William, 109, 126, 137, 145.

Robertson—George, 110; William, 132.

Robinson—Angelina, 53; Ann, 5, 15, 123; Benjamin, 35, 123; Caroline, 53; Charles, 123, 127, 133, 142; Elizabeth, 53, 133; Emaline, 53; George, 127; Hannah, 98; Henry, 123; James, 81, 98, 123. 125; John, 45, 91, 92, 117; 123, 127, 152; Joseph, 15, 34, 53, 96, 109, 130; Mary, 107; Mary Emma, 98; Noah, 123; Rebecca Ann, 123; Reuben, 33, 147; Robert, 10, 115, 147, 150; Sallie Ann, 96; Sarah, 123; Serena, 91; William, 44, 53, 123.

Rocap—Hannah, 151.

Rodan—Harriet, 74.
Rogers—James, 48; Lydia, 60, 125.
Roork—John, 123.
Rose—John, 93; Prudence, 72.
Rowan—Thomas, 47.
Royal—Hannah, 45; Mark, 45; Peter, 45; Sarah, 45; Susannah, 45; William, 21, 27.
Rudolph—Mary, 57.
Rumsey—Charles, 49; George, 69, 82, 106, 124; Henry, 82, 136; Margaret, 69, 111, 136.
Rusling—T. V. F., 90; Thomas V. F., 77.
Russell—Jeremiah, 21.

S

Sack—John, 30, 36.
Sanderlin—Joseph, 113.
Sanford—William, 46.
Salesbury—Samuel, 77.
Sap—Joseph, 39.
Sarish—Stephen, 143.
Saske—Henry, 127.
Sayre—Ann, 91; Clarissa, 91; Hannah, 6; James, 91; Reuben, 91; Sarah, 91; William, 91.
Scattergood—Jonathan, 142.
Scudder—William, 85.
Scull—Abigail, 24; Ann, 24; Deborah, 60; Gideon, 24; Judith, 24; Mark, 24; Sarah, 24;
Seagrave—Artis, 24; Charles, 24; Clement, 87; George, 87; Israel, 44; John, 87; Joseph, 87; Mary, 37, 87; Robert, 87; Samuel, 24; Sarah, 24; 87; William, 24, 37, 40, 87.
Seasor—James, 125.
Seeds—Alexander, 109; Ann, 109; Benjamin, 109; Catharine, 109; Fithian, 109; Jeremiah, 109; John, 109; Mark, 109.
Seeley—Elias, 45.
Seers—Martha, 44; Samuel, 44; Sarah, 44; William, 44.
Sembes—Absalom, 78.
Shallcross—Morris, 26.
Sharp—John, 25; Joseph, 7; J. T., 97.

GENERAL INDEX 195

Shaw—Ruth, 19.

Sheets—David, 115; Isaac, 127.

Shelton—William, 16.

Shepherd—Enoch, 97.

Sheppard—Albert, 147; Ann, 129, 130; Benjamin, 46; Charles, 17, 141; Clarkson, 80; Ebenezer, 122; Edmund, 142; Elizabeth, 41; Emeline, 147; Gilbert, 147; Henry, 147; I. N. C., 17; Isaac. 18, 147, 111; John, 41, 147; Joseph, 18. 64, 142, 147; Leander, 147; Margaret, 136; Margaretta, 111; Mary, 9, 41; Moses, 39; Noah, 146; Phebe 41; Providence, 105, 114, 122, 146; Rachel, 16, 23, 39, 88. 89, 146; Richard, 42, 71; Robert, 42, 141; Samuel, 75; Sarah, 124; Sylvanus, 129; Theodore, 147; Thomas, 124; William, 17, 141.

Sherron—Albert, 102; Catharine, 102; Charles, 102, George, 102; Gervas, 102; Samuel, 102; Sarah, 102; William, 23, 42, 102.

Shields—Andrew, 21.

Shimp—Ann, 54; Archibald, 108; B. R., 58; Christiana, 129; Daniel, 108; David, 108, 112; Edmund, 54; Eliza, 30; George, 108; Jacob 171; John, 108. 129, 131; Lydia, 54; Margaret, 10, 108; Peter, 10; Philip, 69; Richard, 69; Samuel, 58, 120; Simon, 103; William, 34, 54.

Shinn—William, 7, 66;

Shockley—Edward James, 148; Margaret, 148; Robert Henry, 148.

Shoemaker—Elizabeth, 16, 22; Hiram, 127; John, 65, 104; Mary Ann, 104; Sarah, 127.

Shough—Daniel, 44; David, 128, 129; Jacob, 128; William, 129.

Shourds—Benjamin. 51; Clara, 110; Martha, 51, Mary, 51, 109, 110; Rachel, 51, 109, 110; Sarah, 38; Thomas. 74, 111; William, 51.

Shull—Thomas, 17.

Shultz—Eliza, 20; John Christian, 20.

Shute—Ann Elizabeth, 90; Atley, 104; Isaac, 126; Lydia, 64; Mary, 142; Rebecca Ann, 64; Samuel. 104; Sarah, 64; Seeley, 90; Thomas, 64.

Sickler—Francis, 81; Mary, 130; William, 112.

Siger—Lewis, 138; Peter, 138.

Simkins—Abraham, 18; Caroline, 18; Casper, 76; Eliznbeth, 76; Ellis, 18, 42; Hannah, 18; James, 85; Joel, 83; John, 99; Mary, 86; Rebecca, 86; Reuben, 18; Richard, 19; William, 18, 84, 86.

Simms—Gervas, 36, 60; Mason, 105.

Simpkins—Alfred, 56, 63; Joseph, 56; Mary, 123; Samuel, 56; William, 96.

Simpson—John, 13.

Sims—Ann. 84; Hannah Ann, 84; Hedge, 84; John, 84; Mason, 84; Mary, 84; Smith, 84.

Singley—Ann, 107; Edward, 105.

Sinnickson—Andrew, 93, 95, 109, 126, 153; Ann, 81; Clarissa, 125; Clement, 37; John, 37, 62, 78, 81, 96, 136; John Howard, 36; Maria, 125; Mary, 135, 136; Ruth, 125; Sarah, 62; Thomas, 6, 19, 23, 25, 56, 62, 69, 77, 78, 82, 95, 109, 126, 136; William 56.

Sithen—George, 94; Hosea, 18; Mary, 83; Mary Ann, 83.

Sithens—Benjamin, 43; Enos, 19; Lucy, 83, 116; Mary, 19; Mary Ann, 116; Sarah, 83, 116; Sedgwick, 83, 116.

Sivil—Nathan, 65.

Slape—Charles, 87; William, 24.

Smart—Ann, 25; Deborah, 25, 93; Hannah, 25; Isaac, 24, 25, 32; John, 93; Mary, 24, 25; Rebecca, 24, 25; Ruth, 25; Tamson, 72;

Smashey—James, 52.

Smith—Abigail, 75; Abner, 30, 130; Andrew, 85; Ann, 55, 71; Attila, 33; Azariah, 25; Benjamin, 111, 121; Chamblis, 37; Charles, 74; Clarissa, 30; Daniel, 47, 71; Daniel Ashton, 78; David, 75, 122, 127; Ebenezer, 65; Edward, 144; Eleazar, 25; Elikim, 78, 87; Elizabeth, 41, 52, 130; Emily, 71; Hannah, 78, 118; Henrietta, 111; Hugh, 25; Isaac, 43, 148; Israel, 38, 42, 111; James, 33, 44, 46, 144; Job, 87; John, 25, 34, 75; Jonathan, 26, 118, 120, 121, 146; Joshua, 44, 68; Josiah, 151; L. P., 111; Lucy, 11; Margaret, 12, 130; Maria, 126; Martha, 75, 86; Mary, 62, 82, 122, 127, 144; Mary Ann, 83; Mary Jane, 58; Oliver, 14, 30, 36, 84, 125, 130; Phineas, 14, 130; Priscilla, 44; Rachel, 25; Rebecca, 132; Samuel, 124, 132; Samuel Asa, 75; Sarah, 33, 144, 153; Stephen, 84, 94; Thomas, 56, 75, 85, 94, 97, 116, Thomas, 31, 56, 85, 94, 97, 116, 125, 126; William, 14, 33, 43, 75.

Snell—Phebe, 132.

Snitcher—Eliza, 27; George, 27; H. W., 8; Isaac, 22.

Somers—Albertus, 40, 91, 92; Chalkley, 63; Deborah, 109; Edith, 65 Hannah Ann, 99; Jacob, 25; Japhet, 61; John, 81; Joshua, 91; Mary, 53, 81; Richard, 9, 12, 15, 36, 77, 91, 120, 129, 134, 145; William, 63, 65.

Souders—George, 18.

Spackman—George, 66.

Sparks—Charlotte, 64; David, 144; Edward, 58; Jane Anna, 144,

GENERAL INDEX 197

145; Margaret, 144; Ebenezer, 58; Eliza, 135; Gerard, 75, 140; Hannah, 130; John, 64, 127; Mayhew, 130, 148; Phebe, 64; Richard, 22, 110, 125; Robert, 57, 58; Samuel, 58, 145; Sarah, 143.

Springer—Alfred, 144; Anna, 121, 147; Christiana, 48, 121; Cornelia, 121, 147; Hudson, 12, 25, 65, 70, 77, 93, 110, 120, 129; James, 30, 48, 99; John, 15, 121, 127, 128, 129, 144, 147; Lavina, 25; Lydia, 121; Maria, 121, 147; Mary Jane, 121, 147; Richard, 48; Wilber, 121, 147.

Sprogell—Caroline, 133; Mary, 125.

Stackhouse—Archer, 90; Charlotte, 140.

Stalcup—John, 79.

Stanger—Elizabeth, 81; Harriet, 50; Margaret, 14; Mary Ann, 50; Peter, 14.

Stanton—David, 44; Jacob, 44, 50; James, 24; Josiah, 44; Leonard, 30; Mary, 129, 153; Mary Ann, 44;.

Stearley—Jacob, 93.

Steelman—Abigail, 41; Isaac, 41; John, 41; Jonathan, 41; Mark, 41; Sarah, 40.

Stelle—Maria, 147,

Sterling—Edith, 68; Thomas, 68:

Steward—Maria, 78; Stacy, 78.

Stewart—Ann, 12; Deborah, 24; Elizabeth, 49, 151; John, 12; 111, 151; Joseph, 151; Mark, 21; Mary, 151; Sarah, 18, 53, 120; Samuel, 24, 151; Thomas, 53; William, 151.

Stevenson—Elizabeth, 100.

Stiles—Jacob, 121; James.

Stilley—William, 133.

Stokes—Benjamin Franklin, 98; Luella, 98.

Stokely—Frederick, 74.

Stokes—Mary, 98.

Stoughten—E. B , 19; O. B., 108; Margaret, 126; Mary, 125, 126.

Stout—Beulah, 63; Joseph, 50, 63.

Stow—T. B., 69; Thomas, 82.

Strang—Harrison, 72.

Stratton—Anna, 61; Eleazar, 144; Isaiah, 61; John, 144; Rachel, 144; Sarah, 144; William, 5, 68.

Straughn—Mary, 137.

Stretch—Anna Maria, 132; Beulah, 12, 132; Daniel, 63; David, 82; Deborah; 79; Elizabeth, 26, 79, 132, 133; George, 111; Hannah, 132;

James, 132; Joanna 79; Job, 12; John, 120, 132; Joseph 97, 132; Joshua, 12, 110; Margaret, 132; Mary, 12, 26, 111; Mary Jane, 132; Nathaniel, 54; Richard, 56; Robert, 133; Samuel, 132; Sarah, 12, 132; Tamson, 79; Thomas, 132, 133; William, 12, 120, 128.

Strickland—Rachel, 62; Rebecca, 55; William, 55, 62.

String—Elizabeth, 33; Jane, 10; Mary Elizabeth, 10; Peter, 10, 53, 103; Rachel, 100; Sarah, 103.

Strimple—William, 9, 44.

Stull—Jeremiah, 30; John, 98; Juliana, 98.

Stutly—John, 32.

Sullivan—Job, 140.

Summerill—Ann, 120; Christiana, 119; Garrett 100, 120; Hannah, 85; Hannah Ann, 59; John, 23, 56, 85, 119; Joseph, 52, 56, 120; Mary, 20; Naomi, 120; Rebecca, 120; William, 59, 85, 99, 100, 120, 140.

Surran—Andrew, 91.

Suttenger—Sarah Ann, 121.

Sweaton—Benjamin, 73.

Sweetman—Martha, 113.

Swing—Abraham, 13; Charles, 8, 60, 148; Elizabeth, 128, 138; Hannah, 148; John, 25, 105; Leonard, 13; Margaretta, 148; Martha, Nathaniel, 86, 114; Samuel, 13.

T

Tatum—Joseph, 45, 80; Josiah 7; William, 45.

Taylor—Catharine, 45; Daniel, 44, 63; Jonathan, 45; Margaret, 46; William, 45, 89.

Teel—Isabella, 20, 82,

Test—Hannah, 97, 103; John, 97; Joseph, 72, 103, 120, 151; Thomas, 97.

Thackara—Frances, 56; George, 56; Hannah, 56; James, 56; William, 56, 62.

Tharp—Job, 7.

Thomas—Elizor, 35; James, 153; John, 113, 133; Lydia, 98; Moses, 113, 116.

Thompson—Andrew, 135; Ann, 135; Ann Elizabeth, 94; Anna Maria, 66, 153; Caroline, 103; Charles, 12; Clement, 37; Daniel, 99, 135; Edith, 135; Elizabeth, 22, 51, 74, 94, 96, 99, 108; Esther, 108;

GENERAL INDEX 199

Hannah Ann, 21; Hedge, 129, 153; Isaac, 37; Isabella, 98, 153; James, 99, 135; John, 82, 99, 135; Joseph, 6, 22, 39, 41, 55, 66, 77, 98, 123, 129, 153; Joshua; 5, 47, 94, 103, 133; Josiah, 42, 82, 88, 94, 103, 110; Lewis, 94; Mary, 6, 55, 135, 153; Mary Ann, 146; Rebecca, 6, 55, 153; Richard, 6, 18, 66, 129; R. P., 66, 98, 111, 146, 153; Samuel, 37, 73; 135; Sarah Ann, 37; Sarah Hall, 135; Sarah Jane, 135; Susan, 129; Thomas, 6, 94, 153; William, 5, 37, 38, 53, 60, 81, 94.

Tice—Hannah, 30.

Tidmarsh—Anna Margaret, 57; Joseph, 58.

Till—Rebecca, 133.

Tindall—Rachel, 47; Thompson, 33.

Tinker—Dudley, 61; Silas, 17.

Titus—Thomas, 133.

Tomlin—Baker, 145; Clement, 145; Henrietta, 145; Hiram, 145; Jacob, 142; Joseph, 142; Kitturah, 25; Robert, 145.

Tomlinson—Sarah, 99.

Torton—Sarah, 118.

Townsend—Adam, 88; Charles, 88; Ellen, 88; Hannah, 81; Jonathan, 88.

Tracy—Daniel, 81; Jeremiah, 88; Sarah, 62.

Treadway—Aaron, 75, 141; Samuel, 75; Sarah, 75.

Treen—John, 132.

Trenchard—Curtis, 56; George, 62; James, 55, 100, 119, 151; John, 113.

Trullenger—David, 123; Elizabeth, 123.

Truss—James, 22; Josiah, 22; Mary, 22; Samuel, 22.

Tuft—Annie, 52; Eliza, 37; John, 52, 68; Josiah, 74; Mary, 117; Sarah, 37, 130; Thomas, 92; Thompson, 37, 112; William, 37.

Turner—David, 107; Ephraim, 16, 74; John, 44; Joseph, 14; Richard, 118.

Tusse—Sarah, 149.

Tussey—David, 115; John, 115; Joseph, 99; Samuel, 99, 115; Sarah, 115; William, 115.

Tyler—Beulah, 154; James, 18, 120; Job, 21, 94, 110; John, 128, 154; Rachel, 120; Ruth, 18.

U

Underwood—Elizabeth, 77; Emily, 77; Mary Ann, 77; Nathan,

77; Sarah, 77.

Urban, Eunice, 131; John, 131.

Urion—Jacob, 146; Joseph, 131; Samuel, 142; Sarah, 97.

V

Valentine—Aaron, 23; Ann, 138; Anna, 23; Asa, 23, 138; John, 23, 138; Lewis, 23; Samuel, 23; Silas, 23, 138.

Vallance—Ann. 56.

Vanlewdener—Ann, 45.

Vanlier—George, 32, 132; Hannah, 132; Samuel, 50.

VanMeter—Abraham, 15, 35; Ann, 7; Anna, 61; Benjamin, 61; Caroline, 137, 149, 154; David, 15, 18, 35; Edward, 102, 103, 113, 119, 122, 134, 135, 137, 141, 149, 154; Emma, 34; Enoch, 18, 94; Harriet, 34; Hiram, 18; Isaac, 15, 18, 35; Jacob, 18; James, 8, 18, 56, 61, 142; John, 142; Joseph, 15, 35, 142; Lewis, 18; Mason, 34, 90, 136; Mary, 43; Nancy, 43; Phebe, 18, 35; Rachel, 15; Robert, 8, Ruth, 18; Sarah, 34, 142; Sarah Ann, 142; Susannah, 18; William, 22.

Vaneman—Abigail, 74; Amanda, 74; Mary, 74; Richard, 74.

Vanneman—Caroline, 120; Daniel, 34, 36, 59, 66, 74, 105; Hannah, 44, 85, 105, 106, 120; John, 85; Mary, 33; Sarah, 12; Sarah Jane, 85; William, 20, 68, 100, 104, 120, 124, 137; W. S., 79.

Teal—Enos, 130.

W

Waddington—Aaron, 11; Aaran Bradway, 48; Ada, 149; Anna, 76; Edward, 12, 22, 24, 39, 48, 57; Eliza, 103, 119; Frances, 103, 119; Franklin, 149; Hannah, 119; Jane, 48; Jesse, 62; Joseph, 60, 148; Joshua, 48; Lydia, 48, 60; Martha, 85; Mary Ann, 76; Rachel, 85; Rebecca, 60; Richard, 24, 39, 60; Robert, 48; Sarah, 85; William, 63, 85, 103, 119.

Waithman—Rachel, 153.

Walker—Anna, 90; Charles, 90; Charles Pitman, 20; David, 90, Edward, 20; Emma Jane, 90; James, 21; Joseph, 20; Margaret, 20; Maria, 129; Mary, 20; Michael, 20; Rebecca, 21; Sarah, 90; Thomas, 90; William, 8, 90, 91.

Wallace—Allen, 102; Christiana, 120; Clarissa, 120; Henry, 24; James, 120; Wesley, 120,

GENERAL INDEX 201

Wallen—Samuel, 83, 128.
Walmsley—Ann, 146.
Walters—Ephraim, 118.
Wam3ley—George, 149.
Ward—Ann, 43; George, 32, 37, 43, 51, 55, 60, 62, 67, 71, 72, 73, 76, 80, 83, 88, 98, 101, 107, 116, 126, 129, 134, 143, 145.
Wardsworth—James, 147; Jacob, 147.
Ware—Ann, 6, 125; Anna Jane, 109; Benjamin, 66, 74, 101; Beulah, 49, 51; Caroline, 144; Charles, 144; Clement, 71; Dan, 88; Edith Ann, 135; Elijah, 49, 69, 71, 107, 139, 152; H. B., 106, 153; James, 106; Jane, 139; Job, 38, 139; Mary, 37 38; Maskell, 139, 147; Rachel, 101; Rebecca, 55, 72, 106; Richard, 125; Samuel, 19; Smith, 66, 74.
Warner—Elizabeth, 34, 35; Hannah, 107; Nathaniel, 34, 35.
Warrington—John, 126.
Waters—Clement, 65; Elisha, 17, 45; Ephraim, 92; Hannah, 65; Job, 65; John, 65; Moses, 65; Rachel, 17, 127.
Watson—Ephraim, 5; Matilda, 45; Thomas, 16; Tyler, 16.
Wattson—Charles, 22; Charlotte, 22; George, 22; Isaac, 22; Louisa, 22; Mary, 22; Rebecca, 22.
Wayman—Abigail, 24.
Welch—Anderson, 97.
Weatherby—David, 77; Jeffery, 35; J. C., 146; Mary, 41.
Webb—Samuel, 24.
Webber—Henry, 41.
Webster—Clark, 18; Elizabeth, 18.
Weiss—Catharine, 133.
Welch—Elidabeth, 60; Maurice, 64.
Weldon—Jeremiah, 153; Lydia, 153.
West—Emily, 151; Joseph, 151.
Wheaton—Rosanna, 142; William Henry, 142.
Whitaker—Ambrose, 25, 31, 33, 86, 94, 105; Andrew, 22; Deborah, 35; J. S, 88; Mary Ann, 109; Sheppard, 109; Susannah, 13; Thomas, 31, 32, 44.
White—David, 149; Elizabeth, 79; Gertrude, 149; Hannah, 54; Isaac, 45, 79; James, 148; Jerusha, 118, 149; Jonathan, 100, 127; Joseph, 26, 63; Lewis, 22; Lydia, 149; Margaret, 79; Mary, 11, 24, 26, 40; Rebecca, 79, 127; Samuel, 26, 79; Sarah, 79, 127; Walter Wilson, 149; William, 11, 24, 40, 101, 118.

Whiteman—David, 24.

Whitesall—Thomas, 34, 36.

Whitsel—Benjamin, 36; Conrad, 36; David, 36; Elizabeth, 36; Jacob, 36; Jamima, 36; Joseph, 36; Matilda, 36.

Whitsell—Elizabeth, 137.

Wible—David, 116; John, 116; Joshua, 116, 117; Ruth, 116; Samuel, 116; Thomas, 116.

Wick—David, 43; Jacob, 26, 43; James, 43; James Lawrence, 30.

Wiley—George, 137; John, 136, 137; Joseph, 79, 136; Lydia, 92; Mary, 136.

Willetts—Samuel Abbott, 81.

Williams—Atlantic, 65; David, 145; Elizabeth, 48, 20, 80: Fidelia 48; Hannah, 8; John, 47, 80, 82, 91, 113; Joseph, 20; Maria, 145; Mark, 33; Mary, 33; Mary Jain, 49; Moses, 80; Sarah, 48, 80; R., 89; William, 80.

Williamson—Thomas 89.

Willis—Clement, 32; George, 115; Sarah, 72; William, 142

Willits—David, 69; Edmond, 69; Francis, 69; George, 69; Leah, 69; Martha, 60, 67, 68; Matilda, 69; Samuel, 60, 68; Sarah, 69; Tamar, 69.

Wilson—Hannah, 71; Jane, 41; Joseph, 13; Rebecca, 13; Ruth, 71; Sarah, 13, 33, 69; William, 13.

Winder—Joseph, 29.

Winner—William, 46.

Wintzell—Levi, 49.

Wiser—James, 16.

Wistar—Casper, 16, 21, 28, 29, 37, 38, 52, 107, 117, 123; Catharine, 42; Charlotte, 123, 124; John, 42, 106; Josiah, 42, 128; Martha, 42; Rebecca, 60, 76; Richard, 42, 123.

Wood—Aaron, 57; Auley, 104; Bathsheba, 66; Belford, 140; Benjamin, 148; Caleb, 83; Eli, 72; Elizabeth, 61; Hannah, 12, 36, 53, 81; Henry, 36; John, 12, 87, 95; Jno., 135; Joseph, 66; Joseph Henry, 96; Mary, 9; Rebecca, 26; Sarah, 61; Sarah Ann, 87; William, 66.

Woodnutt—Anna, 150; James, 82, 150; Janathan, 19, 150; Margaret, 150; Mary Emily, 150; Richard, 93, 150; Sarah, 150; William, 54, 144, 150.

Woodruff—Daniel, 73; John, 73.

Woodsides—John, 43, 152; Sarah, 43.

Woolf—James, 49.

Woolman—James, 114, 146; John, 134.
Woolston—Joshua, 48.
Woster—William, 48.
Wright—Ann, 73, 116; Benjamin, 125; Charles, 124; David, 30; Ebenezer, 125; Edward, 125; Elizabeth, 60; George, 124; Harriet, 22; Harrison, 125; Holmes, 54; Job, 40, 60, 125; John, 30, 128; Joseph, 125; Letitia, 125; Martha Ann, 149; Nathan, 60; Priscilla, 127; Richard, 95, 125; Sarah, 126; Stephen, 60, 125, 149; Thomas, 60, 124; William, 124.

Y

Yarrow—Eliza, 46; Hannah, 46; Sarah Ann, 46; Thomas, 5, 6, 8, 10, 11, 12, 15, 17, 34, 35, 42, 46, 50, 55, 79, 108, 130.
Yoken—J. B., 142.
Yonker—Joseph, 134.
Yorke—Lewis, 78; Mary, 25, 78; Thomas Jones, 56, 78.
Young—Elizabeth, 36; James, 12, 36; Louvisa, 36; Martha Jane, 36; Mary, 113; Rachel, 113; Robert, 114.

Z

Zane—William, 122.
Zantzinger—Harriet, 119; William, 119.

www.ingramcontent.com/pod-product-compliance
Lightning Source LLC
Chambersburg PA
CBHW020650300426
44112CB00007B/317